"*Words That Matter* is a must-read for anyone interested in presidential campaigns and media influence. Drawing on an impressive array of traditional media and social media data along with survey responses over the course of the 2016 election, the authors provide ample evidence about how and why media may have affected the outcome even when citizen perceptions were not reflective of news attention."
—ERIKA FRANKLIN FOWLER, *director, Wesleyan Media Project;*
associate professor of government, Wesleyan University

"The authors have compiled the authoritative account of what journalists wrote, and what voters heard, about Hillary Clinton and Donald Trump throughout the 2016 presidential election campaign. They document the very real effects of media coverage on the campaign and show how reporters who shaped the coverage of big stories, such as James Comey and the FBI investigation into Hillary Clinton's email, could have shaped the outcome. Every political reporter in the country should read this book and grapple with the crucial role that they play in American democracy."
—G. ELLIOTT MORRIS, *data journalist*

Words That Matter

Words That Matter

How the News and Social Media Shaped the 2016 Presidential Campaign

Leticia Bode
Ceren Budak
Jonathan M. Ladd
Frank Newport
Josh Pasek
Lisa O. Singh
Stuart N. Soroka
Michael W. Traugott

BROOKINGS INSTITUTION PRESS
Washington, D.C.

The Brookings Institution is a private nonprofit organization devoted to research, education, and publication on important issues of domestic and foreign policy. Its principal purpose is to bring the highest quality independent research and analysis to bear on current and emerging policy problems. Interpretations or conclusions in Brookings publications should be understood to be solely those of the authors.

Library of Congress Control Number: 2020934356
ISBN 9780815731917 (cloth : alk. paper)
ISBN 9780815731924 (ebook)

9 8 7 6 5 4 3 2 1

Typeset in Freight Text Pro

Composition by Elliott Beard

Contents

Acknowledgments

Any project involving a large, interdisciplinary, multi-institutional team working on a project like this is indebted to many people and sources of support. We'd like to start by thanking Bob Groves for bringing our research team together. As a former longtime Michigan faculty member and current Georgetown Provost, he connected us with each other and told us he thought that it would be a great idea if we pursued a new project examining the consequences of the emergence of social media. The rest, as they say, is history.

We are very grateful to our collaborator Frank Newport at Gallup. His work with us began with a pilot study in August 2015 and then became a full-fledged partnership during the 2016 presidential campaign. Our team provided rapid analysis to support Gallup as they collected their daily surveys, not only in the manipulation of the data to produce results, but also in the development of a variety of visualization techniques to facilitate the presentation of information on their website and as a way to facilitate the interpretation of the results for consumers.

Our research was supported by both the University of Michigan and Georgetown University. The University of Michigan (UM) team was supported by a grant from the Michigan Institute for Data Science (MIDAS) with funds provided by the University of Michigan Provost (Brian Athey and Alfred Hero, MIDAS co-directors). Additional cost sharing at Michigan was provided by the Institute for Social Research (ISR) (David Lam, ISR director), the Center for Political Studies (CPS) at the Institute for Social Research (Kenneth Kollman, CPS director), and the Survey Research Center (SRC) at the ISR (Trivellore Raghunathan, SRC director). The School of Information (SI) (Thomas Finholt, SI dean) also provided monetary and mentoring help.

The Georgetown University team was supported by two grants from the Massive Data Institute (MDI) in the McCourt School of Public Policy. In addition to Provost Bob Groves, we are grateful for support throughout this process from Ed Montgomery, dean of the McCourt School during the 2016 election; Michael Bailey, director of MDI; Maria Cancian, current dean of the McCourt School; Bala Kalyanasundaram, chair of the Department of Computer Science in 2016; and Nitin Vaidya, current chair of the Department of Computer Science.

This book project is part of work by a larger research team studying social media at Michigan and Georgetown called the Social Science and Social Media Collaborative (S3MC; see S3MC.org). We thank the other members of the S3MC research group (who are studying social media in other areas of American life) for providing valuable feedback on initial results and various conference presentations. Jule Krueger (CPS) gave a careful read of an initial draft of the manuscript, and Julia Lippman (CPS) assisted with the production of the final book.

We presented earlier versions of these analyses at the Annual Meeting of the American Association for Public Opinion Research, the Annual Meeting of the Midwest Association for Public Opinion Research, the Big Data Meets Survey Science (BigSurv) conference, the University of California, Berkeley's Research Workshop in American Politics, the University of Virginia's American Politics Speaker Series, Georgetown University's American Government Seminar, and the MIDAS 2019 Annual Symposium "Embracing the Challenge: Data

Science for the Next Ten Years" at the University of Michigan. We are thankful for the extremely helpful feedback that we received at all of these presentations.

A number of other people contributed to our efforts through data management, analysis, or writing. Andrew Dugan at Gallup provided significant assistance in the preparation of chapter 6, and he is credited as a co-author. We thank Caitlin Chamberlain at the McCourt School for providing crucial research assistance in the writing of chapters 1, 2, and 3. We thank John Maguire, who edited the book for style and greatly improved the writing. We would also like to thank Department of Computer Science members and MDI software developers, including Yanan Zhu for participating in the data processing during the campaign, and Yiqing Ren and Lingqiong Tan for their support creating some of the visualizations. In addition, we are grateful for the help of several graduate students at Michigan, including Mei Fu (SI), Lia Bozarth (SI), Colleen McClain (SRC), and Fernanda Alvarado-Leiton (SRC). We are also grateful for valuable research assistance from Anthony Zheng, a UM undergraduate student in engineering.

Finally, we want to thank our families for supporting us in our work generally and also for being understanding and supportive of the twice-a-year in-person meetings in D.C. and Ann Arbor that have made this collaboration work. Thank you so much.

1

The Changed Information Environment of Presidential Campaigns

What information do citizens get from the mass media during presidential campaigns? This question has been studied in the past, yet is more important than ever. Since America's first competitive presidential election in 1796, the technology of mass media has been constantly changing. It has evolved from small partisan newspapers in the 1700s, to mass-circulation broadsheets in the 1800s, to radio and television in the 1900s. But mass media seem now to be more omnipresent than ever before, augmented over the last fifteen years by social media, transforming how news is created, disseminated, and consumed. This is the starting premise of the book that follows. Traditional and social media content is a central feature of modern election campaigns; indeed, for most citizens, election campaigns occur *entirely* through traditional and social media. It follows that accounting for both the nature of media content and the nature of media effects is central to understanding presidential election campaigns.

This book seeks to understand what information is produced, how that information gets to voters, and what information voters actually absorb in our new and complex information environment. In any national-level democratic election, there is a long list of issues and candidates that the media can focus on, and innumerable ways in which those issue and candidates can be presented. Most citizens' experiences of a presidential campaign are fundamentally affected by these journalistic decisions.

In 2016, in addition to many pressing national policy concerns that might have demanded attention regardless of the candidates, both major party nominees had unprecedented characteristics, and the fall campaign was particularly eventful. The Democratic nominee, Hillary Clinton, was the first woman ever nominated for president by a major American political party. She had a long history in national Democratic politics that included losing a hotly contested primary battle against Barack Obama when she ran for president in 2008. In the 2016 cycle, she faced an unexpected fight for the nomination from Senator Bernie Sanders of Vermont, an Independent who caucused with the Democrats. Donald Trump, in contrast, defeated a large number of other candidates and won the Republican nomination rather handily. He became his party's presumptive nominee well before Clinton did, and he was successful despite having no prior electoral experience and indeed little previous connection to the Republican Party. On Election Day, for the second time in the last five presidential elections, the Republican nominee won despite receiving fewer votes than the Democrat. What were the nature and content of the information environment—that is, the words conveyed by and recalled from mass and social media—in this historic election? This is one central concern in the chapters that follow.

Even as media content is increasingly available in digital format, examining media content is in some ways more challenging than it was in the past. Changes in media technology mean that people encounter information about a presidential campaign in many different ways. In addition to hearing directly from friends and family, reading written publications in print or online, listening to news-oriented radio, or watching an increasing number of different network and cable television news programs, citizens encounter political news through various social media platforms. These platforms interact with more traditional forms of media and with interpersonal communication, amplifying certain messages more than others. Capturing this increasingly multivariate media environment is difficult, to say the least.

Thus another ongoing theme of this book is that advances in media technology call for new ways of measuring the information environment. Thankfully, corresponding developments in survey and content-analytic research techniques facilitate new approaches to measuring the information that reaches and is absorbed by the mass public. Put more succinctly, there is an increasingly complex system by which political information reaches voters, and an increasingly complex set of research methodologies to match. In this book, we rely on new ways of measuring information flow and reception during political campaigns, focusing on language and words, toward understanding the 2016 presidential election. We believe that some of the approaches outlined will be valuable for political communication scholars trying to understand the nature of campaign information in the context of a new and complex media environment.

The chapters that follow paint a detailed picture of one of the most notable political campaigns in the postwar era. Our work suggests that the pre-election period was characterized by particularly negative messaging, a shifting but largely uninfluential series of scandals for Donald Trump, and a single, stable, and influential scandal for Hillary Clinton. The impact of email-related news on Clinton's election prospects is readily apparent in our data. But the effects of that scandal were not, as some have suggested, only driven by late-campaign interventions from FBI Director James Comey. Our data make clear the *long-standing* salience of email, in news content but especially in the public mind. Even when there was other news about Hillary Clinton, the public thought about "her emails"—for months and months—indeed, starting before the election campaign was even underway. The end result was a close enough election outcome that Donald Trump won the Electoral College vote. Considered narrowly, these findings highlight the importance of email scandals to the 2016 election outcome. Considered more broadly, our results highlight the importance of considering not just the content of the (increasingly diverse) media environment but also the ways in which that content circulates across media platforms, and over time, and "sticks" in the minds of prospective voters.

The Impact of Campaign-Period News

American presidential campaigns are unusually long by international standards. Candidates start to run for their party's nomination sometimes two years in advance, and often the nominees are effectively decided well over six months before Election Day. In 2016, overall, approximately $2.4 billion was spent on the presidential campaign by candidates, parties, and independent groups (Sultan 2017). But, of course, attention to the campaign does not come only, or even primarily, from electioneering. Most people never meet a candidate or attend a campaign event; they hear about the campaign at least as much through the news media as through campaign advertising; and overall, the publicity surrounding U.S. presidential campaigns is massive by any reasonable measure.

This book is premised on the idea that campaign-period media content can matter to election outcomes. In spite of the magnitude of U.S. campaigns, however, there are reasons to question this assumption. Political scientists have focused a lot of attention on how and when news coverage reaches voters. Many have concluded that the impact of news coverage is limited. Instead, they often say campaigns mostly reinforce citizens' existing predispositions, making them more certain that they prefer the same type of candidates they had voted for in the past (e.g., Lazarsfeld, Berelson, and Gaudet 1948; Berelson, Lazarsfeld, and McPhee 1954; Klapper 1960; Kinder 2003; Bartels 2006). Other work finds that one can predict the presidential popular vote margin fairly reliably without knowing *anything* about the campaign coverage.

Just knowing the economic growth rate in the election year, whether the United States was engaged in an unpopular foreign war, and how many terms the current president's party had held the White House enables one to predict, if not the exact vote totals, at least which elections were landslides for one party or the other and which were close (e.g., Abramowitz 1988; Bartels and Zaller 2001; Hibbs 2000, 2007; Bartels 2008; Wlezien and Erikson 2012; for more on this, see chapter 2).

While many political scientists and communication scholars believe that media coverage during presidential campaigns has only minor effects on voting, many journalists and pundits believe the opposite: campaign messages matter a lot. We suspect that reality is somewhere in between. Indeed, even as there is work that makes accurate election predictions in the absence—and indeed largely before—any campaign-period media coverage, there is also work that finds small but significant media effects throughout election campaigns (Sides and Vavreck 2013). Some work suggests that small errors in long-term predictions may be accounted for by media content—that even as long-term macroeconomic factors matter, so too does media content, albeit at the margins (Belanger and Soroka 2012).

Other work demonstrates media effects in the context of election campaigns. Studies find that those who consume more news prefer different candidates than those who consume less, for instance, holding partisanship and other background characteristics constant (Bartels 1993; Hetherington 1996). Other work finds that, even if media content does not change people's vote choices, it changes their beliefs about which topics are salient (i.e., at the top of the head) and the issues people base their voting decision on, phenomena called "agenda setting" and "priming" (e.g., Iyengar and Kinder 1987; Krosnick and Kinder 1990; Johnston et al. 1992; Iyengar and Simon 1994; Johnston, Hagen, and Jamieson 2004; Ladd 2007; McCombs 2014).[1]

The activation of predispositions, especially partisanship, appears to be stronger when people are exposed to media coverage that emphasizes partisan themes; and the influence of the economy on voting appears to be stronger when campaign media coverage primes economic considerations and less when the economy gets less coverage (Bartels 2006; Vavreck 2009; Sides and Vavreck 2013). The agenda-setting and priming that happen during campaigns may thus augment the impact of predispositions and the economy on voting preferences. Put differently, it may be that in many cases the impact of campaign-period media is simply to engage the fundamentals (e.g., Campbell 2008; Gelman and King 1993; Erikson and Wlezien 2012), reminding voters about their predispositions and preferences in time for Election Day.

Who is most influenced by these media messages? Some people enjoy following politics and pay a lot of attention to political news, whereas others have little interest. While campaign interest among the American public varies greatly (Zaller 1992; Delli Carpini and Keeter 1996; Prior 2018), for the portion interested in politics, there is almost unlimited coverage of the campaigns in the media environment. Indeed, the seemingly never-ending growth in media and entertainment choices over the past several decades has only exacerbated the differences in exposure to political communication between those who enjoy it and those who don't (Prior 2005, 2007). These long and heavily publicized presidential campaigns don't necessarily break through to the less politically engaged. Those who are addicted to political news consume most of it.

Since political engagement is strongly correlated with partisanship and ideological consistency, those who consume the most political messages are the least likely to be moved by those messages. Instead, persuasion usually occurs in the uncommon event that those with moderate levels of political engagement encounter political information, or the very rare event that those with low political engagement do (Zaller 1992).

The fact that middle- and low-engagement voters are the most susceptible to influence when they encounter political information also helps us understand why the topics given heavy attention in the media environment can be consequential. First, stories that are covered heavily and repeatedly over a long period of time are most likely to break through and actually get noticed even by people without strong pre-

existing political commitments. Second, it is easier to change preferences (and the intensity of preferences) by changing the subject than
by directly telling people to vote for or against a candidate. Persuadable
voters who don't follow the details of politics may be more likely to
notice when one issue is getting heavy coverage, and thus think more
about that issue in the voting booth.

In short, media effects needn't draw citizens away from their initial preferences; and effects should not be distributed evenly across all
citizens. These facts have led to what we would characterize as a new
consensus about the likely effects of media coverage in election campaigns. Media content *can* shift support for candidates, for some voters
at least, either through the introduction of new information, or through
the reinforcement and intensification of "fundamentals" and preexist-
ing partisan preferences. In a close election like 2016, these effects can
be of real consequence.

Identifying when and which mass-mediated information matters
is of course relatively complex. This book examines some possibilities
by focusing on the information that was both disseminated in media
and actually absorbed by the public (i.e., the content of traditional and
social media), and the public's recollections of that content. Our data
point to a storyline that sits somewhere between what we might call the
campaign-period-information and *engaging-the-fundamentals* perspectives of media effects. On the one hand, it seems clear that campaign-
period coverage of email scandals related to Hillary Clinton and the
Democrats were highly salient for survey respondents. On the other
hand, these email-related scandals were not "new" to the campaign—
they were prominent before the campaign began, and their impact
seems to have stemmed in part from their enduring salience, spurred
on by campaign events. In short, "email" was a *pre-campaign* issue for
Hillary Clinton, the election impact of which may have been augmented
by campaign-period news coverage.

The Plan for This Book

This book examines how information flowed through various forms of media to the public in the 2016 presidential campaign. The chapters that follow reflect complementary but also somewhat different approaches to analyzing full-text news content, social media posts, and survey responses. These differences reflect the fact that we are eight coauthors, each of whom brings a slightly different approach to the study of campaign media. That said, each chapter aims to characterize which issues and candidates get covered or neglected during presidential campaigns, how the coverage of those issues and candidates differs in traditional media versus social media, and the relationship between the information in both of these venues and the information citizens actually report hearing about.

As already noted, the issues and candidates in this election were unusual in multiple ways, and the 2016 campaign was particularly eventful. It is difficult to interpret what we are seeing in the media content without some understanding of the candidates and the events of the campaign. Thus chapter 2 briefly provides some basic background on the candidates, the state of the country in 2016, and the events of the fall general election campaign. It gives special attention to explaining Hillary Clinton's email scandal, which persistently dominated much of the 2016 media environment. We think this chapter serves as a useful review of many of the details of the 2016 campaign that may now have been forgotten. The reader might also refer back to this chapter when reading later chapters for a refresher on an event to which the media system is reacting.

Chapter 3 introduces the main datasets we use in this book and provides a brief description of what the media, journalists, and the public were focused on throughout the campaign. Using topic models that analyze the words used in each of these datasets throughout the fall campaign, we consider when and how topics emerged from the background into focus and then faded.

Chapter 4 looks at media reaction to the first Republican primary debate in the election season in August 2015. This was the national introduction to Donald Trump, how he would behave on the stage of national presidential politics, and how the media system would react to him. We find, very early on, patterns that would be echoed in the fall 2016 campaign information environment. Trump dominated news coverage of the debate. And, despite it rarely coming up from Republican candidates in this debate, people were nevertheless hearing about Clinton's email scandal during this time.

Chapter 5 examines the tone of coverage in the fall 2016 campaign. It finds that overall news coverage was more negative than in recent previous presidential campaigns, consistent with these candidates being the most personally unpopular nominees in polling history. We also find that the tone of media content became more negative when moving from newspaper coverage to Twitter content to personal recollections of what people had heard about the campaign.

Chapter 6 closely examines what people reported hearing about the candidates in the open-ended survey questions during the campaign. We find a persistent and large focus on Clinton's email scandal throughout the campaign. Interestingly, Republicans tended to recall hearing more about Hillary Clinton than Democrats did.

Chapter 7 examines major events of the fall 2016 campaign and how information about them got out to the public. We give special attention to examining how long coverage of events lasts in the media system and how long people report hearing about it. We find that what people reported hearing about during the campaign was largely not long-standing challenges facing the country but short-term campaign events generated by the candidates themselves. These candidate-generated stories temporarily displaced the Clinton email scandal in the public's thinking; but after a short period they faded, and the email story returned. This created a contrast between the information people received about Clinton and Trump. While topics in coverage of Trump were very inconsistent over the weeks of the campaign, Clinton coverage kept returning to the same narrative over and over. We also find that what the public reported hearing is not a mirror image of what was covered in our media datasets—what the public reported hearing was both more responsive to recent events and more dominated by the email scandal.

Chapter 8 takes a careful look at fake news stories on social media. We find that there were a lot of fake news stories circulating on social media, but, in general, high-quality news tended to be shared more than low-quality news. However, Republican voters were more likely to remember information that was in fake news stories about Clinton than what was in traditional news coverage of Clinton.

Chapter 9 sums up the lessons we learned about the information the mass public encounters in a modern presidential campaign, and uses those lessons to think about future campaigns. We discuss the implications both for scholarship on campaign messaging in future elections and for media practitioners who will be covering elections in 2020 and beyond.

Many of the figures in this book have dynamic features built into them that can be viewed from the website Words That Matter Supplemental Files (https://dx.doi.org/10.17605/OSF.IO/JS7FT). For example, running a mouse over some of the charts that show a specific pattern of survey or Twitter responses will indicate key dates or activities in the campaign.

2

What Might Have Made News

Big Issues, Historic Candidates, and Hillary Clinton's Strange Email Scandal

This chapter serves as a brief retelling of the major events and potential news topics in the 2016 U.S. presidential campaign and election. The messages in the media information environment don't come from nowhere. We can only analyze and evaluate the information environment surrounding the campaign in relation to some measure of reality. The most relevant components of the information environment include the national context at the time of the election, the candidates in the race, and the events of the campaign. What is the relationship between the campaign information environment, and what people get from it, to these realities? The sections that follow review the candidates themselves, the national issue context, and the events of the campaign itself.

This overview serves the important purpose of reviewing major events, topics, and characteristics that *could* have been covered in the information environment during the campaign, shown up in tweets about the candidates, or been cited by survey respondents as things they had recently heard about each candidate. Having a sense of what could have surfaced in each of these information streams gives greater insight into what actually broke through. This overview of the potential content of the campaign information environment thus lays a foundation for the rest of the book, allowing us to consider which topics from this universe became salient in the information environment and in what ways, and which topics gained little traction.

The Candidates
Hillary Clinton

Hillary Clinton has been a controversial and highly prominent national figure since her husband Bill Clinton ran for president in 1992. During his presidency, she chaired the task force that wrote the administration's health care reform proposal, which at the time was considered its most significant policy initiative—though it ultimately failed in Congress. She is the only presidential spouse ever to have an office in the West Wing of the White House. Her role as a policy adviser was controversial among those who preferred that she follow the example of past first ladies and stick to less controversial projects.

During her husband's presidency, she was also connected to numerous real scandals, conspiracy theories, and a series of news stories in the gray area between the two. The most investigated scandal of the Clinton presidency was Whitewater. It began as an investigation of an investment that the Clintons made in the late 1970s in a real estate company called the Whitewater Development Corporation. The question was whether Hillary's work for the Rose Law Firm, which was employed by a savings and loan that also invested in Whitewater, constituted a conflict of interest, given that, as Arkansas's governor, her husband was responsible for regulating the savings and loan. The Independent Counsel's investigation of Whitewater eventually led to Bill Clinton's impeachment in 1998, after it discovered that he had engaged in an affair with a White House intern.

There were other minor scandals directly involving Hillary Clinton during her husband's administration. There was the case of the missing billing records: when the Independent Counsel's office requested her Rose Law Firm billing records, she said they were lost, but then found them in the White House two years later. There was "Travelgate": the accusation by the independent counsel's office in its final report that she made false statements about the firing of the White House travel staff, which critics claimed was done to fill the jobs with Clinton loyalists. And there was "Filegate": the Clinton administration improperly acquiring the FBI files of 900 former White House employees, including many from Republican administrations, which some accused Hillary of requesting, although the Independent Counsel's final report cleared her. In this period, the media also reported that Hillary made large profits buying and selling cattle futures in 1978 and 1979, which some conservatives suggested may have been the result of unethical conduct.

In the 1990s, Hillary Clinton was the subject of conspiracy theories around the suicide of Vince Foster in July 1993. Foster was a longtime Clinton family friend and Hillary's partner in the Rose Law Firm who served as deputy White House counsel at the start of the Clinton administration. Right-wing conspiracy theorists suggested that Foster's suicide was related to the Whitewater scandal and that Bill and Hillary might have arranged to have Foster murdered. The Whitewater Independent Counsel's office (twice), the House of Representatives, and the Senate each conducted investigations, all concluding that Foster's death was indeed a suicide and had no connection to the Whitewater Development Corporation.

After her husband left office in 2001, Hillary Clinton was elected senator from New York, serving from 2001 to 2009. Reporters often wrote that she was relatively well liked by her Senate colleagues (Chaddock 2003). One of her most prominent early roles was advocating for aid to New York City to help it recover from the 9/11 terrorist attacks. In her eight years as senator, she was generally viewed as a Democratic Party team player and one of the most liberal senators. In her last Congress (the 110th, 2007–2009) she was the twelfth most liberal senator, placing her voting record very close to that of her 2008 primary opponent, Barack Obama, who was the eighteenth most liberal senator according to DW-NOMINATE roll call voting scores (see Enten 2015, but also verified by the authors from the DW-NOMINATE data at vote-view.com). In her Senate career, Clinton voted against most of President George W. Bush's major domestic initiatives; exceptions were the 2001 USA PATRIOT Act (supported by every senator from both parties except Russ Feingold), the 2001 Authorization for Use of Military Force (AUMF) against terrorists responsible for 9/11 (passed with unanimous Senate support, with two abstentions), and the 2002 Authorization for Use of Military Force Against Iraq (supported by 29 of 50 Democrats and 48 of 49 Republicans).

Then, after losing a close presidential nomination battle to Barack Obama in 2008, she served as secretary of state during his first term. In those four years, she spent a total of 401 days traveling around the world and visited 112 countries, more than any previous secretary of state (Landler 2013). She was involved in, and supportive of, all of Barack Obama's international initiatives, including the use of "soft" power (e.g., engaged participation in international organizations and agreements) and "hard" power (e.g., the use of military force in Libya and Syria) around the world. After leaving the State Department in 2013, she worked for the Clinton Foundation and gave a series of paid speeches for business groups, including several for Goldman Sachs, typically receiving around $225,000 per speech. Together, Hillary and Bill Clinton received well over $25 million in speaking fees between the time she left the State Department and when she began her 2016 presidential campaign in earnest. All of Hillary Clinton's experiences over her long, eventful, and very public career were potentially relevant topics of news coverage during the 2016 presidential campaign; so too were the lessons these experiences revealed about her temperament and ability.

Donald Trump

Donald Trump had been a national celebrity since the 1980s, when he gained fame for his building projects in Manhattan, especially his epony-mous Trump Tower, and for his casinos in Atlantic City. Trump began his career with money given to him from his father, who repeatedly provided additional cash infusions when his son hit financial hard times. Overall, in the course of his career, he received $413 million from his father to fund his various businesses (Barstow, Craig, and Buettner 2018).[1]

Unlike most real estate developers, he sought publicity and culti-vated his personal brand. As described in his 1987 memoir, *The Art of the Deal*, Trump's strategy for dealing with the media and generating press coverage involved being "different" and "outrageous" as well as engag-ing in "bravado" (Trump and Schwartz 2015, 56–58).

In fact, the two things Trump showed a consistent talent for were getting publicity and losing money. He became a widely known pop cul-tural figure in the 1980s and 1990s, appearing on talk shows, making cameos in movies, appearing on the covers of *Time*, *Newsweek*, and *Play-boy* magazines, and entering a variety of other businesses beyond his core of real estate and casinos, all with his name prominently attached. He owned a team in the U.S. Football League, the New Jersey Generals, and started his own airline, Trump Shuttle, which operated for three years before defaulting on its debt and being sold to U.S. Airways. Over this period, Trump lost a staggering amount of money. A 2019 *New York Times* investigation found that, in the 1980s and early 1990s, "Year after year, Mr. Trump appears to have lost more money than nearly any other individual American taxpayer." Between 1985 and 1994, Trump lost ap-proximately $1.17 billion of his and his investors' money (Buettner and Craig 2019). The losses eventually caught up to him. Six businesses he controlled went legally bankrupt over the years (three Atlantic City Ca-sinos in 1991–1992, the Plaza Hotel in New York in 1992, Trump Hotels and Casinos Resorts in 2004, and Trump Entertainment Resorts in 2009), although he managed to avoid personal bankruptcy (Qiu 2016; O'Harrow n.d.; M. Lee 2016).

Despite all his financial problems, he maintained a reputation for wealth among the broader public, likely due to the extensive media attention his personality and lifestyle cultivated (Koury and Raspa 1999; Wooten 2009). In the later years of his business career, he profited off this reputation by licensing the Trump name to numerous products, such as Trump ties, Trump steaks, Trump bottled water, and even Trump University, which operated as an unaccredited educational institution from 2005 to 2010. (One month after the 2016 election, Trump settled two class action lawsuits and one suit from the New York attorney general for a total of $25 million for defrauding Trump University students.) In 1996, he purchased the Miss Universe Pageant and operated it until selling it in 2015. This also traded on and perpetuated his glamorous image.

In 2004, Trump reached a new level of fame by playing a rich, successful businessman in the NBC reality TV show *The Apprentice*. It was a hit and ran for fourteen seasons. Since the winning contestant's prize at the end of each season was not cash or merchandise but a job in the Trump Organization, he and the organization were depicted as being glamorous (Foreman, Roth, and Moriarty 2017; Schrodt 2016; Grynbaum and Parker 2016).

Though he had previously been a registered Democrat, and over the years had donated to both political parties and took a wide variety of policy positions, Trump became more politically active before the launch of his own presidential campaign by frequently criticizing President Barack Obama. He prominently and repeatedly spread the conspiracy theory that Obama had been born in Kenya (Krieg 2016; Barbaro 2016). This only came to an end when Trump admitted Obama was born in Hawaii at a press conference in the middle of the general election campaign on September 16, 2016 (Collinson and Diamond 2016; Haberman and Rappeport 2016).

The Issue Context
The Issues That Political Scientists Think
Influence Presidential Election Results

As we note in chapter 1, political scientists have found that, without even considering candidates or campaign tactics, American presidential election results are correlated with three things: (1) national economic growth during the election year; (2) how many years the current president's party has occupied the White House; and (3) whether the United States is engaged in an overseas war where large numbers of American soldiers have died (Abramowitz 1988; Hibbs 2000, 2007; Bartels and Zaller 2001; Bartels 2008; Mayhew 2008; Sides and Vavreck 2013). Collectively, these are often referred to by political scientists as "the fundamentals." The influence of each of these conditions can be enhanced or reduced depending on media emphasis (Bartels 2006; Vavreck 2009). Because these conditions are so important, it is natural to consider the state of the fundamentals in 2016, which party they favored, and then how much attention each received in the media information environment.

What, then, did the fundamentals look like in 2016? America was engaged in a wide range of overseas military activities. While these activities were arguably morally important, they didn't involve the types of large casualties that have historically hurt the incumbent party in presidential elections. The number of troops in Afghanistan steadily shrank during the later years of the Obama administration, until fewer than 10,000 remained in Afghanistan at the start of 2016; this dwindled to 8,400 by the end of the year (Martinez 2015; Collinson and Kopan 2016; Lee and Schwartz 2016; McLeary 2017).

Collectively, military engagements in Afghanistan and Iraq generated fewer than 30 U.S. casualties in each of 2015 and 2016, very small amounts by historic standards and therefore relatively unlikely to foster a great deal of journalistic attention.[2] This was far from the high rates of death in the Korean and Vietnam Wars that seem to have hurt the electoral performance of the incumbent president's party's in the post–

World War II era (Hibbs 2007). Although journalists could have decided to cover these conflicts during campaign because of their moral importance, the number of recent American war deaths seemed unlikely to have large consequences on the election.

In American politics, parties usually win a second term in the White House, but rarely a third. Since World War II, the only example of a party winning three consecutive terms was the Republicans in 1988. Yet while this pattern is useful for prediction, it is not itself an explanation. Political scientists are unsure why parties have so much difficulty attempting, as the Democrats did in 2016, to win the presidency a third consecutive time. Scholars have speculated that the pattern may be a function of incumbency or simply Americans' sense that it is "time for a change" (Abramowitz 1988; Mayhew 2008). Yet, whatever the reason, it was realistic to expect the Democratic Party to face a more challenging election in 2016 than they had in 2012.

The final background condition that is correlated with presidential election outcomes is economic growth in the election year. Many studies have examined economic voting, and several consistent patterns emerge (e.g., Lewis-Beck 1990; Lewis-Beck and Stegmaier 2000; Bartels and Zaller 2001; Hibbs 2007). First, it appears that change in the economy, rather than the level of economic prosperity, is correlated with election outcomes. That is, determinations on objective indicators of the state of the economy, such as the unemployment rate and GDP per capita, do not seem to matter. Nor does it matter whether the economy has fully recovered from an economic slump. The consequential information is the rate of growth in the election year itself.[3]

Finally, although economic considerations account for important variations in electoral choice, they do not yield a precise prediction of the vote (Silver 2011; Gelman 2011, 2016). When the GDP growth rate is over 2.5 percent or the real disposable income (RDI) growth rate is over 3 percent, the incumbent party does quite well, as in 1964, 1972, 1984, and 1996. When the GDP is shrinking, or RDI growth is less than 1 percent, the incumbent party is in trouble, as in 1980 and 2008. When the economy is in between these extremes, either candidate could win the popular vote.

Some political scientists argue that news coverage of the economy during the campaign increases economic influence on the vote (Gelman and King 1993; Bartels 2006). This priming of economic considerations is enhanced when the campaigns themselves emphasize the economy in their messaging (Vavreck 2009). In 2016, the growth rates of GDP and gross domestic income (GDI) were 1.6 percent and 1.2 percent, respectively.[4] This is within the range of economic conditions where either party could win (Sides 2016). However, other economic statistics that historically have a lower correlation with election results reflected a more positive economic situation. The national unemployment rate varied between 4.7 and 5.0 percent every month of 2016.[5] Inflation was historically very low: 2.1 percent for the first ten months of 2016.[6]

Given these moderately positive economic conditions, one could imagine the campaigns conducting a fierce argument about whether economic conditions were good or bad and the media covering this controversy. Both campaigns did refer to the economy—including related issues like jobs and employment, wage stagnation, wealth inequality, and others—but this was not the major issue of either campaign. Still, the economy was undeniably a potent political issue that could have influenced voters if the campaigns or news media chose to emphasize it.

Other Challenges Facing the Country
That Received Little Attention

We also want to mention two topics that didn't get much attention in the campaign information environment and why that happened. The first is wage stagnation. And the second is climate change. Long-term wage stagnation is a possible explanation for why low-education, white voters in northern midwestern states were open to voting for an outsider like Trump, yet we find almost no evidence that the media environment emphasized it. Similarly, there are many reasons to believe that mitigating climate change was the most important policy challenge facing the United States government in 2016. This issue was also essentially ignored in campaign coverage.

Because Trump won the Electoral College as a result of surprise victories in Pennsylvania, Michigan, and Wisconsin, and his rhetoric was viewed as more populist than previous Republican nominees, much postelection punditry focused on whether postindustrial populism driven by frustration with poor economic opportunities had fueled Trump's support (Kramer 2016; Vance 2018).

The unemployment rate and wage growth had recovered very slowly from the 2008 recession (Desilver 2018), compounding long-standing worries about increased income inequality (Picketty and Saez 2003). Overall median household income (adjusted for inflation) had increased only from $40,000 in the early 1970s to $52,000 by 2014, very slow growth by historical U.S. standards (Leonhardt 2014). The situation was even worse if you consider people in the lower half of the income distribution. The average earnings of hourly nonsupervisory employees in the United States showed no net growth from 1970 to 2014 (Krugman 2014). The situation has been especially disappointing for less-educated men. The median incomes of men from ages 30 to 50 actually declined 29 percent between 1969 and 2009 (Lowrey 2014). While the experience of this "secular stagnation" (Summers 2013) may have influenced some low-education and/or midwestern voters, future chapters show little evidence that the campaign information environment reminded them of it.

Finally, the campaign information environment paid virtually no attention to arguably the most serious problem facing the United States and the world in 2016: the threat of climate change. In 2014, the UN Intergovernmental Panel on Climate Change's Synthesis Report had reiterated its conclusion that climate change and (related) ocean warming were happening and that human activity was the cause. It estimated that global temperatures would rise more than 1.5 degrees Celsius by 2100, perhaps even more than 2 degrees in some plausible scenarios (Intergovernmental Panel on Climate Change [United Nations] 2014). In 2015, more than two hundred nations, including the United States, adopted the Paris Agreement, under which, starting in 2020, nations would institute policies to limit carbon emissions so that global temperatures rose less than 2 degrees (and ideally 1.5 degrees) Celsius above preindustrial levels. This would entail net zero global carbon emissions by the second half of the twenty-first century (Goldenberg et al. 2015). In 2016, the National Aeronautics and Space Administration (NASA), the National Oceanic and Atmospheric Administration (NOAA), and the Japan Meteorological Association each separately published reports concluding that global temperatures were at all-time highs and rising. In the summer of 2016, NASA reported that arctic sea ice accumulation was at its lowest point since 1979, when satellites began tracking its measurement, and that 2016 was virtually assured to be the hottest year on record. Yet none of this received more than trivial amounts of coverage in traditional or social media, nor did the public hear much about it, as reported in our Gallup surveys. It was virtually absent from the campaign.

The Events
Hillary Clinton's Strange Email Scandal

One topic dominated the 2016 media information environment more than any other: the connection between Hillary Clinton and email. There were several distinct email-related scandals, and they all came together in the 2016 campaign in a way that was likely indistinguishable in many voters' minds. This topic played such a crucial role in the 2016 election that it is worth providing a brief explanation here.

In October 18, 2011, while Hillary Clinton was secretary of state, Kevin Lamarque (of Reuters) and Diana Walker of *Time* magazine took photos of her staring down at her BlackBerry while sitting on a plane flying from Malta to Tripoli (Schwarz 2015). In the moment, which would become a popular meme and two of the most well-known photos ever taken of Clinton in her long career, she wears sunglasses, sits in a large, cushioned chair with a pile of briefing books in front of her, and peers down at her BlackBerry phone, apparently checking her email. She has a serious, no-nonsense expression that people quickly picked up on. Two days later (on October 20), Kevin Lamarque's picture, which was in color, appeared online in a blog post for Reuters by Robert

Basler (2011). On November 7, Diana Walker's picture, which was black and white, appeared in *Time* (Zengerle 2015). A Tumblr blog called *Texts from Hillary* was opened in 2012, which paired Lamarque's color photo with imagined email conversations Clinton was having with various celebrities and political leaders. Clinton and her staff liked the meme. Diana Walker said that, "the Secretary seemed to have thought it was funny and all the reaction to it around the world was she looked cool" (Zengerle 2015). When Clinton opened her own personal Twitter account after leaving the state department in 2013, she used Walker's black and white photo as her profile picture (Jackson 2013; Schwarz 2015).

In the original Tumblr page, and for many people who shared these photos and added their own captions imagining what Clinton was writing, she was usually depicted positively. She appeared calm, cool, and in command in the photo, which is how she was often portrayed in her imagined email messages.

Following the October 18, 2011, BlackBerry photo's rise to viral status, Clarence Finney (director of the Correspondence and Records office under the Executive Secretariat), who had been told when Clinton first took office that she was not initially using an official State.gov email account, became curious about whether this was still the case. In response to an inquiry from Finney, the State Department's internal IT office confirmed that Clinton still did not have an official email account (Gerstein 2016; Hattem 2016; Tacopino 2016). Yet at this point, the situation seemed to be politically neutral or even positive for Clinton. A *Washington Post* blog playfully mentioned in 2012 that, "when Hillary Rodham Clinton checks her phone, she's probably reading top-secret emails—but one blogger would prefer to imagine that she's sending goofy texts instead" (Judkis 2012). As Jason Zengerle (2015) wrote in *GQ*,

> The photo pointed to what will serve as a cornerstone of Clinton's 2016 campaign: her State Department years, during which she transformed herself from the haughty, bumbling presidential candidate of 2008 into

the hyper-competent, take-no-prisoners political ninja who was capably running the world. In a way, the picture managed to capture everything that accounted for Clinton's impressive favorability rating when she left the State Department in 2013.

But her connection to email did not remain so flattering. On March 18, 2013, the website thesmokinggun.com first reported that Romanian hacker Marcel Lehel Lazăr (known as Guccifer 2.0) had hacked Sidney Blumenthal's AOL email account and released emails regarding the Benghazi attack sent to and from Clinton's personal email account clintonemail.com (The Smoking Gun 2013). The State Department later discovered several emails related to Benghazi originating from the clintonemail.com account during the course of an investigation directed by the House Select Committee on Benghazi. But no other news outlet followed up on the story.

On March 2, 2015, a front page *New York Times* story by Michael Schmidt broke the news that Clinton had exclusively used a private email account while serving as the secretary of state, which, although not unprecedented, was in violation of federal law (Schmidt 2015). Clinton's personal staff had only in the previous two months reviewed all of her emails from her time at the State Department and turned over 55,000 pages of selected emails to the department for archiving. While reporters for national outlets continued to pursue the story, the next month, on April 12, 2015, Clinton formally announced her candidacy for president (Karni 2015).

On July 24, another front-page *New York Times* story (Schmidt and Apuzzo 2015) reported that, despite Clinton's previous denials, there was classified information in her private email account, which was stored on the email server she had set up in her house. Her campaign claimed that all the classified information had been assigned that status after they were saved on the email server, but "inspectors general of the State Department and the nation's intelligence agencies said the information they found was classified when it was sent and remains so now" (Schmidt and Apuzzo 2015).

On September 8, 2015, fourteen months before Election Day, Clinton for the first time apologized for her private email setup (Kreutz 2015), telling ABC News that "What I had done was allowed, it was above board. But in retrospect, as I look back at it now, even though it was allowed, I should have used two accounts. One for personal, one for work-related emails. That was a mistake. I'm sorry about that. I take responsibility."

In October, the first Democratic primary debate occurred. (A week later, Clinton was scheduled to appear before the House Select Committee investigating the death of two American diplomats in Benghazi, Libya, in 2012.) In response to a question about her email server from CNN's Anderson Cooper, she took responsibility for using a private email server:

> Well, I've taken responsibility for it. I did say it was a mistake. What I did was allowed by the State Department, but it wasn't the best choice. And I have been as transparent as I know to be, turning over 55,000 pages of my e-mails, asking that they be made public. And you're right. I am going to be testifying. . . . But let's just take a minute here and point out that this committee is basically an arm of the Republican National Committee. It is a partisan vehicle, as admitted by the House Republican majority leader, Mr. McCarthy, to drive down my poll numbers. (*New York Times* 2015)

Yet the email-related answer that got the most news coverage after the debate came from Senator Bernie Sanders, who said, "Let me say— let me say something that may not be great politics. But I think the secretary is right. . . . the American people are sick and tired of hearing about your damn e-mails" (New York Times 2015; Summers 2015).

On October 15, Clinton testified for 11 hours before the House Select Committee on Benghazi. The official topic of the hearing that day was investigating the 2012 terrorist attack that killed two American diplomats and two CIA contractors in Benghazi, Libya, while Clinton was secretary of state. Yet the questions frequently turned to Clinton's email habits.

Consistent with Bernie Sanders's stated preference to avoid focusing on Hillary Clinton's emails, the topic was not a major focus of their long and heated battle for the Democratic presidential nomination in the winter and spring of 2016. However, the email issue did still percolate over this time in conservative media outlets. On January 14, 2016, Alex Jones released a video on his InfoWars website titled "Hillary Clinton Could Be Indicted within 60 Days." On January 29, the *Washington Examiner* ran a story under the headline "Former House Oversight Chairman: 'FBI Director Would Like to Indict Clinton and Abedin,'" in which it quoted California Congressman and former House Oversight Chairman Darrell Issa saying,

> I think the FBI director would like to indict both Huma and Hillary as we speak. I think he's in a position where he's being forced to triple-time make a case of what would otherwise be, what they call, a slam dunk. . . . You can't have 1,300 highly sensitive emails that contain highly sensitive material that's taken all, or in part from classified documents, and have it be an accident. . . . There's no question, she knew she had a responsibility and she circumvented it. And she circumvented it a second time when she knowingly let highly-classified material get onto emails in an unclassified format. (Morrongiello 2016)

On March 3, Fox News "senior judicial analyst," former New Jersey Superior Court judge Andrew Napolitano went on multiple Fox News programs to say repeatedly that because Clinton's former aid Bryan Pagliano, who set up her personal email server, was granted immunity by the Department of Justice, indictments in the case were coming "very soon, like May, in terms of somebody getting indicted. . . . Hillary should be terrified." Napolitano's predictions were covered in an InfoWars article under the headline "Judge: FBI Is Ready to Indict Hillary over Emails" (Goldman 2016; Watson 2016).

On April 1, Ed Klein, a former editor of the *New York Times Magazine* (1977–1987) and the author of the 2005 book *The Truth about Hillary*, said on the Fox Business channel show *Varney & Co.* that "I think [FBI Director James] Comey realizes that he's got to wrap this [investigation] up well before the conventions, otherwise he's going to disenfranchise millions and millions of people. So I think this is going to be wrapped up in around six more weeks." Klein said that if Clinton wasn't indicted, James Comey and "a lot of other FBI agents" would resign in protest (Guest 2016).

On May 25, the State Department's inspector general issued its report on email practices by the past five secretaries of state, an investigation that was prompted by controversies over Hillary Clinton's use of her private email server. It found that former secretaries Colin Powell and Hillary Clinton had used personal email accounts for State Department business, and that this practice was not "the appropriate method" for electronic communication because of "security risks" and was part of "long-standing systemic weaknesses" in State Department record keeping. At the same time the *Washington Post* quoted anonymous officials as saying that "FBI investigators have so far found little evidence that Clinton maliciously flouted classification rules" (Helderman and Hamburger 2016).

Meanwhile in the GOP primary campaign, Donald Trump won the Indiana Republican primary on May 3, leading Ted Cruz and John Kasich to withdraw from the race. This essentially clinched the nomination for Trump because no viable contenders remained in the field. Five weeks later, on June 7, Clinton won the Democratic primaries in California, New Jersey, and New Mexico and declared victory in the Democratic presidential nomination contest.[7]

On July 5, James Comey held a press conference to announce that the FBI had recommended no criminal charges for Clinton for her handling of emails as secretary of state. In a break with the common practice of providing few details about matters where charges were not brought, Comey called Clinton's email use "extremely careless" and specifically contradicted some of her past statements on the topic. Attorney General Loretta Lynch had, a week before, said that she would accept whatever the FBI's recommendation was in the case (Landler and Lichtblau 2016).

Two days later, on July 7, Comey was called to testify about the matter before the House Judiciary Committee. Under intense questioning from both parties, Comey stated that Clinton's email server in her home, which she used to run her private email account, was an "unauthorized location for the transmitting of private information." He went on to say that "I think she was extremely careless. I think she was negligent. That I could establish. What we can't establish is that she acted with the necessary criminal intent. . . . [Yet] we did not find evidence sufficient to establish that she knew she was sending classified information beyond a reasonable doubt to meet the intent standard" (Gass 2016). At the time, this seemed to mark the end of the FBI's investigation of Hillary Clinton's use of her personal server and email account while secretary of state, setting the stage for the fall campaign.

Other Major Events of the Fall Campaign

Finally, as in any contemporary political campaign, there were a large number of events during the election season that could have reverberated through the media information environment. We define the campaign period as the four months from July through Election Day (which in 2016 fell on November 8), the same period our datasets cover. This period includes not only the traditional central events in most presidential campaigns—such as the party conventions and debates—but also a number of other major news stories related to the candidates that were seen at the time as likely to influence attitudes toward the candidates. These campaign events were often topics of news coverage, things discussed on social media, and ideas that crept into the public perception of the candidates. We outline here what we see as the major events of the campaign.[8]

The data analyzed in this book mostly (except for chapter 4) focus on the fall 2016 campaign, from the beginning of July through Election Day. On July 15, Trump announced that Indiana governor Mike Pence would be his running mate, just before the Republican National Convention in Cleveland (July 18 through 21). Our newspaper and Gallup open-ended data (see chapter 3) indicate that the RNC convention was heavily covered in conventional media, and the public reported hearing about it. Trump did receive a convention "bump" in the polls.[9] As illustrated in figure 2-1, he trailed Clinton by 3.6 points when he gave his acceptance speech on July 21 (40.9 to 37.3 percent), yet eight days later, on July 29, he had opened up a small lead of 1.2 percentage points on Clinton (40.0 to 38.8 percent). This was Trump's strongest performance in the RealClearPolitics polling average throughout the whole campaign.

On July 22, two days before the Democratic National Convention was set to begin in Philadelphia, Clinton announced that Senator Tim Kaine of Virginia would be her running mate. On the same day, Wikileaks (an international organization dedicated to exposing government and business wrongdoing by leaking private documents) released a large number of private Democratic National Committee emails, which were hacked by an unknown source. These emails included negative commentary about Bernie Sanders from DNC staffers, leading to criticism of the DNC and its chairwomen, Representative Debbie Wasserman Schultz, from Sanders supporters. From July 25 to 28, the DNC held its convention. Despite some continued acrimony from his delegates, Sanders endorsed Clinton, and she accepted the nomination on July 28. The polls seemed to indicate that the convention was well received by the public. The polling average went from even (40.4 to 40.2 percent) the day of her acceptance speech to a 6.6-point lead a week later on August 4 (43.5 to 36.9 percent, see figure 2-1). Her lead in the polling average stayed between 4 and 7.5 points through all of August.

On September 11, she had to leave commemoration ceremonies for the 2001 terrorist attacks because she felt ill. She stumbled walking to her car. It was later reported that she had been diagnosed with pneumonia. This dominated cable news coverage for several days, and Clinton's lead in the polling average shrunk during this time, from 2.2 points (41.8 to 39.6 percent) on September 11 to a low of 0.7 points on September 18 and 19 (41.0 to 40.3 percent). But her poll standing did recover, and she led by 2.4 points (42.7 to 40.3 percent) the day before the first official presidential debate on September 26.

Clinton was perceived as having won the first debate in postdebate

Figure 2-1

Average of Vote Intentions in Publicly Available Polls

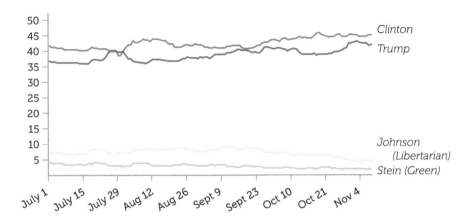

Source: Calculated by RealClearPolitics presidential horserace polling average (Trende 2016).

polls and by most pundits (Klein 2016). She was also able to put the Trump campaign on the defensive, in one of her last speaking turns, by criticizing Trump's treatment of a Miss USA Pageant winner, Alicia Machado, when he owned the pageant. Trump had criticized Machado for not being thin enough in her year as reigning Miss USA. Trump drew further attention to this four days later by sending a series of tweets attacking Alicia Machado, including one in which he falsely implied she had released a sex tape (DelReal 2016). In more bad news for Trump, on October 1 the *New York Times* reported on its own major investigation, concluding that Trump "could have avoided [federal income] taxes for nearly two decades" (Barstow, Craig, and Buettner 2016).

Yet an even more prominent Trump scandal broke a week later on October 7, when reporters discovered a videotape of backstage footage of Trump before appearing on the entertainment news show *Access Hollywood* in 2005. In the tape, Trump bragged to the show's host about attempting to seduce a married woman while he was married to his current wife, saying:

> I did try and fuck her. She was married. . . . I moved on her like a bitch, but I couldn't get there. And she was married. Then all of a sudden, I see her, she's now got the big phony tits and everything. She's totally changed her look.

Later he went on:

> You know I'm automatically attracted to beautiful—I just start kissing them. It's like a magnet. Just kiss. I don't even wait. And when you're a star, they let you do it. You can do anything. Grab them by the pussy. You can do anything. (Fahrenthold 2016)

In the days after the video release, more than half a dozen women came forward with claims that they had been assaulted by Trump.

Later on the same day as the *Access Hollywood* tape came to light (and one month before the election), Wikileaks released another batch of emails hacked from Clinton's campaign manager John Podesta. These included controversial excerpts from closed-door speeches Clinton had given to Wall Street executives after leaving the State Department but before beginning her campaign for president (Koran, Merica, and LoBianco 2016).

These weren't the only stories competing for attention during the last intense month of the campaign. The second debate occurred on October 9, only two days after the *Access Hollywood* tape story broke. In another attempt to distract attention from the tape, Trump held a press conference in the hours before the debate with a series of women who had accused Bill Clinton of sexual harassment or assault over the years and invited them to sit with his family during the debate. Postdebate polls indicated that more people believed Hillary Clinton had won the second debate than Trump.

The third and final debate took place ten days later on October 19, just about the time that "harassment scandal" stories about Trump were fading out of newspaper coverage. As in the previous ones, this debate again featured unorthodox rhetoric from Trump, with Trump calling Clinton a "nasty woman," saying he would rid the United States of "bad hombres," and referring to abortion as "ripping the baby out of the mother." For the third straight time, Clinton was perceived to have won the debate in polls conducted afterward (Klein 2016).

Overall, Clinton's position in the race seems to have improved considerably during the period of the three debates. The night of the first debate on September 26, Clinton had led Trump in the polling average by only 1.6 points (43.1 to 41.5 percent). By the day of the third debate on October 19, Clinton led in the polling average by 6.2 points (45.3 to 39.1 percent). Even a week later, on October 26, her lead remained at 5.6 points (45.7 to 40.1 percent). The only signs of concern for Clinton were that the email story had not entirely gone away. During the weeks of the second and third debates, email had remained a minor topic of newspaper coverage of her campaign, and it returned again to be the most frequently mentioned topic respondents said they had heard about her in the Gallup open-ended responses.

This brings us to the tumultuous final days of the campaign. To everyone's surprise, on October 28, just eleven days before the election, FBI Director James Comey penned a letter to eight members of Congress informing them that additional emails were discovered that were pertinent to the FBI's previous investigation of Clinton's use of her private email server while she was secretary of state. It appeared that Comey was reopening the email investigation that he had said was closed at his press conference on July 5. In the assessments of some pundits, as well as Clinton (2017) herself, this letter and its subsequent politicization may have turned the tide of the election in favor of Donald Trump's eventual victory.

Then, in the final major event of the campaign, on Sunday November 6, nine days after the first letter and just two days before the election, Comey released a second letter to Congress about the FBI investigation of Clinton's emails. In this second letter, Comey stated that there was no evidence in the additional emails indicating that Clinton should face charges over handling of classified information. On its face, this letter appeared to restore the circumstances to what they had been after Comey's press conference on July 5, clearing up the cloud of doubt about Clinton's culpability raised by his first letter. Indeed, what was described in the first Comey letter from October 28 turned out to be a relatively inert affair. No substantive new information related to the investigation had been found. Clinton would never be criminally charged for the classified information that made its way onto her private email server. This jolting "October surprise" turned out to be all smoke and no fire.

Although logically the second letter might have told readers to disregard the concerns raised in the first, the effect of both letters was to raise the salience of the email issue again, right before Election Day and during a period when many early and absentee voters were already casting their ballots.[10] The RealClearPolitics polling average shows a modest tightening of the race over the last two weeks of the campaign. Clinton led by 5.6 points (45.7 to 40.1 percent). on October 26, and her lead had been between 5 and 6 points for the previous week. Two days later, when the first Comey letter was released on October 28, Clinton's lead had narrowed to 3.9 points (44.9 to 41.0 percent). Clinton's lead shrunk a bit more in the few days after the Comey letter, to 2.2 points on November 2, then stayed at around 2 points for the next five days. After the second Comey letter, Clinton's lead seems to have actually grown slightly, but not all the way back to the 5-point lead she held before the first Comey letter. She led the RealClearPolitics polling average by 3.3 points on both November 7 and November 8 (45.5 to 42.2 percent on November 8).[11]

Other prominent polling averages, calculated with slightly different smoothing and weighting formulas, told a similar story at the end of the campaign. On Election Day, Clinton led by 3.6 points (48.6 to 45.0 percent) in the FiveThirtyEight.com polling average and by 5.3 points (47.3 to 42.0 percent) in the Huffington Post Pollster polling average. When the returns came in on Election Day, Clinton had slightly underperformed the polling averages, but she still won the national popular vote by 2.1 points (48.0 to 44.9 percent), a difference between the polls and the national vote that is not unusual by historical standards.

However, it became clear early on election night that the Electoral College would be extremely close. As the evening progressed and returns came in, Trump had outperformed the Republican nominees in 2008 and 2012 by narrowly winning Florida, a perpetual swing state, by 1.2 points (48.6 to 47.4 percent), and even more narrowly winning three rust-belt states that Democrats had won the previous six presidential elections: Pennsylvania (by 0.7 points, 48.2 to 47.5 percent), Michigan (by 0.2 points, 47.3 to 47.0 percent), and Wisconsin (by 0.8 points, 47.2 to 46.5 percent). At 2:29 a.m. Eastern Time, Wednesday, November 9, the Associated Press declared Donald Trump the election winner (Colby 2017).

Conclusions

This chapter has outlined the underlying context of the 2016 campaign: the candidates, the national conditions, and the major campaign events. The campaign information environment is best analyzed and evaluated in relation to this underlying reality. In any election year, the list of possible topics is much longer than the list of those that actually receive attention from the media and the public. Which of these potential topics received heavy attention in the information environment, which did not, and why? Chapter 3 introduces the datasets used in the rest of this book. Then it looks in more detail at three of those datasets, to present which issues and events actually did receive attention from journalists, traditional news media, and the public.

What the Media Covered, Journalists Tweeted, and the Public Heard about the Candidates

This book uses a variety of different types of evidence, but there are five datasets that we come back to repeatedly, all of which we collected over the course of the entire fall campaign. The point of this effort is to use these five datasets to study changes in the information environment and public perception during the 2016 campaign. We describe each briefly in this section, and further details on each database are included in the appendix.

The first is the Twitter Daily Random Sample Database. This consists of a random draw of 5,000 tweets about Donald Trump, and 5,000 tweets about Hillary Clinton, each day of the campaign, from July 4 until Election Day. The sample was collected using the Sysomos Application Programming Interface (Sysomos 2018). In total, the Twitter Daily Random Sample Database includes over 760,000 tweets per candidate. The topics mentioned in these tweets are presented in figures 3-1 and 3-2.

The second is the Twitter Journalist Database. These data include all campaign-period tweets from over 930 journalists and bloggers who had an influential social media presence, as identified by StatSocial (2015).[1] We used the Twitter Application Programming Interface to collect these data; from July 4, 2016, until Election Day. The database includes 1.97 million tweets from these journalists and bloggers. Figures 3-3 and 3-4 illustrate the topics in political journalists' tweets mentioning Clinton and Trump, respectively, from July 1, 2016, through Election Day.[2]

In 2016, journalists regularly tweeted about events as they were happening, when most or all of them had not yet produced news covering the event. Journalists also followed and interacted with each other on Twitter. We believe that the topics they mentioned in their tweets are, among other things, a measure of the issues journalists were thinking about, as well as the information they shared with, and got from, their peers while the campaign unfolded.

During the campaign, Twitter provided a much more representative sample of political journalists than of the mass public. Almost all national political journalists had some Twitter presence (Lawrence et al. 2014). Many merely tweeted out links to their own articles, but others replied to other Twitter accounts and shared information from journalists and other sources. News organizations often encouraged or required journalists to have an active Twitter account as a way of publicizing and building an audience for their work.

For these reasons, journalists' tweets about the candidates during the campaign may tell us as much or more about the national information environment than tweets about the candidates from the general public. Although Twitter was a place where many voters shared and consumed political messages, a small and unrepresentative sample of the mass public used Twitter. In 2016, only 24 percent of online adults reported in polls that they regularly used the site (Greenwood, Perrin, and Duggan 2016; Desilver 2016), and only a small portion of these users were likely to be tweeting about politics (see e.g., Pasek et al. 2019). Indeed, people posting political content on Twitter were more politically active than the average citizen or even those posting political content on Facebook (Bode and Dalrymple 2016).

The only social media platforms that a majority of the public used at the time were Facebook and YouTube (Shearer and Gottfried 2016).

Of the two, Facebook was by far the dominant source of political information for ordinary Americans. In January 2016, well before the election had reached its full pitch, 37 percent of Americans reported that they had received election information on the platform in the prior week compared to 11 percent for YouTube and 9 percent for Twitter (Gottfried et al. 2016). The relatively low attention to politics on YouTube can likely be attributed to the design of the site, which was not well suited to following politics on a daily basis. Unfortunately for research in this area, information about what people were posting and reading on Facebook is not available for scholarly analysis (Gramlich 2019).

Our third main dataset is a collection of representative news coverage about general election candidates from July 4, 2016, until Election Day. We compiled all articles that mentioned Hillary Clinton and/or Donald Trump in a series of national prestigious newspapers. Articles were drawn from LexisNexis using the Web Services Kit (WSK), based on a full-text search on both candidates' names. This resulted in 40,842 newspaper articles retrieved between July 2016 and November 2016, from the following newspapers: the *Chicago Sun-Times*, the *Denver Post*, the *Houston Chronicle*, the *Los Angeles Times*, the *New York Times*, the *Philadelphia Inquirer*, the *St. Louis Post-Dispatch* (Missouri), *USA Today*, and the *Washington Post*. Further details of the news database are provided in the appendix (see the section "Data Source and Data Collection"). These newspapers were selected for use in constructing the dataset because (1) the full text of their articles was available in LexisNexis, and (2) they were high-profile newspapers that likely influenced and were influenced by the topics covered by other newspapers and on national and local television programs.

Figures 3-5 and 3-6 show substantial variation in the topics discussed in the newspaper articles mentioning Clinton or Trump over time. While this might be quite different than what is covered in more ideological or tabloid news sources, these prestige outlets tend to set the agenda for smaller mainstream television stations and newspapers across the country (Gans 2004; Graber and Dunaway 2017), making this a reasonable proxy for the traditional news media writ large.

It is worth considering the pluses and minuses of measuring the content of media coverage with a selection of prominent newspapers. A benefit is that, because it is a medium where information is primarily communicated through text, it provides a relatively clear point of comparison with our other datasets. Throughout this book, we try to develop text analysis tools to make realistic, valid comparisons across these different information streams, so that differences and similarities we observe can teach us how information compares across streams, and suggest how dissemination may occur. In this endeavor, we focus on data that are produced in a textual format. We adopt this limitation in part in an effort to homogenize some of the central ways that information is communicated and mitigate the potential that differences we find between the streams are driven solely by media format and our different measurement methods.

Notably, there are also weaknesses to this approach. We do not engage directly with streams of information in cable news and conservative talk radio despite the fact that these are common conduits for political news (Gottfried et al. 2016). Further, there are reasons to expect that these formats provide very different types of messages from less overtly ideological news sources, such as newspapers, national broadcast networks, or National Public Radio. It is therefore possible that some differences between the contents of Twitter, newspaper text, and what people report that they remember reading, seeing, or hearing in polls (to be discussed) may be because people are hearing about things on cable news programs and talk radio or from discussions with friends and family.

Our fourth main dataset comes from Gallup's "read, seen, or heard" survey questions. As part of their nationally representative telephone surveys, every day from July 11 through Election Day[3] Gallup asked a random sample of approximately five hundred American adults: "What specifically do you recall reading, hearing or seeing about Hillary Clinton in the last day or two?" and "What specifically do you recall reading, hearing or seeing about Donald Trump in the last day or two?" The two questions were asked in a random order, and verbatim responses to each were recorded by the interviewers. There were no constraints placed on length, but in general the responses were very short—consisting of a few words, such as *email*, or short phrases, such as "he wants to keep America safe."[4] We used automated natural language processing techniques to analyze the topics as well as the (positive/negative) valence of these comments. As you see in figures 3-7 and 3-8, the topics that the Gallup respondents report hearing about vary dramatically over time, much more than the content of the newspaper articles and the journalists' tweets.

Fifth and finally, because Donald Trump raised the specter of "fake news" so frequently, and there were concerns about foreign intervention in the campaign through the spread of misinformation and disinformation, we also created three related datasets to analyze the existence and prevalence of such elements on the Internet. From our archive of over 5 million sampled tweets and retweets, we retrieved a set of URLs and linked back to their source. We used automated web scrapers to extract the content from these sources. A second dataset uses a list of fake news sites (Zimdars 2016) and their coding as fake news, satire, extreme bias, and the like, to associate each tweet with the same classification. We collected the third of these datasets from Alexa (Alexa Internet 1996), which provides commercial web traffic data and analytics based on the web-browsing behavior of a panel of millions of Internet users. This source was used to identify traditional news sources. We analyze these data in detail in chapter 8.

Together, these five datasets provide an unparalleled record of information flows during the 2016 campaign. For more information on our datasets and how we analyze them, please refer to the appendix at the end of the book. The remainder of this chapter and the chapters that follow examine them to understand what information people encounter in the information environment created by the modern media system, made up of traditional and social media. We compare the information provided to the public, and the information left out, to the challenges facing the country in 2016, the candidates' qualifications for office, and the events of the campaign itself.

Figure 3-1

Random Tweets about Clinton

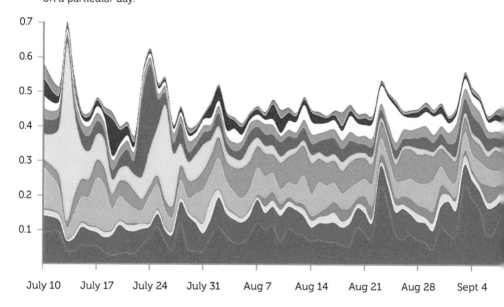

Proportion or fraction of tweets
associated with each topic
and across all of the topics
on a particular day.

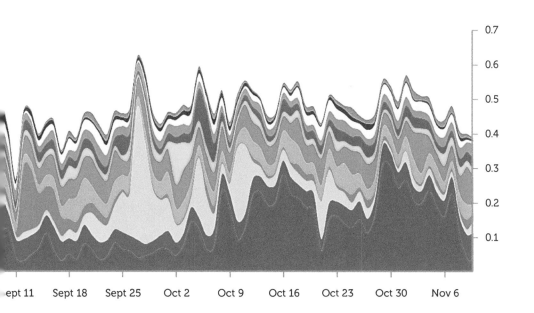

Clinton Color Legend

- ◼ Email Scandal
- ◼ Clinton in the Media
- ◻ Debates
- ◼ Clinton Health Issues
- ◻ Clinton Dishonesty
- ◼ Attacks on Trump
- ◼ Vice President
- Clinton Corruption
- ◼ Democrats Convention
- ◼ Benghazi Scandal
- ◻ Domestic Policies
- ◻ Bernie Sanders
- ◼ Positive Remarks
  about Clinton
- ◼ Crime and Shootings
- ◻ Terrorism Policy

0.7
0.6
0.5
0.4
0.3
0.2
0.1

ept 11   Sept 18   Sept 25   Oct 2   Oct 9   Oct 16   Oct 23   Oct 30   Nov 6

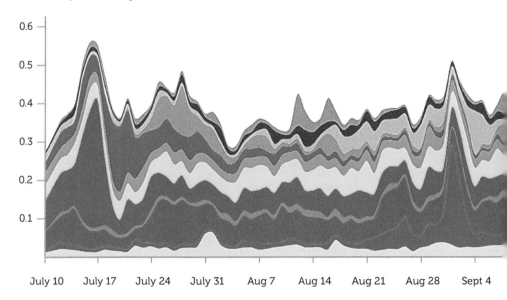

Figure 3-2

Random Tweets about Trump

Proportion or fraction of tweets
associated with each topic
and across all of the topics
on a particular day.

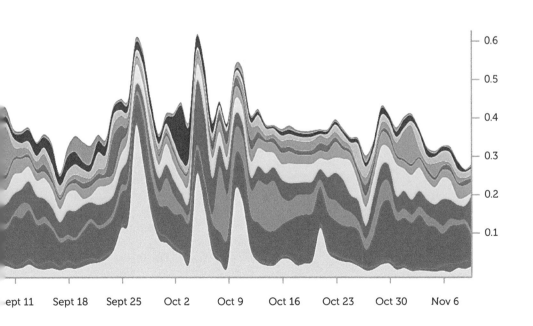

Trump Color Legend

- Debates
- Immigration
- Attacks on Hillary
- Harassment Scandal
- Vice President
- Republican Convention & GOP
- Trump in Media
- Terrorism Policy
- Negative Remarks about Trump
- Positive Remarks about Trump
- Trump's Tax Returns
- African American Community
- Economy Policy
- Crime & Shootings
- Russia & Korea

Figure 3-3

Journalists' Tweets about Clinton

Proportion or fraction of tweets
associated with each topic
and across all of the topics
on a particular day.

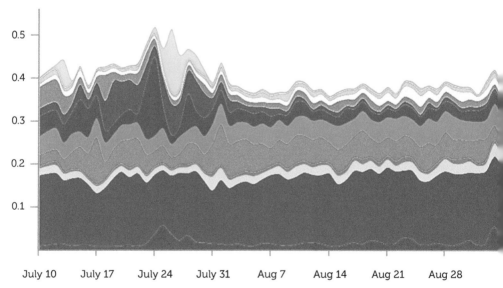

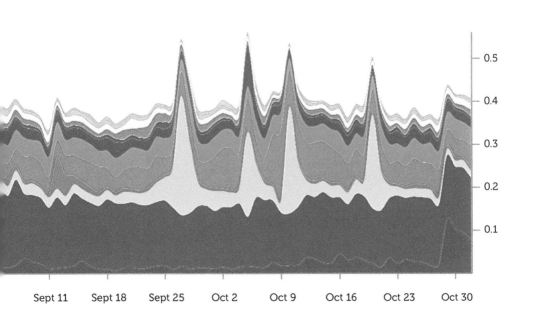

Clinton Color Legend

- Email Scandal
- Clinton in the Media
- Debates
- Clinton Health Issues
- Clinton Dishonesty
- Attacks on Trump
- Vice President
  Clinton Corruption
- Democrats Convention
- Benghazi Scandal
- Domestic Policies
- Bernie Sanders
- Positive Remarks
  about Clinton
- Crime and Shootings
- Terrorism Policy

Figure 3-4

Journalists' Tweets about Trump

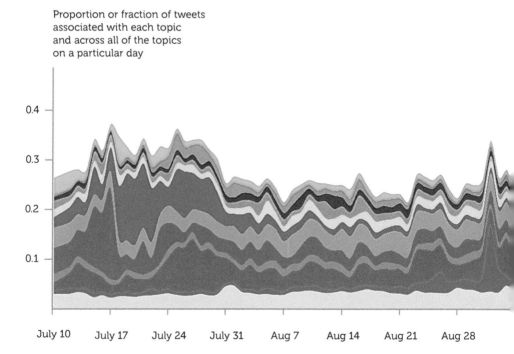

Proportion or fraction of tweets
associated with each topic
and across all of the topics
on a particular day

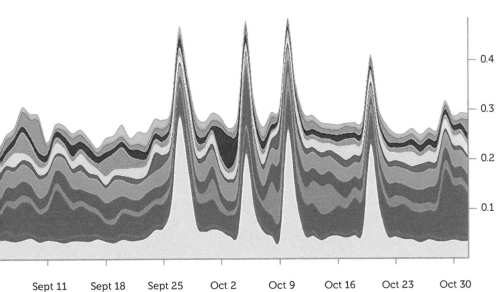

Figure 3-5

Newspaper Coverage of Clinton

Proportion or fraction of newspaper articles
associated with each topic and across
all of the topics on a particular day

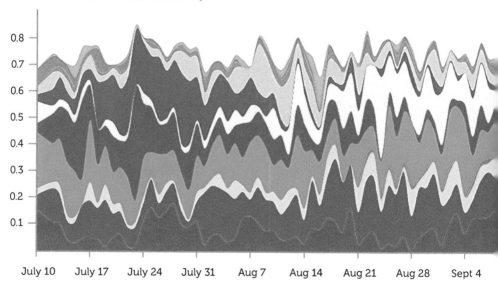

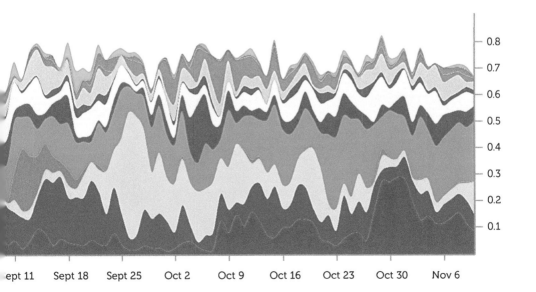

Clinton Color Legend

- Email Scandal
- Clinton in the Media
- Debates
- Clinton Health Issues
- Clinton Dishonesty
- Attacks on Trump
- Vice President
  Clinton Corruption
- Democrats Convention
- Benghazi Scandal
- Domestic Policies
- Bernie Sanders
- Positive Remarks
    about Clinton
- Crime and Shootings
- Terrorism Policy

ept 11   Sept 18   Sept 25   Oct 2   Oct 9   Oct 16   Oct 23   Oct 30   Nov 6

0.8
0.7
0.6
0.5
0.4
0.3
0.2
0.1

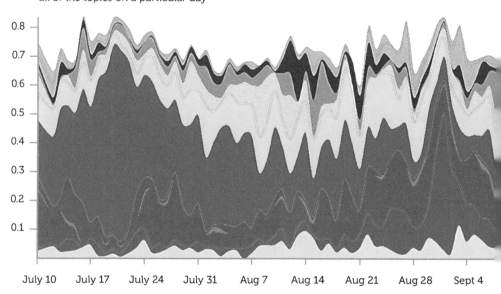

Figure 3-6

Newspaper Coverage of Trump

Proportion or fraction of newspaper articles
associated with each topic and across
all of the topics on a particular day

| 0.8 |
| 0.7 |
| 0.6 |
| 0.5 |
| 0.4 |
| 0.3 |
| 0.2 |
| 0.1 |

July 10   July 17   July 24   July 31   Aug 7   Aug 14   Aug 21   Aug 28   Sept 4

Trump Color Legend

■ *Debates*

■ *Immigration*

■ *Attacks on Hillary*

■ *Harassment Scandal*

■ *Vice President*

■ *Republican Convention
   & GOP*

■ *Trump in Media*

■ *Terrorism Policy*

   *Negative Remarks
   about Trump*

■ *Positive Remarks about
   Trump*

■ *Trump's Tax Returns*

■ *African American
   Community*

■ *Economy Policy*

■ *Crime & Shootings*

■ *Russia & Korea*

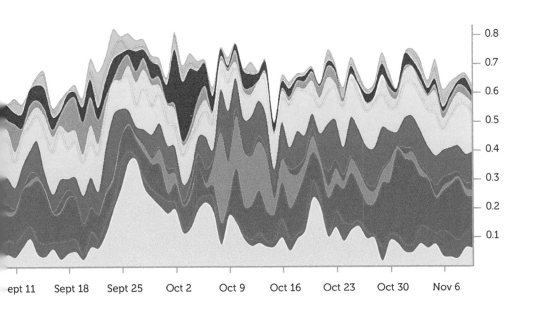

ept 11   Sept 18   Sept 25   Oct 2   Oct 9   Oct 16   Oct 23   Oct 30   Nov 6

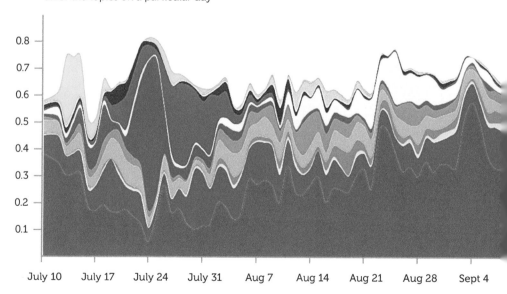

Figure 3-7

What the Public Heard about Clinton (Gallup data)

Proportion or fraction of Gallup responses
associated with each topic and across
all of the topics on a particular day

Clinton Color Legend

- ■ Email Scandal
- ■ Clinton in the Media
- ▒ Debates
- ■ Clinton Health Issues
- ▒ Clinton Dishonesty
- ■ Attacks on Trump
- ■ Vice President
- Clinton Corruption
- ■ Democrats Convention
- ■ Benghazi Scandal
- ▒ Domestic Policies
- ░ Bernie Sanders
- ■ Positive Remarks about Clinton
- ▒ Crime and Shootings
- ░ Terrorism Policy

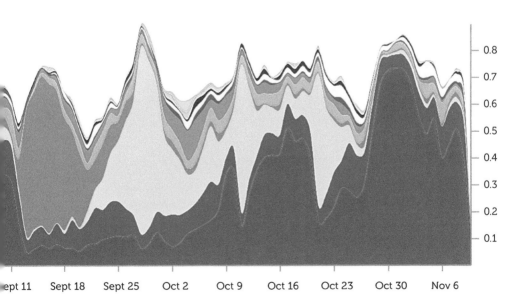

Figure 3-8

What the Public Heard about Trump (Gallup data)

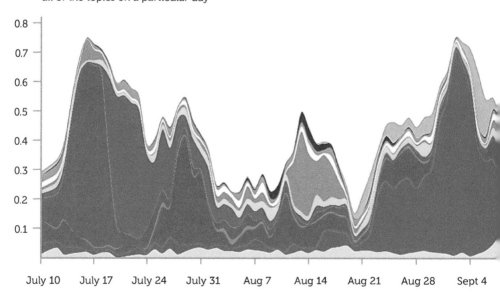

Proportion or fraction of Gallup responses
associated with each topic and across
all of the topics on a particular day

Trump Color Legend

- ■ *Debates*
- ■ *Immigration*
- ▨ *Attacks on Hillary*
- ▨ *Harassment Scandal*
- ■ *Vice President*
- ■ *Republican Convention & GOP*
- ▫ *Trump in Media*
- ▨ *Terrorism Policy*
- *Negative Remarks about Trump*
- ▨ *Positive Remarks about Trump*
- ■ *Trump's Tax Returns*
- ▨ *African American Community*
- ▨ *Economy Policy*
- ▫ *Crime & Shootings*
- ▨ *Russia & Korea*

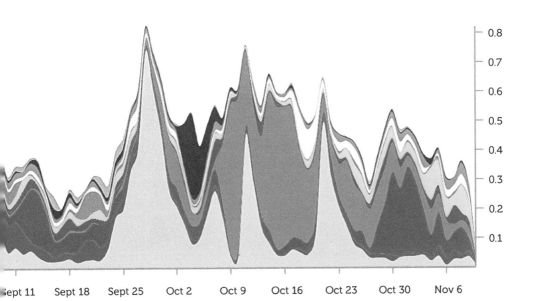

What the Media Covered, Journalists Tweeted, and the
Public Heard about the Candidates during the Campaign

To begin this process, the remainder of this chapter looks in more detail at three of the data streams: the text of journalists' tweets (figures 3-3 and 3-4), newspaper content (figures 3-5 and 3-6), and responses to Gallup open-ended questions (figures 3-7 and 3-8). The newspaper content provides a proxy measure of what traditional media covered. The journalists' tweets allow us to see what political elites were discussing during the campaign. And the Gallup open-ended questions, asking respondents what they have "read, seen, or heard" about each candidate in the past day, provide a measure of what topics got through to the public during the campaign.

These three streams were measured daily throughout the campaign. This allows us to see the relationship between these measures and how they each move over the course of the campaign. We analyze the topics featured in each stream using automated topic modeling, looking for predictable associations of words and labeling the resulting categories.

Journalists' Tweets

The content of journalist tweets about Hillary Clinton throughout the campaign was fairly consistent over time (figure 3-3). In general, the most common topic was "Clinton in the Media"—a generic category capturing day-to-day campaign content about Clinton, including appearances, rallies, speeches, and interviews (the dark blue color seen as a consistent band at the bottom). Similarly, there was persistent discussion of positive remarks about Clinton (light blue), as well as Clinton's attacks on Trump (orange). There were also four predictable spikes corresponding to each of the four debates (September 26, vice presidential debate October 4, October 9, and October 19, seen in yellow). Finally, journalists' tweets responded briefly to Clinton naming Tim Kaine as her running mate (pink, in July), the Democratic National Convention (purple, in July) as well as protests by Sanders supporters at the convention (light green), Clinton's collapse and pneumonia announcement in September (dark green). Note that the email category (dark red on the bottom) did not represent a large portion of journalists' tweet content.

Journalists' tweets about Donald Trump (figure 3-4) shared some characteristics with those about Hillary Clinton but also behaved quite differently. They also responded predictably to Trump naming Mike Pence as his running mate (pink, in July), to the Republican National Convention (purple, in July), and to the four debates (yellow, in September and October). There was fairly consistent coverage of attacks on Clinton throughout (maroon, toward the bottom of the graph). And there were also notable spikes related to major events, including Trump's speech on immigration (August 31, blue), the *New York Times* story on Trump's taxes (October 1, brown), and the release of the Access Hollywood tape (October 7, green).

Newspaper Coverage

We now turn to what topics were covered by the traditional news media. We use newspaper content as a proxy for traditional news media content. These topics are shown in figure 3-5 for Hillary Clinton and figure 3-6 for Donald Trump.

As might be expected, newspaper coverage seems to be even more driven by events than journalists' tweets were. Different topics— naming a running mate, the Democratic National Convention, concerns about corruption, Clinton's health, and the debates, to name a few—tended to "take over" throughout the campaign, as they became most salient. Again, emails (dark red) were not terribly prominent in newspapers throughout most of the campaign, although this topic did spike in response to James Comey's letter about reopening the investigation on October 28.

Newspaper coverage of Trump was similarly very event driven, prominently featuring the Republican National Convention, Trump's immigration speech, the debates, scandals, and the *Access Hollywood* tape. Coverage frequently spikes when he attacks Clinton. It is worth noting that research on television coverage of the election did find a marked, though not dramatic, difference in scandal coverage of Clinton (about 21 percent) as compared to Trump (about 13 percent; Searles and Banda 2019).

What People Read, Saw, or Heard

Finally, we believe that our dataset of what people report having "read, seen, or heard" each day about each candidate, courtesy of the Gallup Daily tracking survey, is crucial to understanding what information in the campaign information environment broke through and was remembered by the mass public. This is shown in figure 3-7 for Hillary Clinton and figure 3-8 for Donald Trump.

These data show not just what content existed, but what topics people encountered, accepted into their mind, and then remembered when asked by a pollster. One of our crucial findings is that *this data stream looks radically different from the two media-related streams described earlier.*

For Hillary Clinton, the topic that resonated with the public throughout the campaign was her emails. The maroon bar at the bottom of the figure rises and falls as other events take over (especially her health issues and the debates), but it's prominent throughout the campaign. It also spiked at the end of the campaign, following Comey's October 28 letter. After that, almost everyone reporting that they read, saw, or heard something about Hillary Clinton were saying *the thing they had heard was related to her emails.*

For Trump, on the other hand, what people had read, seen, or heard appears much more event driven (more similar to the previous two information streams). Topics—immigration, debates, tax, and harassment scandals—often took over the entirety of what people report having read, seen, or heard, but were displaced quickly (for more on this, see chapter 7, on events). This "Teflon" quality of Donald Trump—no scandal seems to persist in the public mind—is something that journalists have pointed to as an unusual aspect of 2016 (Boydstun and Van Aelst

2018; see also Sides, Tesler, and Vavreck 2018, 135–144).[5] Indeed, there was no underlying topic that voters returned to in the way that they gravitated to Clinton's emails.

Conclusions

This chapter introduces the five major datasets that are used in this book: newspaper coverage, a random sample of tweets from all users, journalist tweets, our Gallup "read, seen, or heard" survey questions, and our three related datasets tracking fake news on Twitter. These data streams provide an overview of the campaign information environment throughout late summer and fall of 2016. The chapter briefly summarizes the topics that were salient throughout the campaign for journalists, in newspaper coverage, and for the public. We think it is useful to see how these streams differ—how they respond to events, and how they mirror (or don't mirror) one another. While there are clear connections between events, media coverage, and what the public reports having read, seen, or heard, there is a substantial disconnect as well.

Several patterns stand out, which we interrogate further in future chapters. First, there is much more variation over time during the campaign in the topics people report hearing about than in the topics appearing in newspapers or that journalists are discussing on Twitter. Second, in general, when an event leads to a spike in the public's attention to a topic, it is short-lived. With the exception of Clinton's email scandal, after a campaign event induces people to start hearing about a campaign topic, mentions of that topic quickly dissipate. Yet people reported hearing about Clinton's emails even when there was no event to draw attention to them and newspapers were not really covering them much. This implies that Clinton's email scandal was unusually memorable to ordinary people, that there was a meaningful alternative information flow not captured here that consistently drew attention to the email story, or some combination of both. The remainder of the book dives deeper into these different flows of campaign information.

The August 2015 Republican Debate

A Study of Information Flow in the 2015–2016 Republican Nomination Contest

Information flow in a political campaign varies by the stage of the campaign and can be a function of broad themes supported by various news media or the coverage of specific events. Identifying the sources and patterns in these trends, however, can be difficult in the cacophony of a typical campaign environment. Hence we start exploring key questions of information flow not by focusing on the many competing claims of the general election but instead by examining how these general processes worked at a time when the messages available to ordinary citizens could be more easily isolated. To this end, this chapter focuses on how messages from a single primary debate in August 2015 percolated through the various data streams we examine.

The Republican primary debate on August 6, 2015, serves as the key focal point for this chapter for a variety of reasons. At this point in the campaign, more than a year before Election Day and almost six months preceding the Iowa caucuses, there was little general public attention to the election. Seventeen candidates were attempting to get their messages to resonate in the media and break through to public awareness. And the lack of other campaign events around the time ensured that the debate and subsequent coverage of the debate were the primary vehicles through which candidates' messages could influence the public. It was also the first occasion we could assemble data from a variety of sources—a transcript of an event, journalists' Twitter-based discussion of the event as well as press coverage of it, and survey responses after the event containing information about the visibility of the candidates and the information that survey respondents recalled about them.

The analysis reported in this chapter served as a pilot study for the larger project we pursued during the general election campaign using many of these same data sources. Then we had longitudinal information about press coverage, public Twitter reactions to the campaign and the candidates, and a representative sample of public reactions to the candidates and events of the campaign. This provided a perspective on the ebb and flow of responses to broad themes in the campaign as well as to specific events. It also enabled us to reconceptualize information flows beyond previous measures of attention to and reliance on specific media for political news and information.

This chapter looks at public perceptions of a large field of Republican candidates seeking their party's nomination to oppose Hillary Clinton, the presumptive frontrunner for the Democratic Party nomination. We compare the topics covered in the debate to those in the subsequent news coverage, and we focus on the substance of the coverage compared to its emphasis on the dynamics of the performances and the relative allocation to the candidates involved. We do this through the lens of journalists' tweets and the characteristics of the network that connected them at the time. Then we look at whether the event had any impact on assessments of the candidates shortly thereafter. This debate was Donald Trump's first appearance among other more experienced Republican candidates, and for many citizens their first exposure to him as a candidate. This case study provides insights into how Trump would be covered and evaluated in the general election campaign.

The Role of Debates in a Presidential Campaign

Debates play an important role, especially early in the campaign cycle, as candidates strive to develop a positive image, especially in a crowded field. Such an image is composed of two parts: a combination of name recognition and high levels of candidate favorability. Name recognition has important direct and indirect effects on developing candidate momentum (Kam and Zechmeister 2013) as knowledge of a candidate's name can increase support as well as improve perceptions of a candidate's viability. At the same time, if a candidate's name becomes linked to particular issue positions that members of the public weigh heavily in distinguishing their choice among multiple candidates, that is a benefit as well. From the perspective of electoral politics, having high name recognition associated with a positive image linked to issues that are important to the voters is a formula for success at the ballot box. Bartels (1988) argues that mere exposure can increase familiarity, while candidates and their campaign managers distinguish between name mentions that appear in the news (earned media) from those that they can produce by advertising (paid media). In the primary campaign, debates help partisans determine their preferred choice for the nomination, and in the general election they can affect the eventual vote choice for president.

Though televised debates in general elections are ubiquitous around the world now, they began in the United States in the 1960 campaign between John F. Kennedy and Richard Nixon; but they did not become a regular feature of presidential contests until 1976. Because Kennedy's narrow victory was related in part to his strong performance on television, in comparison to Nixon's poorer showing, there were no subsequent televised presidential debates until 1976 because Lyndon Johnson (1964) did not feel television was his medium, and Richard Nixon (1968 and 1972) did not get over his poor performance in the original encounter (Kraus 1979; Greene 2012).

The Democratic Party's McGovern–Fraser Commission, in its 1972 report, proposed revisions to the presidential nominating process that resulted in our current system of mandatory participation in primaries and caucuses in order to assemble binding delegate votes at the convention. The 1976 election—the first to be run under the new system in both parties—was an unusual kind of open contest involving two relatively unknown candidates who each wanted all the media coverage they could get. Gerald Ford was an appointed vice president who had ascended to the office upon Nixon's resignation after Watergate. He had never run a national campaign at the top of the ballot. Jimmy Carter was a former southern state governor with little national exposure. The initial debates were organized by representatives of the Democratic and Republican parties along with the League of Women Voters. In 1987, the establishment of the Commission on Presidential Debates regularized presidential and vice presidential debates in the general election campaign with the cooperation of the national broadcast networks.

Primary debates between candidates contesting for their party's presidential nomination started in 1968, but they were less well organized because the national parties were not involved in arranging them until the 1980s. The national parties have limited influence over the state parties, the calendar of the primaries and caucuses, or the rules and regulations that govern candidate eligibility and citizen voting. Furthermore, the state parties began to negotiate arrangements with news organizations—principally network television—for the organization of and access to debates. The courts have recognized debates as public events but the parties as private organizations. The parties have always had significant discretion to establish eligibility criteria for participation, but their arrangements with television stations and networks gave certain weight to production considerations, of particular relevance to the number of participants appearing on stage.

In a bid to foster the appearance of transparency, the debate organizers established an external eligibility criterion of standing in a selected set of public polls. For the 1980 presidential debates, the floor was an average of 15 percent support, which was met by Republican congressman-turned-Independent candidate John Anderson. When Jimmy Carter refused to appear with him, Anderson appeared on the stage alongside Ronald Reagan. By the second and final debate, Anderson's support had fallen below that level, and Carter went head-to-head with Reagan. By the end of that campaign, the use of poll standing to determine eligibility was established, although the level of support and the particular polls used varied from election to election and sometimes from event to event.

The 2016 Cycle Primary Debates

Although presidential debates have been around for a long time, researchers have never had the data and computing resources available to understand how news coverage of them is developed and how the public absorbs information about them. At the very start of the campaign for the Republican Party's nomination, we had access to unparalleled resources to investigate this process. They consisted of the first debate transcript—the actual questions asked and responses offered. From a list of political journalists' Twitter accounts, we had information they exchanged with their followers about what they observed and thus how they were going to frame the subsequent coverage. We had examples of the coverage produced by those journalists. And we also had the messages people tweeted about the debate itself and the subsequent media coverage. All of this information was accessible and amenable to modern computer science software for natural language processing, sentiment and topic analysis, and an inspection of the networked relationships among journalists. These combined resources allow us to map the way that debate content was translated into news and how citizens processed that information, based on exposure to the news, social circles, and interactions on social media.

In the elections from 1972 to 2004, one party nominated either its incumbent president or vice president, so there was serious competition for the presidential nomination in only one party. But 2008 was an open contest on both sides, and the number of candidates seeking the nomination in each party was large. In 2016, there was again an open contest in each party since Joseph Biden decided not to seek the Democratic nomination. The Democratic field was relatively small because of Hillary Clinton's frontrunner status, but the Republican field was quite large.

In the run-up to the 2016 presidential election, the fields of candidates from each party were crowded. On the Democratic side, Hillary Clinton was assumed to be the frontrunner, and she had planned to announce formally in summer 2015. However, she was prompted by the activities of another candidate to get in early, and she formally announced her candidacy on April 12 through a YouTube video. This opponent, who would prove to be her most formidable challenger for the nomination, was Senator Bernie Sanders from Vermont. The Republican field was much more crowded. By the time of its first televised debate on August 6, 2015, the field had become so large that television production values limited the number of candidates that the sponsoring news organizations would allow on the stage. Fox News sponsored the first debate, as well as half of the twelve events endorsed by the Republican National Committee. As in the past, they proposed to use the "objective" criterion of a candidate's standing in the national polls as a ticket to the main debate stage. Those faring worse in the polls were allowed to participate in a less viewed debate earlier in the evening among the weaker Republican candidates.[1] Therefore, it was important for candidates in such a large field to enter the race as soon as possible, in order to raise enough money and obtain enough endorsements to begin advertising to build name recognition. If they could do this, their standing in the polls would presumably increase as a result.

Table 4-1 provides the declaration date of each of the seventeen formally declared candidates for the Republican presidential nomination and the date when they suspended their campaign or withdrew from the contest. Most of the candidates (fourteen) were in by the end of June 2015, whereas the last three entered in July. Ted Cruz, the senator from Texas, was the first to declare, on March 23, closely followed by Rand Paul and Marco Rubio. Donald Trump did not declare until June 16.

Five of the candidates (Perry, Jindal, Walker, Graham, and Pataki)

Table 4-1

Declaration of Candidacy and Withdrawal or Suspension of Campaign Dates for Republican Candidates in the 2016 Presidential Campaign

Candidate	Declaration Date	Withdrawal/ Suspension Date
Ted Cruz	March 23, 2015	May 3, 2016
Rand Paul	April 7, 2015	February 3, 2016
Marco Rubio	April 13, 2015	March 15, 2016
Ben Carson	May 4, 2015	March 4, 2016
Carly Fiorina	May 4, 2015	March 10, 2016
Mike Huckabee	May 5, 2015	February 1, 2016
Rick Santorum	May 27, 2015	March 3, 2016
George Pataki	May 28, 2015	December 29, 2015
Lindsey Graham	June 1, 2015	December 21, 2015
Rick Perry	June 4, 2015	September 11, 2015
Jeb Bush	June 15, 2015	February 20, 2016
Donald Trump	June 16, 2015	**NOMINEE**
Bobby Jindal	June 24, 2015	November 17, 2015
Chris Christie	June 30, 2015	February 10, 2016
Scott Walker	July 13, 2015	September 21, 2015
John Kasich	July 21, 2015	May 4, 2016
Jim Gilmore	July 30, 2015	February 12, 2016

could not sustain their campaigns through the end of the year and dropped out before any votes were cast. When the primaries and caucuses started on February 1, the winnowing process intensified (Aldrich 1980; Orren and Polsby 1987). Candidates not winning many votes or delegates saw their funding dry up and their press coverage dwindle and turn more negative. By the end of February five more had dropped out (Bush, Paul, Huckabee, Christie, and Gilmore). Four more were out by the end of March (Carson, Fiorina, Santorum, and Rubio). Trump essentially clinched the nomination when he won the Indiana primary on May 3 and his main rivals—Cruz and Kasich—dropped out over the next two days.

In the 2016 cycle, the Republican Party scheduled twelve debates across an extended period that started in August 2015 and ran on until March 2016, down from the twenty they scheduled in 2012.[2] Their purpose was to introduce the candidates to the public and especially to those who potentially would vote in Republican primaries and caucuses. The locations were geographically dispersed across the country and generally in Republican-leaning territory. Even when one was held in the Democratic stronghold of California in September 2015, the site was the Reagan Library in Simi Valley with a retired *Air Force One* airplane providing the backdrop.

Candidate Visibility Prior to the Debate

Gallup collected data on the name recognition and favorability of each of the candidates during the summer of 2015.[3] Information is presented in table 4-2 that gives the recognition levels and favorability scores for the Republican candidates among all Americans based on data collected between June 22 and August 4. Just before the first Republican debate, Gallup found that 95 percent of adults were familiar with the name of Donald Trump, while Jeb Bush had the second-highest familiarity among this group at 87 percent. At the bottom of this distribution were Jim Gilmore (38 percent), Carly Fiorina (39 percent), John Kasich (43 percent), and Ben Carson (45 percent).

Gallup also computed a net favorability score for each candidate, calculated by subtracting the percent unfavorable from the percent favorable. Among *all adults*, only six Republicans had a positive net favorability score, but the values were very low. The highest value was for Ben Carson (+12), followed by Marco Rubio (+5). The most recognized candidate, Donald Trump, had a net favorability score of –22. Among *Republicans* in summer 2015, the candidates' net favorability scores ranged from a high of +38 for Marco Rubio and Scott Walker to a low of

Table 4-2

Recognition Levels and Favorability Data for the Republican Candidates among All Adults in Summer 2015 Prior to the First Republican Debate

Candidate	Percent Favorable	Percent Unfavorable	Net Favorability	No Opinion	Heard About, Other
Jeb Bush	35	39	−4	13	13
Donald Trump	33	55	−22	7	5
Mike Huckabee	29	31	−2	14	26
Marco Rubio	29	24	+5	14	33
Rand Paul	28	28	0	13	30
Rick Perry	28	32	−4	14	33
Chris Christie	27	37	−10	12	23
Ted Cruz	26	31	−5	13	31
Ben Carson	24	12	+12	9	55
Scott Walker	23	20	+3	12	45
Rick Santorum	22	29	−7	16	33
Bobby Jindal	20	19	+1	11	50
George Pataki	18	20	−2	19	43
Lindsey Graham	18	27	−9	14	41
Carly Fiorina	16	13	+3	10	61
John Kasich	16	13	+3	14	57
Jim Gilmore	6	19	−13	13	62

−9 for George Pataki. Donald Trump ranked 11th out of 17, with a net favorability of +15 percentage points. By comparison, Hillary Clinton was recognizable to 99 percent of the adult population, but her net favorability score was 0. The only other Democratic candidate familiar to a majority of adults was Bernie Sanders, and at this point in the campaign his net favorability score was +1.

The Gallup Survey Experiment

At the end of August, Gallup tested a new form of data collection about the presidential candidates that they subsequently would use extensively in the general election campaign. In the week from August 24 to August 30, they interviewed a random sample of about 500 adult Americans each night, for a total of 3,556 interviews. For each of the seventeen Republican candidates and five Democratic candidates, they asked two questions:

1. Have you read, seen, or heard anything about Candidate X in the last day or two?

2. (IF YES) What was that?

The interviewers recorded verbatim the responses to this open-ended question. This question is not a measure of name recognition per se, because the names are provided, but rather, an indicator of retained information about a candidate that might have been gleaned from exposure to recent news, social media content, or conversations with friends or family members, for example. Sometimes respondents provided little information, whereas other respondents provided quite a bit in their responses. The Gallup interviewers recorded up to three distinct statements (or "mentions") that respondents made in response to this question about each candidate.

The statements by each respondent about a candidate can be categorized in two ways: by topic and by valence or sentiment—the context in which a respondent remembered something about a candidate, and the effect of the retained information that can be coded as positive, negative, or neutral. As shown in table 4-3, about one-fifth of the survey respondents had heard something about Donald Trump, about the same level as had heard something about Clinton (21 percent). One in six had heard something about Jeb Bush. Levels of information about Chris Christie, Marco Rubio, Rand Paul, Ted Cruz, Mike Huckabee, Ben Carson, Rick Perry, Scott Walker, and Carly Fiorina were slightly lower, with Bobby Jindal, Lindsey Graham, Rick Santorum, John Kasich, George Pataki, and Jim Gilmore following. Fiorina did not make the cut for the main event, and she and those below her in recognition appeared in the less-watched second-tier debate.

For comparison, the situation was much different in the last week of the 2016 general election campaign. Of the 3,552 respondents inter-

Table 4-3

Percent Recalling Something about the Republican Candidates, August 24–30, 2015*

Donald Trump	20%
Jeb Bush	16%
Chris Christie	13%
Marco Rubio	11%
Rand Paul	10%
Ted Cruz	10%
Mike Huckabee	10%
Ben Carson	10%
Rick Perry	9%
Scott Walker	9%
Carly Fiorina	8%
Bobby Jindal	7%
Lindsey Graham	7%
Rick Santorum	7%
John Kasich	6%
George Pataki	4%
Jim Gilmore	2%

*The denominator here is the total number of interviews conducted (N = 3,556).

viewed in that final week, 83 percent could report on something they had read, seen, or heard about Donald Trump in the previous couple of days, while 78 percent could do the same for Hillary Clinton.[4]

The First Republican Debate

As noted in chapter 2, controversies over email were a consistent source of negative news stories for Hillary Clinton. However, the Republican candidates never focused on that during their first debate. Table 4-4 shows the topics of the questions asked of each candidate. The number of questions asked of each candidate ranged from four to eight, with Chris Christie and Ted Cruz getting the fewest and Donald Trump getting seven. The topics ranged from domestic to foreign policy, including direct questions to some candidates about their fundraising success and electability. A highlight of the debate was a request from the moderator for an indication that each candidate would support whomever won the nomination. In the first of many news-making gambits, Donald Trump was the only candidate on stage refusing to make such a pledge (Schwartz 2015).

During the debate itself, the most frequent question topics were immigration (six references), Iran, the economy, and references to God (five references each). There were only two references to email. A question from Fox News's Bret Baier to Senator Ted Cruz mentioned the hacking of the chairman of the Joint Chiefs of Staff's email. Governor Scott Walker made a reference to "Hillary Clinton's email server" late in the debate when he answered a question about how he would react to any attempts by Vladimir Putin to destabilize new NATO members in Eastern Europe. There were no questions about Hillary Clinton's server or emails during the debate. It was not a campaign issue in either primary contest, even though the Office of the Inspector General of the Department of State had reported in June and July that it was likely there were some classified exchanges in her emails.

There was also some attention to Trump's treatment of women. Megyn Kelly, a moderator from Fox News, opened the debate by asking

Table 4-4

The Number and Focus of Each Candidate's Questions in the First Republican Debate

Donald Trump (7 questions)

Pledge, women, illegal immigration, Obamacare, political donations, entitlement reform, abortion, name calling, Iran

Ben Carson (6 questions)

Electability, waterboarding, size of government, taxes, respond to Clinton, Syria, God, race relations

Marco Rubio (6 questions)

Preparation, illegal immigration, Common Core, growth of the economy, abortion, God, veterans

Jeb Bush (6 questions)

Political dynasties, illegal immigration, invade Iraq, Common Core, economy, name calling

Ted Cruz (5 questions)

Electability, illegal immigration/amnesty, ISIS, Iran deal, hacking, God

Chris Christie (4 questions)

Financial management, opposition to Paul's security concerns, entitlement reform, military strength

Scott Walker (8 questions)

Abortion, immigration reform, partners in the Middle East, economy and job growth, Iran deal, policing NATO, word from God

Mike Huckabee (5 questions)

Electability, size of government, entitlement reform, Iran deal, transgenders in military

Rand Paul (5 questions)

ISIS, rebuttal to Christie, Iran deal, gay marriage, foreign borrowing

John Kasich (5 questions)

MEDICAID, government expansion, illegal immigration, respond to Clinton, gay marriage, God

Donald Trump a question about his attitudes and behavior toward women, pointing out that he had referred to women as "fat pigs, dogs, slobs, and disgusting animals." Beyond the answer he gave to that question, Trump reacted further by attacking Kelly for days afterward in interviews—including the infamous line to CNN that "there was blood coming out of her eyes, blood coming out of her . . . wherever"—and on Twitter (an illustrative tweet from January 27—demonstrating the persistence of Trump's attacks against Kelly—reads, "I refuse to call Megyn Kelly a bimbo, because that would not be politically correct. Instead I will only call her a lightweight reporter!"). Some of this exchange seemed particularly misogynistic, and the follow-up became newsworthy in itself.

Next, we reviewed the candidates' responses in the debate transcript using the Linguistic Inquiry and Word Count (LIWC) program. In its simplest form, after the removal of common words and linking terms, we counted the total number of words spoken by each candidate, a rough measure of how equally the time was allocated to them by the debate moderators and whether or not they extended their allotted time when answering questions. Given that there were 10 candidates on the stage, each candidate could be expected to have used 10 percent of the total words spoken. Rand Paul spoke less than expected (7.0 percent), while Donald Trump spoke considerably more (14.9 percent). Across all the candidates, Rand Paul and Ben Carson had the lowest proportion of all the topical speech, while Donald Trump (13.2 percent) and Jeb Bush (12.1 percent) had the highest.

The Interactions of Journalists in and around the Debate

This analysis focuses on the social network of the journalists and the topics they were tweeting about during the Republican debate. This provides one indicator of the topics journalists mentioned live during the debate, before any reporting or analysis had been done. Scholars have a growing interest in how digital journalism impacts the way journalists and political commentators cover political events and produce news content. This research has looked at the social networks that journalists form on Twitter, how that is related to their own ideology, and the slant of the content they produce (Wihbey et al. 2017), as well as the content of their tweets, as an indicator of their use of such networks to share information, push their own stories, or focus on their perceptions of campaign dynamics (Lawrence et al. 2014). Underlying a lot of this work is the degree to which such electronic networks of interaction have replaced the pack journalism associated with past campaigns, which Crouse (1973) identified in his book *The Boys on the Bus*.

We assembled a list of 1,249 Twitter handles of journalists and commentators who cover politics in order to look at their Twitter behavior around the time of the Republican debate to see how well they were connected as a social network of people who followed each other and to get further insight into what topics from this debate spread through the media to the public (see appendix A for more details). These political journalists, bloggers, and commentators share a common set of topical interests, even if they do not all have the same political perspective, so it is not surprising that they form a fairly cohesive network. In this network, there were more than 75,000 edges linking the individuals. The diameter of the network was 5, indicating that the flow of information was rapid. The clustering coefficient for the network was 0.44, indicating a high degree of association among groups of journalists. For a more detailed explanation of the network metrics used, see appendix A.

During the month of August, the number of tweets they produced ranged from 2 to 4,305. Two conservative-leaning commentators—@RadioFreeTom (Tom Nichols) and @redsteeze (Stephen Miller)—were by far the most frequent tweeters, with 4,305 and 4,159 tweets, respectively. Two political journalists lagged them by a wide margin—Ron Fournier (@ron_fournier) with 2,247 tweets in that month, followed by *Commentary* magazine editor John Podhoretz (@jpodhoretz) with 1,825. Our primary focus is on those who tweeted on August 6, and that list is shorter—only 945 accounts whose activity ranged from 1 to 154 tweets. Again, the list was topped by @redsteeze, followed closely by @jpodhoretz, with @ron_fournier in fourth place. There were 521 individuals from this list who produced fewer than 10 tweets on that day and another 216 who sent between 10 and 20, leaving 196 who produced between 21 and 129.

In the 24-hour period that began at the 9 p.m. Eastern Time (ET) start of the debate, there were 802 journalists and commentators who tweeted, 54 percent of the total set we identified. As an active subset of the larger network, the characteristics of their network are very similar to those for the full set of journalists. The density of the network was slightly higher (0.097 compared to 0.074) as was the clustering coefficient (0.47). The group produced 40,423 tweets in total, of which 5,320 were sent by the end of the debate at midnight ET. Of those, 825 contained the word *debate* or one of the participating candidates' names. The eleven high-visibility journalists who had at least 100,000 followers are television or social media talent. A majority represent the right, not unexpected since the event was a Republican debate; but both sides of the political spectrum were represented, along with straight news reporters.

The tweets were analyzed for the most frequent words they contained also after deleting filler text or stop words. Few of them contained references to any of the main topics candidates were asked about during the debate, as shown in table 4-4, indicated by limited references to abortion (11 tweets), Iran or Medicaid (10 tweets each), pledge (7 tweets), women (6 tweets), and ISIS, gay marriage, and taxes (5 tweets each).

Press Coverage of the Debate

The August 6 debate, the first time that Donald Trump appeared on the stage with the other GOP candidates, had the largest audience ever for a televised primary debate (Stelter 2015). Understanding how this debate was covered in national and local news can help us see how patterns of how Trump would be covered began to form. We examined news coverage of the debate by retrieving relevant content from a variety of newspapers. These content analyses were drawn from the three days leading up to and including the debate and for three days after-ward.[5] We had two measures of the national news stream coverage of the debate: content in national newspapers like the *New York Times*, the *Washington Post*, and *USA Today*, as well as in a geographically dis-tributed set of sixteen other papers from major metropolitan areas. The most obvious results of the content analysis shown in table 4-5 is that Donald Trump received a disproportionate amount of coverage in the national news stream as well as in the regional press.[6] He received about one-fifth of all of the candidate name mentions and at least 50 percent more than the group of four next most frequently mentioned—Jeb Bush, John Kasich, Ted Cruz, and Marco Rubio. Also, as expected, most of the candidates received more coverage in their local media than they did in the national news stream (Darr 2018; Milita and Ryan 2018).

A number of presidential election scholars (Fallows 1997; Patterson 1993, 2016b) have lamented the neglect of coverage of issues in favor of personalities and the dynamics of campaigning. The 2016 campaign was no different in this regard (Patterson 2016a, 2016b). We were inter-ested in whether these trends were present in the very earliest stages of the 2016 presidential campaign, when reporters were getting used to covering Donald Trump and his very unconventional approach to poli-tics. Table 4-6 presents the most frequently mentioned debate-related topics in the week leading up to the debate (August 1–6) and for the three news cycles after it (August 7–9) in these same news sources. The vast majority of coverage was about the candidates themselves and their performance in the debate, including how that affected their chances of success in pursuit of the nomination. Donald Trump received the most coverage in the *New York Times* and the *Washington Post*, and Clin-ton and Obama also received a high level of mentions as the coverage turned to possible matchups in the general election against any Repub-lican nominee. The most frequently mentioned topic in the immediate postdebate coverage was Donald Trump's refusal to take the pledge the candidates were asked about, indicating they would support whomever the eventual Republican nominee would be. Discussions of women and Trump's reaction to Megyn Kelly were also highlighted. Matters of per-

Table 4-5

Candidate Name Mentions in the Press following the Debate

| Candidate | National Media | | | | Local Media |
	Los Angeles Times (%)	Washington Post (%)	USA Today (%)	New York Times (%)	Local Paper (%)
Donald Trump	23.7	20.3	20.8	21.2	21.2
Jeb Bush	14.6	13.6	12.6	14.1	5.3
John Kasich	13.2	12.3	11.5	12.2	11.5
Ted Cruz	12.1	12.3	11.9	12.5	16.2
Marco Rubio	10.5	11.4	12.3	12.5	18.3
Ben Carson	6.5	7.5	9.5	7.0	–
Chris Christie	5.6	6.8	7.9	6.6	10.3
Rand Paul	5.9	6.4	6.1	6.5	11.5
Scott Walker	4.0	5.0	4.1	3.8	15.7
Mike Huckabee	3.9	4.5	3.4	3.7	1.0

sonal style outweighed the coverage of specific issues that were raised and discussed during the moderators' questioning, a pattern that has consistently been observed in presidential campaign coverage (Patterson 2016b).

Finally, we add a third information stream: what people reported hearing from the news in open-ended poll questions. This allows us to see which topics broke through into the public consciousness. In Gallup's interviews in the last week of August 2015, two weeks after the Republican debate, 11 percent of the respondents who had "read, seen, or heard" anything about Clinton in the previous few days (21 percent of all respondents) mentioned "emails" or the "server" as the most frequently mentioned topic. This was undoubtedly due to a crimi-

Table 4-6

Topic Mentions in Republican Debate Coverage, Before and After the Event in Two Representations of the National News Stream

	New York Times and *Washington Post**			Regional Sample[†]		
	Before	After	Increase	Before	After	Increase
Trump	313	521	66%	574	690	20%
Clinton	89	124	39%	126	139	10%
Women/Woman	23	123	434%	59	132	81%
Fiorina	9	119	1,322%	73	118	62%
Megyn Kelly	9	77	756%	19	125	558%
Rubio	44	71	39%	126	139	10%
Obama	157	47	–70%	101	75	–39%
Polls/pollsters	134	80	–39%	348	141	–68%

*Based on articles retrieved from the *New York Times* and the *Washington Post* in the period from August 1 to 6 (before the debate) and August 7 to 9 (after the debate).

†Based on articles retrieved from sixteen regional newspapers in the period from August 1 to 6 (before the debate) and August 7 to 9 (after the debate). The individual papers are listed in the appendix.

nal referral from two inspectors general to the Department of Justice for a review of her use of a private email server as reported in national media (Schmidt 2015). For Donald Trump, on the other hand, no topic similarly dominated. The most frequently mentioned topic people had "read, seen, or heard" about Trump was "immigration," offered by only 4 percent of the respondents. An equivalent proportion of respondents mentioned that he was "running" or "a candidate." Only 1 percent made a reference to the first debate. For most respondents, then, there appears to have been little retained information about even the most recognizable of the candidates at this early stage of the campaign, not surprising given the limited effort and resources that they were devoting to campaigning and the fact that news coverage contained little information about their issue positions.

Conclusions

Although this book is primarily about the general election, not the primary season, our data collection on all three major information streams around the time of the very first Republican primary debate provides some important lessons. For one, the analyses illustrate the potential values of combining survey data with textual analysis of social media information and content analysis of news media for understanding the flow of information during a presidential campaign. When there is a national contest with highly visible candidates, there is a unique opportunity to learn about how important events and the news coverage of them penetrate the public consciousness. It also highlights the potential for understanding the interplay between elite observations and commentary about candidates and political events and public attention to them.

At the same time, the results of these analyses raise many interesting subjects for future research. The Republican debate in August 2015, although watched by many journalists and political professionals, and with larger than unusual primary debate ratings, had only a fraction of the audience for the first debate between Donald Trump and Hillary Clinton in late September 2016 during the height of that campaign. With its 80.9 million viewers, the largest ever for a political debate, the general election debate audience was more than three times the size of the audience for this first Republican primary debate (24 million viewers). Was the level of journalists' Twitter behavior in the general election debate coverage the same? And were their social networks even larger—with more followers and more frequent exchanges? Obviously, the public's recognition of Hillary Clinton and Donald Trump was greater by then, but it did not seem to become more favorable because of extensive campaigning and news coverage. After the campaign, we learned about the intervention of foreign governments and other creators of "fake news" sites who promoted their content primarily through social media. What was their impact on voters leading up to Election Day? These are all topics covered in subsequent chapters of this book.

Yet so many of the information flow patterns observed even this early on foreshadow what we observe in the general election campaign. First, we see Trump's ability to dominate news coverage, sucking up the news oxygen that might have allowed other candidates to get their message out or at least build name recognition (see also Sides, Tesler, and Vavreck 2013, 47–60). The persistence of this pattern into the fall campaign would lead to negative stories about him, and the Clinton campaign's attacks would last only a short time because the press was eager to move on to coverage of the next Trump story, good or bad.

Second, we see in the polling data the first evidence of the salience and persistence of the Clinton email story in the public mind. Even though the main recent story related to the presidential campaign was the Republican debate, in which Clinton and her emails were barely mentioned, respondents still reported hearing about them. Similarly, through the zigs and zags of the fall campaign, whatever the latest biggest news story was, people would report hearing about Clinton's email problems. It was a stream of thinking among the public that Clinton could not interrupt.

The Language and Tone of
the 2016 Campaign

The 2016 campaign appears to have been one of the most negative presidential campaigns in recent history. Consider some of the major themes of the campaign: bold anti-immigrant claims from Donald Trump, concerns about Trump's past treatment of women, and ongoing attacks related to the content of emails from Hillary Clinton and the DNC. This chapter traces the impact of these and other campaign themes, first by looking at the most-recalled stories during the campaign, and then by focusing on the "tone" or "sentiment" of the campaign.

Using automated content analyses, this chapter explores the language and the tone of coverage for both candidates across several of the datasets that form the backbone of the book: a daily random sample of campaign-related tweets, tweets from journalists about each candidate, a sample of news coverage from nine major U.S. dailies, and Gallup's open-ended responses to the "read, seen, or heard" question about each candidate. The chapter also adds one further database to the analyses: a sample of media stories from the 2012 campaign, built in the same way as the 2016 database. The 2012 data will be important to our exploration of whether 2016 was indeed more negative than a campaign in the recent past. Before turning to those results, however, we review the importance of sentiment in the analysis of campaign communication and introduce our automated content-analytic measure of sentiment.

Language and Tone in the 2016 Campaign

One need not look far to find arguments about the apparently high level of scandal and negativity in the 2016 campaign. Consider the fact that there are almost no events mentioned in chapter 2 that are clearly positive, perhaps with the exception of debate results, at least where Clinton is concerned. Every other major event is deeply negative for either Clinton or Trump. There is little doubt that the major moments of the campaign were about scandal associated with one candidate or the other.

It is not surprising, then, that early interpretations of the election highlighted scandal and negativity. Even at the outset of the campaign, commentators warned of increasing negativity (Blake 2016). A mid-campaign story asked, "Has a presidential campaign ever been as negative as this one?" (Kamarck 2016). The close of the campaign saw arguments that negative ads dominated the end of the campaign (Wallace 2016) and that media coverage had overall been deeply negative throughout the campaign, at least if not more so than in the recent past, and markedly more so than before the mid-1980s (Patterson 2016). In a comparison of negativity in debates, Bayagich et al. (2016) too find that the 2016 debates exhibited more negativity than had been seen since 1984.

Tracking negativity is often associated with critiques of negativity—so note at the outset that this is not the purpose of the current chapter. Negativity may reduce engagement with politics, but it may also increase it (Soroka 2014); whether increasing negative sentiment is actually bad for politics and representation is unclear. That said, there is a rich literature exploring the magnitude and impact of negativity, sometimes focused on election ads in particular, sometimes focused on campaign communication more generally (e.g., Kaid and Johnston 1991; Ansolabehere and Iyengar 1997; Cappella and Jamieson 1997; Freedman and Goldstein 1999; Kahn and Kenney 1999; Lau et al. 1999; Geer 2008). And regardless of whether negativity is likely to increase or suppress turnout, or change attitudes and votes, tone is a central, defining element of political campaigns. Focusing on the tone of a campaign gives us some general sense for what political discussion is like at a given time, it helps characterize the nature of the campaign on a day-to-day basis, and it has also been predictive of aggregate-level election outcomes (e.g., Soroka et al. 2009). For these reasons, it is worth focusing on the tone of Clinton and Trump coverage in 2016. As we shall see, doing so highlights some pivotal moments in the campaign. Comparing the tone of coverage in 2016 and 2012 also helps put the recent campaign in context. And comparing the tone of coverage to the tone of Twitter content and Gallup open-ended responses offers a powerful demonstration of the tendency for negative information about the candidates to circulate more widely and be remembered more easily (or more durably).

Exploring the Language of Campaign Communication

Before turning to analyses of tone, however, let us first take a more qualitative look at the language of the campaign. One advantage of the Twitter and open-ended survey responses on which our analyses are based is that they afford a detailed view of the language that reporters and the public used to talk about the campaign. We needn't jump immediately to methods that aggregate words into topics or dimensions, such as subject codes or sentiment analysis. We can look directly at the words themselves. As we shall see, doing so serves to highlight the prevalence of negative, scandal-focused information during the 2016 campaign.

Figure 5-1 offers a first illustration. The figure shows two word clouds. Each includes the top 100 words in tweets about either Clinton (blue) or Trump (red) over the course of the campaign. We apply some simple prewhitening to the tweets, removing the names of candidates, punctuation, and plurals, and a set of standard stop words (e.g., *the*, *and*, etc.). Otherwise, the text is exactly as it appeared on Twitter. The size of words in figure 5-1 reflects the frequency with which words appear in the corpus. And in this case, our corpus includes all tweets about the candidates over the campaign, based on a daily random sample of campaign-related tweets.

Results in figure 5-1 make a few facts very clear. First, the conversations surrounding Clinton and Trump campaigns were fundamentally different, not just in substance but in consistency. Tweets about Hillary Clinton focus predominantly on email-related scandals. Consider most of the most frequent words, including *email*, *foundation*, *Wikileaks*, and *FBI*—each of these words signals ongoing debates about Hillary Clinton's email. Tweets about Donald Trump, in contrast, produce a less coherent picture. Words such as *liar* and *racist* make the top-100, as do words such as *Russia* and *women*, both of which signal scandals surrounding the Trump campaign. But the most frequent words in tweets about Trump are general political ones, such as *president*, *vote*, *campaign*, and *policy*. These rise to the top in part because, unlike Clinton, the Trump campaign was not faced with a single storyline. To the extent that scandal followed Trump in 2016, it was a series of different scandals (see chapter 7).

What do results look like when we focus on Gallup open-ended responses to the "read, seen, or heard" questions about Clinton and Trump? Figure 5-2 presents similar word clouds, this time based on the open-ended responses. The full-text data here are subjected to the same prewhitening as the Twitter data. The corpus for figure 5-2 includes all available open-ended responses, over the entire campaign.

The language used in these open-ended responses is much narrower than on Twitter. Note that tweets can be about anything related to the candidates; but Gallup responses are focused on the "read, seen, or heard" question. As a result, figure 5-2 presents a somewhat clearer pic-

Figure 5-1

Most Frequent Words in Twitter Content About Candidates over the 2016 Campaign

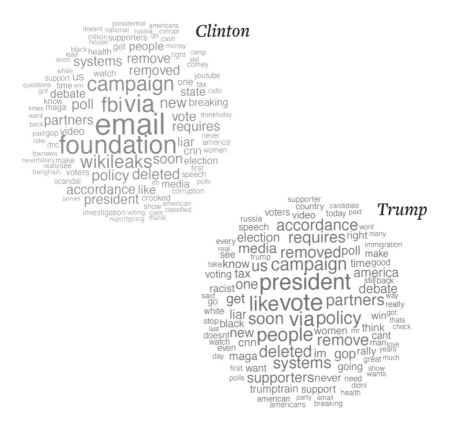

ture of the two campaigns. Recalled content about Clinton was mostly about *email*, to the point where the word overwhelms all other content. Even as other information was swirling about during the campaign, email scandals were the single most enduring component of recalled information about Clinton. Recalled content about Trump was more variable, reflecting a variety of subjects over the course of the campaign. This was already evident in the right panel of figure 5-1, but figure 5-2 illustrates the series of separate scandals a little more clearly.

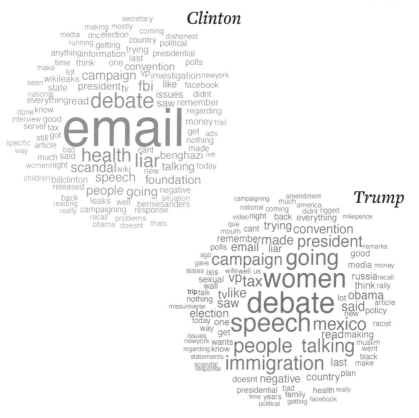

Figure 5-2

Most Frequent Words in Recalled News About Candidates over the 2016 Campaign

Note that results in figures 5-1 and 5-2 fit nicely with Clinton's (2017) own argument about the difficulties she faced in the campaign. Indeed, the word clouds appearing in her book are based entirely on our campaign-period analysis of these data. In those early word clouds, and in the data presented here, it is clear that Clinton faced a much more durable scandal than Trump, who may well have benefitted from changing the scandal facing his campaign on a near-weekly basis.

That said, and somewhat contrary to Clinton's (2017) claim, it does not appear to be the case that the tone of Clinton's coverage was markedly worse than the tone of Trump's coverage. The language surrounding *both* campaigns is quite clearly focused on scandal. The extent to which this is reflected in the tone of coverage generally is the subject of the sections that follow.

Capturing the Tone of Campaign Communication

We examine the tone of the campaign in newspaper content, and then in both Twitter and open-ended survey responses. The tone of the campaign communication is captured here using the Lexicoder Sentiment Dictionary (LSD). This is just one of many dictionaries designed for automated sentiment analysis; it is discussed and tested in some detail in Young and Soroka (2012). Suffice it to say here that the dictionary includes roughly 4,567 entries of positive and negative words. By way of example, negative words include *abandon*, *cheat*, *harm*, *reckless*, and *tainted*, and positive words include *assure*, *dependable*, *honest*, and *resourceful*. The reliability of the word lists is improved through a combination of prewhitening (to remove instances in which otherwise positive/negative words should not be counted), and subtracting out negations (to remove *not happy* from counts of *happy*, for instance). Full details on the design and implementation of the LSD are available in Young and Soroka (2012), and available via lexicoder.com.

The objective here is not to capture the tone of entire articles, however. Rather, the goal is to capture the tone of words associated with either Clinton or Trump. We do so using a hierarchical dictionary count (or proximity count), where we count the positive and negative words that co-occur in sentences that mention either Clinton or Trump. This measure of tone is thus closely (literally speaking) associated with one candidate or the other. This approach is in line with past work that relies on a hierarchical dictionary count to capture the tone of coverage for candidates and parties (see, e.g., Soroka et al. 2009; Belanger and Soroka 2012). The only way in which our measure differs from this past work is that we rely on a slightly different approach to measuring "net tone," that is, the overall tone of candidate coverage based on the difference in positive versus negative words co-occurring with each candidate name. Here, we use a measure suggested in Lowe et al. (2011) and used in Proksch et al. (2019), as follows: log [(pos counts + 0.05) / (neg counts + 0.05)], which is an empirical logit, slightly smoothed toward zero.[1]

Applying this measure to all news stories in our database and then taking the daily average for each of Clinton and Trump produces a time series of mass-mediated candidate-level tone for the duration of the campaign. We add to this a second database, perfectly parallel to the 2016 database, but built for Obama and Romney during the 2012 campaign to provide a point of comparison. We thus have directly comparable measures of candidate-level tone, across four candidates in nine newspapers, and across two presidential elections. Twitter and Gallup data provide another comparison. For Twitter, we rely on exactly the same approach: counts of positive and negative words, co-occurring with either candidate's name, based on daily aggregations of tweets. Where Gallup data are concerned, we needn't use a hierarchical dictionary count—we already have one response for Trump and another for Clinton. But we can apply the LSD in exactly the same way to these open-ended responses. Calculating the number of positive and negative words uttered in relation to each candidate on a daily basis produces a unique, parallel series: the tone of citizens' recalled news about Clinton and Trump.

Note that these time-series data are to our knowledge entirely unique in their parallel measurement of the tone of (1) newspaper coverage, (2) social media content, and (3) what people remember about the candidates. We try to leverage this unique body of data in the next sections, both to explore negativity in 2016 campaign news and to examine differences in the tone of information that is mediated, and recalled, by citizens. First, however, we set the stage using data from 2012.

Candidate Tone in News, Twitter, and
Respondent Recollections

Figure 5-3 shows smoothed (three-day average, centered) daily tone for Romney and Obama from September to November 2012. Recall that the scale of the y-axis is a bit opaque: it is the logged tone measure described earlier. We should also not make too much of the zero line, which is the neutral point mathematically but not necessarily the neutral point for readers. It is unclear whether readers see a single positive or negative word and immediately consider the story positive or negative. Indeed, Young and Soroka (2012) find that the mean LSD-estimated tone for news stories that readers evaluate as being neutral is a little above zero. It follows that there may be some band around (or above) zero that is the neutral point where readers are concerned. That said, variation over time is very clear in the figure and readily interpretable. When the line is going up, there are more positive words, and/or fewer negative words, co-occurring in the same sentences as the candidates' names.

Figure 5-3 offers some useful tests of concurrent validity for the tone measure. Given what we know about the debates, for instance, we expect Obama coverage to benefit from the first and third debates, and suffer from coverage of the second debate. This is exactly what we see here. Obama's coverage is also on balance more positive than Romney's over the course of the campaign, and particularly leading up to Election Day.

How do 2012 results compare with 2016? Figure 5-4 shows the same measures for Clinton and Trump from September to November 2016. Variation over time is somewhat muted for Trump, but the average is clear: whereas lines in 2012 were consistently above zero, the line for Trump is, with only a few exceptions, consistently below zero. Even at the end of the campaign, as it becomes clear that Trump is polling well in the Midwest, there are only a few days when the tone of coverage is on balance over zero.

Results for Clinton are just as illuminating. Clinton's mean is also below the means for Romney and Obama in 2012. Clinton coverage is

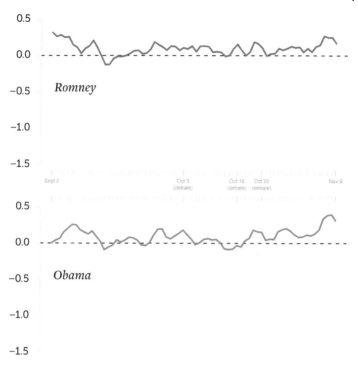

Figure 5-3

Net Sentiment for Candidates in Newspapers over the 2012 Campaign

Note: Net Sentiment is based on the Lexicoder Sentiment Dictionary, applied to all sentences mentioning Obama or Romney in articles in 9 newspapers.

especially negative in the period surrounding the third debate. It trends steadily upward in late October, but it takes a dive at the time of the Comey letter. Even so, Clinton coverage climbs back to its pre–Comey letter level by November 9. On balance, the last week of the campaign looks better for Clinton than it does for Trump. This is true for newspaper content, at least.

What about social media content? Figure 5-5 shows trends in the same tone variables, this time calculated using Twitter content. We cannot easily compare these results to 2012, since that Twitter content

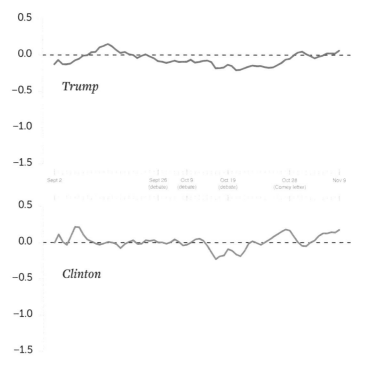

Figure 5-4

Net Sentiment for Candidates in Newspapers over the 2016 Campaign

Note: Net Sentiment is based on the Lexicoder Sentiment Dictionary, applied to all sentences mentioning Clinton or Trump in articles in 9 newspapers.

is no longer available. But in comparison with 2016 newspaper content, Twitter is remarkably negative. There is no point at which daily net tone on Twitter is positive for either candidate. The changes over time seen in Clinton's newspaper coverage are roughly similar in Twitter, though the variability is greater, and the average is lower. There was little variation over time in newspaper coverage for Trump, but there is in figure 5-5. We can see drops in tone at predictable times, including the release of the *Access Hollywood* tape, and comments about immigrants. We can also see an uptick in tone leading up to Election Day—and, moreover,

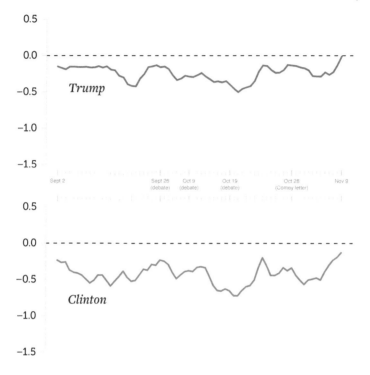

Figure 5-5

Net Sentiment for Candidates in Twitter over the 2016 Campaign

Note: Net Sentiment is based on the Lexicoder Sentiment Dictionary, applied to a random sample of 5,000 Tweets per day mentioning Clinton or Trump.

more positive end-of-campaign Twitter content for Trump than for Clinton.

Recalled information responses (figure 5-6) were the most variable over time and the most negative in net tone. Despite brief moments when Gallup respondents have marginally positive recollections about Trump or Clinton, the bulk of the campaign is characterized by markedly negative informational recall. Trump recollections are impressively low in the third week of October. Our suspicion is that these reflect both contemporaneous and current events and an accumulation of neg-

Figure 5-6

Net Sentiment for Candidates in Gallup "Read, Seen, or Heard" Responses over the 2016 Campaign

Note: Net Sentiment is based on the Lexicoder Sentiment Dictionary, applied to open-ended responses to Gallup's Read, Seen or Heard question.

ative information about Trump since the middle of September. Clinton coverage reflects, we suspect, the same kind of accumulated negative coverage, but in this case across a lengthy political career. There is a period surrounding the first two debates when Clinton recollections are better, but the late October values for Clinton reflect a return to her predebate equilibrium. Put differently: even as Clinton began the campaign with relatively positive newspaper coverage, recalled information about Clinton was predominantly negative. The last week of October sees less negative tone, perhaps (pushed downward briefly by the Comey affair); but even as Clinton is finishing the campaign with a daily average tone that is higher than it was in early September, it is still the case that negative words outnumber positive ones by a factor of roughly 2 to 1.

Discussion

What do we make of results in figures 5-1–5-6? Word clouds make very clear the prevalence of scandal during the 2016 campaign. Analyses of tone also suggest that the coverage of both Clinton and Trump was more negative in 2016 than the coverage of either Obama or Romney in 2012. In comparison to the preceding election, newspaper coverage of the 2016 campaign was, as many have suggested, decidedly negative.

Perhaps more importantly, the magnitude of negativity appears to increase as we move from newspaper content to Twitter to respondent recollections. Why might this be the case? One possibility is that both Twitter and recollections are essentially summaries of news content— they contain only the most critical elements of campaign-period media coverage, and sentiment-laden words are one such element. The end result is that a good deal of content that is not sentiment laden falls away as we move from newspaper coverage to Twitter to respondent recollections.

Another possibility is that both social media and recollections re- flect the information that people pay most attention to, and/or remem- ber the most. This account would fit nicely with work (reviewed earlier) suggesting that humans tend to be more attentive to negative informa- tion than to positive information. In this account, news coverage may include both positive and negative information, but the negative infor- mation is more easily recalled and has a larger impact on readers; the result is that recalled information about candidates will tend to be more negative than the original news coverage.

We cannot easily adjudicate between these two possibilities here, of course. And we probably needn't—both likely contribute to the dif- ferences we see in figures 5-3–5-6. In any campaign, then, we expect that recalled information will be more negative than the original news stories. And in a campaign in which media coverage is already decidedly negative, the sentiment of recalled information will be even more so.

We suspect that these are the generalizable findings from these analyses, but this work highlights some important features of the 2016 campaign as well. First and foremost is the fact that even as Clinton may have started September with relatively positive media coverage, the information that citizens recalled about her was predominantly negative. This may have been the first hint that the campaign would not be an easy Democratic win. Even if Trump was regarded by many as ill equipped to be president, Clinton started the campaign not with a surplus but with a deficit where the tone of recalled information is concerned. Citizens could already cite reasons to be reluctant about Hillary Clinton. The Gallup data in figure 5-4 make this abundantly clear; and subsequent chapters will probe more closely the themes driving this dynamic. (Hint: it's email.)

It is also not clear whether the Comey revelations toward the end of the campaign were deeply damaging to the Clinton campaign. All our time series—newspapers, Twitter, and recalled information—show the same basic dynamic: a Clinton recovery in the third week of October that is reversed, but only temporarily, by the Comey letter. By the time the campaign ends, the tone of Clinton coverage is slightly higher than it was before the Comey letter. And indeed, the Gallup series suggests that the tone of Clinton recollections started to decline *before*, not after, the Comey letter. Of course, we cannot know what the campaign might have looked like without the Comey intervention. But the evidence here is not obviously in line with an account suggesting that Comey played a critical role in the election outcome.

What is perhaps most remarkable about the Trump series is that it is not more negative. It seemed that the campaign was one negative event after another for Trump, and although the data point to a declining tone for Trump from roughly September 20 to October 20, the decline is rather muted in media coverage, barely evident in Twitter content, and entirely reversed by October 25. There is little support here for the idea that Trump scandals accumulated over the campaign, at least where tone is concerned. While the Clinton series appears to be the result of long-term accumulated baggage from continuous Republican attacks dating back to her role in Bill Clinton's White House, the same is not true for Trump. Of course, the ongoing strength of the Clinton email story may lie in its having been repeated, over and over, during the campaign.

The Things People Heard about Trump and Clinton

with Andrew Dugan

This chapter focuses on the ways in which information about the two major party presidential candidates percolated into the consciousness of the average American during the general election campaign. Gallup conducted a rolling cross-sectional survey involving almost 60,000 interviews with average Americans, spread across the crucial last months of the presidential campaign from July to November. These data, described in chapter 2, provide us with an unparalleled insight into not only the level of attention the public was giving to each candidate but also what it was about the candidates that Americans were most easily able to recall on a daily basis.

How much attention did Americans pay to the campaign as it unfolded? This chapter seeks to answer this question, using the Gallup data. In our Gallup data, there was no direct measurement of media exposure or attention to the campaign per se. Rather, we collected responses to a more general measure of whether a respondent had read, seen, or heard anything about each of the candidates "in the last day or two," an indirect measure of reception of campaign-related information. This question measured information obtained from direct media exposure and also the indirect effects that might come from discussions with friends and family members, people at work, or others with whom they might have interacted. Gallup also did not measure the candidate preferences of these respondents in the standard way of asking for whom they intended to vote. Instead the survey measured favorability toward each candidate on a daily basis, permitting the calculation of relative candidate favorability between Clinton and Trump over time.

The question is interesting to answer because past literature suggests that the effect of the media on political interest and hence political participation is one of the most important things to understand about democracy. Since most Americans are not interested in politics most of the time, campaigns are an important source of information for citizens. The candidates' activities and the press coverage of them can serve as stimuli to voting. In recent decades, news sources have proliferated, especially on the Internet, and social media provide another opportunity for citizens to learn about candidates and issues and to discuss them with their friends or through social networks. At the same time, researchers have debated whether media exposure depresses political interest (Robinson 1976; Cappella and Jamieson 1997) or increases it (Norris 2000; Holtz-Bacha and Norris 2001). Strömbäck and Shehata (2010) demonstrated with panel data that there are reciprocal causal effects between media exposure and attention and interest in politics. Of course, there are differences between campaigns in terms of the interest they might engender, and citizens' reactions to the candidates might vary as well. Shaw (1999) found a relationship between campaign events, subsequent news coverage on television and in newspapers, and changes in a candidate's share of the two-party vote in the 1992 and 1996 presidential campaigns.

In the 2016 campaign, Americans were faced with a contest between two of the least liked general election candidates at the stage of becoming presumptive nominees since at least 1980 (Enten 2016). Clinton was about 5 percentage points more likely to have a "strongly unfavorable" view among the public than any prior Democratic candidate, while Trump's unfavorable rating was about 20 points higher than any prior candidate with the exception of Clinton. The candidates were in the same position, relatively speaking, with regard to their net favorability rating (Enten 2016). Just before the conventions, the Pew Research Center (2016) suggested that there were more Republicans who were likely to vote against Clinton in relation to voting for Trump than for McCain and against Obama in 2012. And among Democrats, there were even larger differences between those voting against Trump and for Clinton than equivalent groups voting for Obama and against McCain.[1]

The relationship between relative candidate favorability ratings of the two candidates (henceforth, candidate favorability) and candidate preference or vote choice is of key interest to this chapter. To date, there has been little research in this area due to a primary focus on other factors like party identification, issue preferences and placement of the candidates on those issues, and factors that affect a person's propensity to vote at all. Anderson and Kibler (1978) investigated the multidimensional structure of candidate images and its relationship to candidate preference in a U.S. Senate race. They identified eight dimensions of evaluation, of which attitude homophily (shared positions) was the strongest, followed by assessments of competence. Warner and Banwart (2016) did something similar in a study of the 2012 presidential election and selected 2014 midterm elections for the U.S. Senate. They found that candidate evaluations tend to group into six factors, the most important two being homophily (i.e., the "understanding of a candidate's values and concerns" (Banwart and Warner 2016)) and assessments of character.

On the other hand, some research suggests that candidate preferences get projected onto candidate evaluations (Bartels 1985, 2002; Delavande and Manski 2012). One possible puzzle of 2016 is that turnout was at historically normal levels despite the candidates being so personally unpopular, and the popular vote outcome was about as close as the national pre-election polls suggested. This implies that many citizens voted for a candidate about whom they had reservations or they voted for a third-party alternative.

Attention to the Campaign as Measured on a Daily Basis

Respondents in the daily Gallup sample were asked to what degree they were following the 2016 presidential election. The results show that nearly eight-in-ten (77 percent) Americans interviewed during the general election months of the 2016 campaign said they were following news about the election "very" or "somewhat" closely. Those having "read, seen, or heard" anything about the two candidates provide another measure of attention to the campaign. This proportion is in line with past presidential elections dating back to 2000. Over the last four months of the 2016 campaign, 78 percent of Americans on average said they had read, seen, or heard something about Donald Trump in the last day or two while 75 percent said the same for Hillary Clinton.

Looking at these items on a more granular level, figure 6-1 displays the day-by-day percentage of Americans who reported having read, seen, or heard something about Clinton or about Trump in the few days prior to the interview, based on the Gallup sample of approximately 500 randomly selected adult respondents each day. The overall mean attention score for the two candidates was 77 percent. The highest level came on September 27, when the average value for Clinton and Trump combined was 90 percent. This was the day after the first presidential debate, held at Hofstra University on Long Island, moderated by NBC's Lester Holt, an event that received the highest viewership of any televised presidential debate ever. The lowest level of attention paid to the two candidates between July and Election Day was 65 percent—coming on July 10, in the "lull before the storm" period prior to the opening of the Republican convention on July 18.

As indicated by these high and low days, the day-by-day awareness of information about the two candidates varied according to what was happening on the campaign front. Attention surged during the two po-

Figure 6-1

Visibility Rating of Donald Trump and Hillary Clinton (July 5 to November 8, 2016)

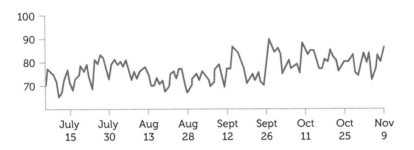

litical conventions, during the fall debates, as a result of major campaign events (such as Hillary Clinton becoming ill during a September 11 remembrance rally in New York City), and as Election Day neared.

Recall of Specific Information about Trump and about Clinton

We now turn to the differences in attention paid to the two major party candidates, as shown in figure 6-2. The naïve conclusion of outside observers might be that Trump dominated the popular consciousness during the campaign because of his unconventional, norm-breaking comments and highly attention-getting self-presentation. But the results showed that Clinton remained almost as much in the public's consciousness during most of the campaign as did Trump. The average recall of having read, seen, or heard something about the two candidates is similar—with Trump having a slight edge over the course of the tracking project: 78 percent overall average for Trump and 76 percent for Clinton.

It is clear that the attention garnered by each candidate varied over the campaign and that Trump generally was more visible than Clinton through much of the campaign. Beyond this, there were several spe-

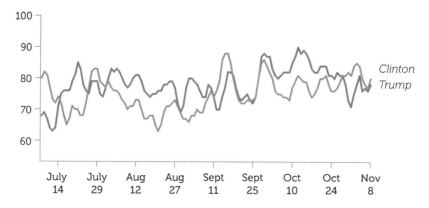

Figure 6-2

Average Three-Day Moving Visibility Ratings of Donald Trump and Hillary Clinton (July 7 to November 8, 2016)

cific periods when the candidate whom people heard the most about switched. First, Trump began with a visibility deficit in early July. During this period FBI Director James Comey announced he was recommending against prosecution of Clinton over her handling of emails while secretary of state. Then Trump gained a clear advantage in attention during the Republican convention, July 18–21, but Clinton regained the attention lead during the Democratic convention, July 25–28.

After the conventions and their immediate aftermath were over, people noticed more news about Trump unless there was a specific event that redirected attention toward Clinton. Trump regained the attention lead during most of August and into early September. Clinton jumped back into the visibility lead after her highly publicized near collapse at a September 11 memorial service, and the subsequent announcement that she had pneumonia. Yet Trump resumed getting higher levels of attention in mid-September and generally held that position, or at the least was tied with Clinton, throughout the period of time in which there were three presidential debates and one vice presidential debate. Clinton regained the lead in attention again only when the Comey letters were released.

What Was Read, Seen, or Heard about the Candidates?

Overall, after the conventions, Trump got more attention in the public consciousness except for during the height of a few big news stories about Clinton. But unfortunately for Clinton, these big stories were mostly bad news for her except for her surge and temporary tie in attention during the debates. What Americans self-reported reading, seeing, or hearing about the two candidates on a daily basis is extraordinarily important information. Presidential campaigns are almost always viewed through the filter of journalistic reportage—that is, based on content analysis of what the media (news outlets and social media) report. In the 2016 campaign, there were more sources of information than ever before, most notably through social media. This undoubtedly stimulated discussion among friends and family. But it has been previously very difficult to analyze what, out of all the streams of information available about a presidential campaign, has actually filtered down into the consciousness of the average American.

Our first conclusion from the analysis of Americans' recollections of what they read, saw, or heard about Hillary Clinton is the extraordinary degree to which they were focused on "emails." The information displayed in figures 3-1 through 3-7 in chapter 3 illustrates the centrality of this issue in the campaign. The data presented in figure 6-3 show the stability of this issue over time during the campaign. In 13 out of the 18 weeks covered in the project, emails were either the first or second most frequently occurring substantive word in response to the question about what respondents had read, seen, or heard about Clinton. Mentions of having read, seen, or heard something to do with the FBI and Clinton were in the second-place slot for the last weeks in November.

The exceptions to the email dominance in the public mind came (1) in the middle of July when Americans' recall about Clinton was focused on her naming of Virginia senator Tim Kaine as her running mate and the Democratic convention generally, (2) three weeks in September when recall was focused on Clinton's near collapse from pneumonia at a September 11 remembrance service, and (3) with the beginning of the presidential debates.

It is important to note that "emails" appeared as a dominant Clinton motif well before the active campaign beginning in July 2016. As mentioned in chapter 4, Gallup's August 2015 poll, when the nominations campaigns were just getting underway, showed that emails were already a factor in Americans' minds when asked what they had read, seen, or heard about Clinton. We summarized the respondents' mentions of topics across each week of the campaign in a sample of about 3,500 interviews each period and then ordered them by their frequency. In figure 6-3, the five most frequently mentioned topics are shown in order, with the relative size of the font indicating the relative frequency of mention of the topic within the week.

At the same time, the recollections of things about Trump were more varied and less consistent across the campaign, reactive to what was happening at that point in the campaign. There was much less of a cognitively dominant motif in perceptions of Trump than there was in perceptions of Clinton. Americans' recollection of what they had read, seen, or heard about Trump moved from initial recall of convention-related topics—including his selection of Mike Pence as his vice presidential candidate and the convention itself—to his criticism of a Gold Star Muslim family that spoke during the Democratic Convention, his trip to Mexico and discussion of immigration, the debates, and to coverage of the infamous *Access Hollywood* tape. Americans often recalled Trump's criticisms of Hillary Clinton, just as Americans often recalled Clinton's attacks on Trump.

The lack of a dominant theme in recall about Trump in part reflects the lack of a conventionally remembered catchphrase or summary term that encapsulated his campaign—in contrast to the easily remembered "email" so readily associated with Clinton. There were so many dramatic stories about Trump during the campaign that didn't fit into one narrative. People's attention moved from one Trump story to the next, and the next. This shifting pattern over time is illustrated in the weekly information displayed in figure 6-4, employing the same representation

Figure 6-3

Most Reported Topics Read, Seen, or Heard
about Hillary Clinton, by Week

as above. A separate analysis by gender shows that the topic of women following the release of the *Access Hollywood* tape was much more salient among female respondents.

What Survey Respondents Read, Saw,
or Heard by Partisanship

The way in which Americans perceived the two major candidates from July 2016 to Election Day was strongly influenced by their partisan orientation. Republicans reported reading, seeing, or hearing substantially different things about the candidates than did Democrats. In line with expectations, each group of partisans tended to recall negative aspects of the opposing candidate and his or her campaign, while recalling

Figure 6-4

Most Reported Topics Read, Seen, or Heard about Donald Trump, by Week

more positive, substantive, and issue-oriented aspects of the candidate from their own party.

With these events in mind, we looked at how Americans of different political stripes followed news about the campaign. As reviewed in chapter 3, Americans regularly talked about email when asked what they recently read, saw, or heard about Hillary Clinton during the campaign. This was true for Americans of all political backgrounds. In each of the final ten weeks of the campaign, the word *email* was the most common or second most common substantive word used by Republicans, Democrats, and Independents to describe information they received about Hillary Clinton. For both Republicans and Independents, *email* failed to be the first or second most commonly used word in answering this question in only one of ten weeks examined, as shown in table 6-1. For

Democrats, *email* was the first or second most frequently used substantive word in all but one two-week period in September.

What other things did people hear about Hillary Clinton besides email? In the week of September 12–18, the word *email* became considerably less salient among all parties, but only because respondents were now discussing Clinton's apparently poor health.

In other instances, such as the week of September 26–October 2, *email* was, for Americans of all political stripes, edged out by another word, *debate*. This was, on the whole, good for Clinton, given perceptions that she had outperformed her opponent in the debate (Gallup found that Clinton was perceived to have won the first debate by the largest margin in polling history.) The other two debates were also frequently mentioned by respondents, though not to the same extent as the first debate.

And in the campaign's closing stretch—October 24 onward—the subject of email again dominated, especially after FBI Director James Comey's letter to Congress on October 29, seeming to relaunch the investigation of Clinton's use of a private email server when she was secretary of state. All political groups—Republicans, Democrats, and Independents—discussed Clinton's email, almost entirely to the exclusion of any other topic. As the campaign came to a close, this was the issue many Americans, regardless of political group, thought of first when thinking about Clinton. From August 2015 and throughout the general election campaign, Americans of all backgrounds consistently reported hearing about Clinton's various problems with email. Her only reprieve was when major good news, like winning the debates, temporarily drowned it out.

While Democrats and Independents were certainly not blind to Clinton's problems involving email, the issue did not resonate as intensely with them as among Republicans, at least as measured by the "read, seen, or heard" questions. Between the period spanning September 5 to November 8, 2016, Republicans used the word *email* about 2.5 times more often than the next most commonly used substantive word (*debate*) when discussing what they recently read, saw, or heard about

Table 6-1

Most Frequently Used Topics when Recalling What They Recently Read, Saw, or Heard about Hillary Clinton during the 2016 Campaign, by Party (Sept. 5–Nov. 8, 2016)

Week of	GOP (word 1)	GOP (word 2)	Independent (word 1)	Independent (word 2)	Democrat (word 1)	Democrat (word 2)
Sept. 5–11	Email	Lie	Email	Scandal	Email	Scandal
Sept. 12–18	Health	Pneumonia	Health	Pneumonia	Pneumonia	Health
Sept. 19–25	Health	Email	Debate	Health	Debate	New York/bombing
Sept. 26–Oct. 2	Debate	Email	Debate	Email	Debate/Saw debate	Email
Oct. 3–9	Email	Debate	Email	Debate	Debate	Email
Oct. 10–16	Email	Debate	Email	Debate	Debate	Email
Oct. 17–23	Email	Debate	Email	Debate	Debate	Email
Oct. 24–30	Email	FBI	Email	FBI	Email	FBI
Oct. 31–Nov. 6	Email	FBI	Email	FBI	Email	FBI
Nov. 7–8 (election week)	Email	FBI	Email	FBI	Email	FBI

Hillary Clinton. Republicans used the word *email* 50 percent more often than Democrats did, and 18 percent more than Independents.

Yet the email issue was not the only perceived Clinton wrongdoing brought up by Republicans during this period. Republicans were deeply distrustful of Clinton, as illustrated by the fact that only an average 6 percent of Republicans said they had a favorable image of her during the fall campaign. They commonly used the words *scandal* or *lie* when talking about her; these words together were used by Republicans more frequently than any single word other than email.

Republicans often referenced Clinton-related scandals that Independents or Democrats were unlikely to bring up, such as allegations of financial misdeeds related to the Clinton Foundation and speculation regarding the events that led to the killing of an American ambassador and three other Americans in Benghazi, Libya, while Clinton was secretary of state.

Unlike the case for Clinton, there was no dominant topic brought up by Americans when discussing what they recently read, saw, or heard about Donald Trump (table 6-2). This is true for Republicans, Democrats, and Independents alike. Instead, the public's focus changed quickly in response to new events.

In the first week examined here (September 5–11), Americans continued to discuss Donald Trump's trip to Mexico on August 31 and his speech in Arizona on immigration later that night, which was widely perceived as hardline. The words *Mexico* and *immigration* were used the most and second most frequently by all groups.

In the next week, Trump raised public questions about his opponent's health after Clinton's collapse at a 9/11 memorial service, and this was brought up frequently by Republicans and Independents. Democrats discussed this somewhat less than those two groups. Additionally, Trump's public acceptance that President Barack Obama was born in the United States (previously contested by Trump) was discussed by respondents, most especially Democrats. From there, partisan responses diverge, and so it is probably more useful to look at each group in turn. But before doing so, we start with three general observations.

Table 6-2

Most Frequently Used Topics when Recalling What They Recently Read, Saw, or Heard about Donald Trump during the 2016 Campaign by Party (Sept. 5–Nov. 8, 2016)

Week of	GOP (word 1)	GOP (word 2)	Independent (word 1)	Independent (word 2)	Democrat (word 1)	Democrat (word 2)
Sept. 5–11	Mexico	Immigration	Mexico	Immigration	Mexico	Immigration
Sept. 12–18	Health (Clinton)	Obama	Health (Clinton)	Obama	Obama	Health (Clinton)
Sept. 19–25	Debate	NY/bombing attack	Debate	New York	Debate	Obama
Sept. 26–Oct. 2	Debate	Miss Universe	Debate	Tax	Debate	Tax
Oct. 3–9	Tax	Woman/women	Woman/women	Tax	Woman/women	Tax
Oct. 10–16	Woman/women	Debate	Woman/women	Debate	Woman/women	Debate
Oct. 17–23	Debate	Woman/women	Debate	Woman/women	Woman/women	Election
Oct. 24–30	Woman/women	Speech/rally/campaign	Woman/women	Email	Woman/women	Email
Oct. 31–Nov. 6	Rally/speech	Email	Email	Campaign/rally/speech	Email	Rally/campaign
Nov. 7–8 (election week)	Rally/campaign	Election	Campaign/speech	Election	Election	Campaign/rally

First, the word used most frequently by all Americans when discussing what they read, saw, or heard about Trump was *debate*. But this may be simply because there was no one specific Trump-related topic for Americans to discuss on a regular basis, leaving the debate to dominate public recall once the debates began in September. Comparing the raw frequency of mentions over this time period, Americans, but especially Democrats, were more likely to discuss Clinton's debate performance when talking about what they recently saw about her than talk about Trump's debate performance when talking about what they recently saw about him.

Second, Americans often mentioned Trump's campaign rallies in some way (in the final two days of the campaign, all partisan groups mentioned these rallies either most frequently or second most frequently). By contrast, respondents of all partisan orientations seldom mentioned rallies or campaign appearances by Clinton. Some respondents might say something about seeing a Trump rally on television, or mention if their city or town recently held or was soon hosting a rally. Some even mentioned attending a rally recently themselves. Trump's rallies attracted attention because of Trump's deliberately provocative comments and allegations, and in the process created interest and buzz among some Americans.

Third, it is not that Trump did not have his own set of issues hanging over his head in the way that Clinton's email problems hung over hers. His refusal to release his tax returns, his treatment of women, and other issues were known, or became known, over the course of the campaign. But no single issue was able to consistently dominate Americans' consciousness on a long-term basis. Even the release of the *Access Hollywood* videotape near the end of October was soon crowded out in terms of the topics or words Americans reported hearing about Trump.

From September 5 to November 8, the most frequently used single substantive word by Democrats when discussing what they had heard about Donald Trump was *woman*. The vast majority of these mentions occurred when the *Access Hollywood* tape was discussed. Uses of the word *woman* (or *women*) shot up by 150 percent among Democrats the week that the recording was released. However, frequent mentions of *woman* initially shot up following the first debate, when Trump spoke in negative terms about a Miss Universe contestant. Democrats were about twice as likely as Independents or Republicans to discuss this topic when answering what they had recently heard about Trump.

The *Access Hollywood* tape commanded Democrats' attention more than it did those with other political affiliations. For instance, the words *sexual* and *assault* were used by Democrats about 30 percent more often than by Independents and about 280 percent more often than by Republicans.

Independents, meanwhile, used the word *debate* most frequently over this time period, though the word *woman* was used almost as frequently. The third most frequently used word was *tax* or *taxes*, in reference to Trump's unreleased tax returns and his boast in one of the debates that not paying taxes would be a sign of his intelligence. Independents actually discussed taxes in relation to Trump about as frequently as Democrats, despite the general tendency for partisans of opposing parties to be those most prone to discuss a candidate's weak points.

Independents also discussed watching Trump's campaign rallies or speeches about as frequently as they brought up his taxes, and the word *campaign* was the sixth most frequent substantive word used by Independents when stating what they recently saw about Trump.

Republicans discussed a smaller range of familiar topics over this time period than either Independents or Democrats. Like Independents, the word *debate* was the most frequently used word by Republicans over this time period, with *woman* coming in second. In frequency, Republicans mentioned the latter term less often than the other political affiliations. Beyond this, Republicans used words that very often indicated they were speaking about a Trump campaign event, such as *speech*, *go see*, and *campaign*. It is clear that different partisan groups were often focusing on very different aspects of the Trump campaign in the final ten weeks, debates and other high-profile events notwithstanding.

Interestingly, in the last week of the campaign this divide narrowed. At that point, what Americans read, saw, or heard about Trump aligned across all three partisan groups, with *email* becoming the most or second most frequently used word for Republicans, Democrats, and Independents when talking about Trump, on top of the fact that these partisan groups mentioned email most often when talking about Clinton. The email issue dominated Americans' thinking about both candidates when they headed to the ballot boxes.

The ongoing tracking surveys conducted by Gallup during the course of the 2016 general election campaign included questions where respondents rated Clinton and Trump on a favorable/unfavorable scale. This enables us to look at the degree to which changes in this measure of affect toward the candidates was, or was not, related to what Americans reported reading, seeing, or hearing about each.

The 2016 presidential campaign provided numerous potential reasons why Americans might reevaluate their opinions about one or both of the candidates. Both battled damaging public revelations in the last weeks of the campaign—Trump with the *Access Hollywood* recording, which echoed long-standing questions about his treatment of women, and Clinton with the release of James Comey's letters to Congress on October 28 and November 6, reminding voters yet again of the email scandals that had been on the public's mind all year, along with many other smaller news stories along the way. All of these were in addition to the normal presidential campaign milestones that generate a lot of media coverage—the conventions and debates.

Despite all of these potential news stories that could have broken into the public's consciousness, opinions about the candidates remained remarkably stable. At the onset of the 2016 presidential campaign, Hillary Clinton and Donald Trump were already well known to the American public, even if he was new to presidential politics. In July 2015, 89 percent of Americans were familiar enough with Clinton to express an opinion about her, and 88 percent were familiar enough to express an opinion about Trump. By the beginning of June 2016, when they were both presumptive nominees, 95 percent of Americans were familiar with Clinton and with Trump. From July 5 onward, the three-day average favorable ratings of both Hillary Clinton and Donald Trump stayed within a tight range of 7 percentage points of each other, with Clinton's favorability rating varying between 38 percent and 44 percent and Trump's between 30 percent and 37 percent.[2]

Familiarity, of course, doesn't mean a person's opinion is immutable. As one example, prior to the campaign, despite her near universal name recognition, Americans' views of Hillary Clinton became significantly more negative, as she transitioned from her tenure as secretary of state to an overtly political role as presidential candidate. The conventions affected the candidates' popular images, with both increasing their own favorable rating during their party's convention as shown in figure 6-5. Additionally, Clinton's favorable rating took a brief nosedive in November, after the Comey letter.

This general stability in favorable ratings is an important caveat to consider in any analysis of the impact of campaign events. Even the smallest movements in public opinion of either candidate could have big consequences when an election is as close as this one was. So how

Figure 6-5

Favorability Ratings for Hillary Clinton and Donald Trump across the Campaign

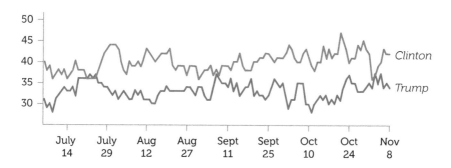

did visibility affect favorability? There is no straightforward answer to this question; the relationship changes over time and for each candidate. Over the course of the July 5–November 8 period in the total sample at the aggregate level, Americans who said they recently read, saw, or heard something about one of the candidates were less likely to have a favorable opinion of them. As shown in table 6-3, respondents who recently read, saw, or heard something about Hillary Clinton were slightly less likely to have a favorable opinion of her than Americans who said they did not recently encounter news about her, at 41 percent compared to 46 percent, respectively. And her net favorability rating was lower among those who recently read, saw, or heard something about her as well.

For Trump, however, this relationship was reversed—Americans who said they recently read, saw, or heard something about him were

Table 6-3

Favorability Ratings of Hillary Clinton and Donald Trump by whether Recently Saw, Read, or Heard Something about the Candidate

	For Clinton		For Trump	
	Recently saw, read, or heard	Did not	Recently saw, read, or heard	Did not
Has a favorable opinion of the candidate	41%	46%	36%	31%
Has a unfavorable opinion of the candidate	59%	54%	64%	69%
Net favorability rating (difference in percentage points)	–18	–8	–28	–38

slightly more likely to have a favorable opinion of the GOP candidate than those who had not recently encountered news about him. While both candidates had negative net favorability ratings, Trump's was larger than Clinton's but smaller among those who had encountered any recent information about him compared to those who had not.

Perhaps as a result of her decades-long status as a conservative bête noire, Americans who identify or lean Republican were more likely to say they had recently read, seen, or heard something about Clinton than were Democrats or those who leaned Democratic, while both groups were equally likely to say they read, saw, or heard something about Trump (table 6-4). Both the findings that those who had read, seen, or heard something about Clinton, and that Republicans were less positive about her, underline the unusual focus that Republicans had on the Democratic candidate in 2016.

Read, Seen, or Heard and the Candidates' Public Image over Time

The statistical correlation between the three-day average of Clinton's visibility and her favorability rating is slightly positive at 0.21, suggesting not all attention was bad for Clinton. The accompanying scatterplot in figure 6-6 displays this relationship graphically, showing the modest tendency for those days when Clinton's visibility was higher to be days when her favorable rating was also higher.

In particular, the days associated with several of the campaign's typical milestones—the three debates—saw Clinton's favorable rating generally rise slightly above its long-term campaign average (39 percent) as did her visibility rating (76 percent). For the last debate on October 19 and the several days afterward, Clinton's favorable rating rose to one of its highest levels throughout the campaign, while the July 25–28 convention and the few days afterward along with the first debate saw Clinton earn her highest visibility rating.

However, two unexpected events that hit the Clinton campaign— her apparent medical emergency at a 9/11 memorial service in New York

Table 6-4

Percentage of Americans Who Said They Read, Saw, or Heard Something about Hillary Clinton and Donald Trump by Party Identification

	% Republican/ Lean Republican	% "Pure" Independent	% Democrat/ Lean Democrat
Clinton	80	63	75
Trump	81	66	80

Figure 6-6

Plot of Three-Day Averages of Hillary Clinton's Favorability and Visibility Ratings (July 5–November 8, 2016)

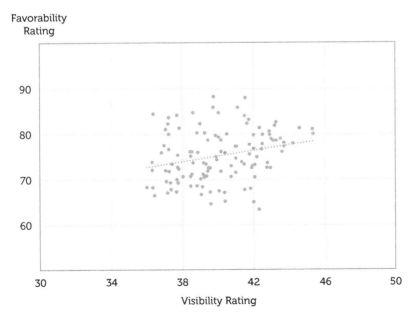

City and the first Comey letter on October 28—had an uncertain effect on the tracking measures. Furthermore, her health problems coincided with the release of her "basket of deplorables" comment, making it difficult to disentangle the effect of each event, although the open-ended responses suggest the medical episode was the more salient of the two unexpected events.

The week of 9/12 recorded several of Clinton's highest visibility ratings of the entire tracking period, with the highest daily rating registering 91 percent on September 14, as speculation about Clinton's health intensified. This speculation was not simply idle chatter—it was so heavily focused that many Americans naming what they recently read, saw, or heard about Trump discussed Clinton's health over this week.

The week of 9/12–9/18 saw Clinton earn her highest *weekly* visibility rating (89 percent) over the tracking period—a 9-point increase in her visibility rating from the week before. But her favorable rating remained static—moving up by 1 point to 38 percent from the week before.

The effect of the attention coming from the Comey letters on Clinton's favorability rating is also difficult to pinpoint. Prior to the release of the first letter, Clinton's visibility and favorability had been relatively positive, with Clinton enjoying a favorability bump from the third debate. Her three-day favorable average climbed as high as 45 percent on October 22, though it then began to fade as attention receded.

But when Comey's first letter was released on October 28 (a Friday), attention to Clinton spiked immediately—her daily visibility rating climbed 8 points to 86 percent on that day, though her favorability rating did not change in any meaningful way. Attention fell slightly over the weekend, with Clinton's daily visibility rating falling below 80 percent, and her favorable rating actually moved up slightly.

However, on Monday, October 31, Clinton's visibility rating moved back above 80 percent as her favorable rating fell. Over October 31 to November 4, Clinton's visibility rating stood at 84 percent—8 points higher than her average rating—and her favorable rating stood at 39 percent. Moreover, of those Americans who said they heard something about Clinton over this time period, 37 percent had a favorable view of Clinton.

It appears that Comey's first letter had a short-term impact on Clinton's favorable rating, but her image recovered quickly. At the time of the second Comey letter on November 6, her favorability rating (based on the November 5–8 moving average) was 42 percent.

Of the two candidates, Donald Trump had the higher three-day average visibility rating (56 percent) throughout the entire July 5–November 8 period. Despite his comparative advantage over Clinton in visibility, his favorability rating was almost always below Clinton's. Although both candidates were unpopular, Trump was more so, and he ultimately became the least popular presidential candidate in Gallup polling history.

These facts alone suggest that, for Trump, visibility and favorability were not necessarily related concepts. A correlation analysis of Trump's three-day average visibility ratings and favorability ratings provides further evidence in support of this notion—there was no correlation between the two (figure 6-7). The correlation between Trump's favorability and lagged visibility rating (one-day lag) is also near zero and not statistically significant.

The major campaign milestones largely did not move public opinion toward Trump, though his visibility rating did, in all instances, exceed 80 percent in the time just following the event. The one major exception is the Republican Convention and the few days after, which saw Trump's favorability rating climb to 37 percent, which was 4 percentage points over the tracking period average. This type of postconvention bounce is quite normal, and Trump's favorable rating fell back down again in the weeks thereafter.

The debates, unlike the GOP convention, failed to move the needle for Trump, with his favorability rating staying near the period average of 33 percent despite the higher-than-normal attention of the American public paid to the Trump campaign. Of course, most Americans judged Trump the poorer debater in these events—so his stable, rather than declining, favorability rating after these events may be considered an

Figure 6-7

Plot of Three-Day Averages of Donald Trump's Favorability and Visibility Ratings (July 5–November 8, 2016)

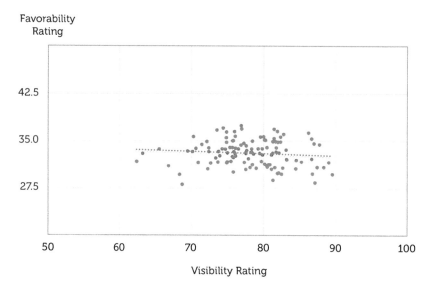

achievement of sorts. Overall, Trump's favorable rating seemed fairly impervious to the ebb and flow of his visibility rating.

Given the richness of the Gallup survey data across the campaign, it was possible to replicate this analysis using the individual-level responses aggregated to a daily total and separately for self-identified Democrats, Republicans, and Independents. Using a one-day lag, the correlation between having read, seen, or heard something about Hillary Clinton and her favorability rating was 0.36 in the total sample, 0.45 among Democrats, –0.01 among Republicans, and 0.01 among Independents. Democrats who said they had recently heard more about Clinton liked her more, but this was not true for Independents and Republicans.

These relationships were quite different for evaluations of Trump. In the total sample, the one-day lagged relationship between having read, seen, or heard something about Trump and his favorability ratings had a correlation of –0.35. Overall, encountering information about Trump lowered his favorability rating. In this case there was no difference between this correlation for Democrats (–0.39) and Republicans (–0.24) except in magnitude. For Independents, this relationship was even weaker (–0.11). Yet for everyone, those who reported hearing more about Trump liked him less.

We also ran a model to estimate favorable opinion for both Clinton and Trump on a given day at the individual level. We began with a set of control variables that included dummy variable measures of gender (male), party identification (Republican and Democratic), race (Hispanic, non-Hispanic black, and non-Hispanic white), and support for the other candidate (favorable toward Trump in the Clinton model and vice versa for the Trump model). As seen in table 6-5, the independent variables behaved in the way we would expect and that other postelection analyses have shown. The most important predictor in each model was party identification; the strongest relationship was a negative one for the membership in the opposition party. The next most important variable was having a favorable attitude toward the opponent, which produced a negative coefficient in each model. Being male was negatively associated with Clinton favorability and positively with Trump favorability. The proportion of black or Hispanic was positively associated with having a favorable view of Clinton, while the proportion of white was negatively associated. The opposite relationships were observed for Trump. In addition, having read, seen, or heard anything about each candidate in the two previous days was positively related to a candidate's favorability. The coefficient was larger for receiving information about the candidate than for the opponent.

An interesting aspect of this analysis is the observation that Trump's visibility declined at the end of the campaign relative to Clinton's and to his own levels of having been read, seen, or heard about earlier in the campaign. This is an aspect of the Trump campaign that bears additional investigation. Researchers need to learn whether the campaign became extremely focused on a limited set of geographical locations at the end of the campaign and reduced their use of traditional campaign

Table 6-5

Predicting Favorability toward Candidates Having Read, Seen, or Heard Something about Them, with Controls

	Clinton Favorability	Trump Favorability
Heard about candidate	0.072	0.066
Heard about opponent	0.046	0.045
Favor opponent	−0.154	−0.168
Party identification		
Republican	−0.122	0.429
Democrat	0.452	−0.082
Male	−0.048	0.024
Race/ethnicity		
Hispanic	0.067	−0.055
Non-Hispanic black	0.085	−0.042
Non-Hispanic white	−0.045	−0.004

Note: Given the large sample size (N = 58,941), all of the unstandardized coefficients are statistically significant with the exception of the one for non-Hispanic whites in the Trump favorability equation.

media while employing more difficult-to-track social media to motivate voters to support the candidate and to get to the polls. Such an analysis may be complicated by the fact that Trump almost immediately announced his intention to run for reelection and his use of nondisclosure agreements with his campaign staff. It is also possible that an element of the strategy was to stay out of the news and let the press focus on the Comey letters. However, there have, so far, been no postelection descriptions of the campaign strategy that were equivalent to what Clinton and her staff have provided since November 2016.

Conclusion

The use of the open-ended questions in the Gallup surveys and of computerized text analysis to make sense of the responses marks a new form of interpreting campaign events and their impact. In combination with the availability of social media data produced and disseminated by political strategists, interest groups, and ordinary citizens, this opens the possibility for new ways to understand and interpret political behavior in an electoral environment.

Hillary Clinton disliked the focus of both the media and her opponent on emails, and generally speaking she attempted to define issues related to emails as peripheral to the campaign and not worthy of a great deal of campaign time. However, regardless of the origin of the focus on that topic, and whether or not that focus was warranted by the underlying reality, the average American closely associated Clinton with emails throughout the campaign. It is also evident that she and her campaign did not solve this problem, at least as evidenced by the open-ended responses and the lack of any meaningful change in her favorability rating. Clinton's association with "emails" became a dominant motif of her candidacy, and as such was likely a pivotal event component of her campaign.

In her memoir of the election, *What Happened?*, Clinton reproduced one of the word frequency graphs we generated for this chapter, employing it to bolster her claim that the news media were obsessed with her emails in an unwarranted fashion. The facts, however, are that if the people defined the situation as real, the consequences were real. Clearly, at the least, the people's continuing focus on Clinton's emails throughout the campaign displaced other messages that she would have wanted to be the focus.

Trump, meanwhile, managed to keep the attention in the campaign moving from one topic to the next, including his series of unconventional moves and typically out of bounds statements, and his constant critique of his opponent. While he was certainly successful in drawing attention to himself for the bulk of the campaign, this attention, even when seemingly for positive reasons, did not make him any more likable in the eyes of most Americans; on the other hand, Trump's darkest moments in terms of attention, notably the release of the *Access Hollywood* recording, did little damage to his image. No story about Trump stayed on the news over the long term or substantially reduced his approval ratings.

Furthermore, Trump's clear strategy of bringing Clinton's (admittedly not spectacular) image down to his level was further aided by the fact that Republicans generally said they paid more attention to Clinton than Democrats did. In general, partisans who said they had heard something recently about the candidate they oppose almost unanimously had an unfavorable view of that same candidate. As such, Clinton's image was to some extent hurt by the fact that a greater share of Republicans were consistently hearing news about her.

Public Attention to Events in the 2016 Election

What Mattered?

Events like James Comey's letters to Congress and the *Access Hollywood* tapes often dominate the way journalists and scholars talk about presidential election campaigns. Each time, the losing candidate's failure is explained by some critical gaffe or societal development. Mitt Romney purportedly lost in 2012 because he suggested that "47 percent of Americans" mooched off the government (Frantzich 2013). Similarly, John McCain was purportedly felled in 2008 by the Great Recession (Kenski, Hardy, and Jamieson 2010). The common narrative is that so-called October surprises and other major events during a campaign can be critical to determining the eventual victor.

But there are reasons to be skeptical about the effects of these supposedly seminal campaign events. For one, the jury is still out on the question of whether electoral campaigns actually have an impact on election results (Holbrook 1996; Iyengar and Simon 2000; Wlezien 2002). In practice, campaign events might have small or nonexistent effects because they are outweighed by other voter considerations (Gelman and King 1993), since their impacts are balanced across candidates (Sides and Vavreck 2013), the effects of these events are fleeting (Gerber et al. 2011; Wlezien and Erikson 2008), or they don't even reach persuadable voters (cf. Zaller 1992). They also might have effects that are conditional in that they appear in some situations but not others. A serious examination of the effects of seminal events on campaigns requires that we consider not only the set of events that generated news attention but also whether, how strongly, and for how long those messages retained their salience.

This chapter first lays out a series of theories articulating the conditions under which campaign events might be expected to influence voters' decisions. This includes both normative questions about what information voters ideally should attend to as well as more pragmatic questions about how that attention might play out in a dynamic election campaign. The chapter then considers a number of events that occurred during the course of the 2016 election and generated media attention. Focusing on these events, we ask questions about which moments captured public attention and how long the media and public attention spans lasted. We then probe the factors that seem likely to distinguish these relations. To accomplish this, we examine the prevalence of event-related words in the newspaper data and responses to the open-ended survey questions on what people had recently read, seen, or heard about the candidates.

When Should Voters Attend to Campaign Events?

At their core, American presidential campaigns are about information. Citizens are expected to learn about candidates by considering the available information about the candidates' character as well as the policies those candidates espouse. Although citizens could be expected to make ideal decisions only if they are fully informed about every aspect of each candidate, such a situation is pragmatically impossible as it would present an undue burden on citizens. The effort to become fully informed in this manner about a single contest (let alone the dozen or so races that may be on a ballot) could easily occupy all of a voter's time over an entire election season.

Scholars have long known that individuals do not need to be fully informed to make choices between candidates in a democracy. Low information cues, such as a candidate's party affiliation, prior occupation, and gender, can allow citizens to use efficient heuristics—or mental shortcuts—to make decisions (Popkin 1991; Lupia 1994). It is a good bet that a pro-life, open-carry supporter will prefer the Republican candidate to the Democratic one in most contests. Similarly, an advocate for universal health care and limiting greenhouse gas emissions should generally favor the Democrat. Knowing a candidate's partisanship can thus serve as a highly reliable, though not perfectly accurate, guide for a potential voter. When cues like partisanship are unavailable, or there are voters whose preferences do not align with a political party, candidate attributes, such as gender, race, or religiosity, might fulfill a similar purpose.

When it comes to information beyond these heuristics, such as the impact of campaign events, political scientists have argued that voters should operate using a "burglar alarm" model (Zaller 2003). That is, institutions in society should provide clear signals about the things voters need to know that may change minds or challenge assumptions. News media organizations, in particular, have been implicated as key actors in letting individuals know what information they should be attending to. In theory, instead of learning everything there is to know about a particular election, individuals should focus on only the most important and relevant facts that might point to errors in their initial assumptions. If voters can bundle low-information cues with the key pieces of information that might upend their decisions, they can vote in favor of their interests without learning everything there is to know about the candidates.

For an individual voter, then, being sufficiently informed to participate in a democratic society does not require "political junkie" status. It simply demands an ability to attend to both key heuristic cues and any sufficiently relevant information that is uncovered during the course of the election campaign. Campaign events that are broadcast in the media should fill this role to the extent that they signal that a candidate is eminently unqualified for office or suggest some larger issue that might undermine their decision. Such evidence may not be common, but it should presumably make a difference.

Do Events Ever Matter?

Despite the long-standing notion that seminal campaign events shape the way Americans vote and a number of reasons to believe that these events should sometimes matter, there is little empirical evidence that what happens in campaigns actually has an impact. Indeed, a large body of research in political science provides reasons to be skeptical. Studies have repeatedly shown that the outcomes of elections are highly predictable long before Election Day (e.g., Wlezien 2002). In 2016, eleven political science models forecast the results of the election with at least sixty days' advance notice. Using variables such as economic performance and primary enthusiasm, they collectively projected that Hillary Clinton would win between 47.5 percent and 52.7 percent of the popular vote (with an average of 50.8 percent) (Campbell 2016). The final certified vote tally had Clinton winning the popular two-party vote by a margin of 51.1 percent, a nearly perfect estimate. This is true even though these models could not account for the *Access Hollywood* tape, the Comey announcements, or any other mediated events that occurred in September or October.

Scholars have attempted to explain the odd juxtaposition of widely varying campaign polls and impressively predictable electoral margins and have presented a series of potential explanations. One possibility is that electoral campaigns simply serve as a vehicle for voters to learn the critical information on which their heuristics rely. That is, voters make their determinations on key factors like partisanship and the economy. The campaign simply serves as a context for learning the relevant economic information, which is presumably imparted by Election Day

(Gelman and King 1993). Another suggestion is that media messages have effects that are fleeting (Gerber et al. 2011). After a few days, voters simply forget what they learned and revert to their previous judgments. A further line of argument posits that campaigns battle in a consistent stalemate (Sides and Vavreck 2013). Although one campaign or another may gain a temporary informational advantage, the messages almost always equalize over the course of a campaign, and this "tug-of-war" renders a net effect that was largely predictable from the beginning.

Reconciling the Ideal Citizen with Stable Predictions

The competing explanations for the stability of American electoral campaigns generally lead to the expectation that campaign events have little net impact, but they differ on whether particular events can matter. This is important, as electoral campaigns are of little value if truly critical events fail to set off the proverbial burglar alarm. A lack of responsiveness to truly critical events should lead us to conclude that elections are effectively predetermined by factors like partisanship and the economy, and that candidate quality and campaign events are inconsequential. If events matter but are fundamentally fleeting, this might represent even more of a normative problem, as only those that occur right at the end of an election campaign would have an impact. But if the reason campaigns have seemed so inert is attributable to each side offsetting the other, citizens may still be responsive to substantive cues.

Our ability to juxtapose news text with the content of open-ended survey responses throughout the campaign offers a new tool for understanding which messages do, in fact, reach ordinary citizens and how long they persist. Further, it is possible to compare the messages that ordinary Americans receive with the media coverage afforded to relevant events. Collectively, these comparisons can allow us to identify the moments that had a disproportionate popular impact, either in magnitude or in duration.

The Psychology of Attention

Media agenda setting is perhaps the most well-known theory to emerge from the study of political communication. In contrast to the "hypodermic needle" model of media persuasion, which was widely refuted in the mid-twentieth century, the agenda-setting account suggests that media guide citizens in their decisions about what topics to think about, though not necessarily what attitudes they should hold about those topics (McCombs and Shaw 1972, 1993; Boydstun 2013). That is, media set the national agenda by focusing attention on some issues and giving short shrift to others. This, in turn, heightens the perceived importance of highlighted issues and the extent to which ordinary people have given serious consideration to their answers.

The basic tenets of agenda-setting theory have been confirmed across numerous studies (see McCombs and Shaw 1993; Scheufele 2000; Boydstun 2013). There is evidence that disproportionate attention to some issues over others is one of the few significant effects of media events on electoral choices (Druckman 2004). Typically, agenda-setting studies involve an attempt to assess how variations in the set of issues covered by the media compare to the composition of issues that individuals think are important (McCombs, Shaw, and Weaver 2014). With respect to election campaigns, a considerable body of work has also associated media messages—through venues such as advertisements, news stories, and debates—with perceptions of the candidates (e.g., Kim et al. 2016).

Much of the work examining the public agenda, however, has been limited by a disconnect between the specificity of the messages communicated by and about the candidates and a relatively crude set of tools that researchers have employed to capture the resonance of those messages. In some studies, scholars have established evidence that attributes of candidates mentioned in the media tend to reinforce those associations in public opinion polls (e.g., Hardy and Jamieson 2005). Others have shown that debates can influence the salience of issues and parties for the public (e.g., Vergeer and Franses 2015). Across studies, however, the topics used to test agenda setting in the mass public have been largely limited to matters that were the subject of routine survey questions. This meant that they were inevitably somewhat more general than the specific messages emanating from specific events that were presumed to account for the agenda-setting process. Indeed, the best evidence for a direct link has come from studies that treated social media as a proxy for public attention (Vargo et al. 2014), which may or may not be a reasonable assumption (Jungherr et al. 2016; see Pasek, Singh, et al. n.d.).

By asking respondents directly about the candidates using open-ended survey questions, the Gallup data used throughout this book offer a new and powerful tool for bridging these gaps. Indeed, unlike for questions about issues or perceptions of candidate traits, these questions can be used to link event-specific information with public attention. And unlike studies that use social media data, we can be certain that the attention we are observing in the data stems from the citizenry at large rather than emerging through some other data-generating process that yields social media mentions (e.g., Kwak et al. 2010; Pasek, Singh, et al. n.d.; Schober et al. 2016).

Identifying Events

To determine how the events Americans found salient during the campaign were related to concurrent news, we selected the substantive moments during the campaign that garnered the most public attention. To accomplish this, we first focused on the Gallup open-ended survey responses. Using these data, we looked for terms that appeared across a number of respondents and that varied in the frequency with which they were mentioned during the campaign period but that were also highly salient, in that they attracted a lot of mentions on some days. Because our goal was to find words that were indicative of events, we looked for terms that were sometimes common and sometimes absent from individuals' answers to the "read, seen, or heard" questions. Our criteria for identifying appropriate words was, on the one hand, that they were mentioned at least ten times on at least one day of the field period of the study and at least fifty times total over the entire election cycle, but that they were also not mentioned on many other days of the campaign.[1] In total, 317 words were extracted from these open-ended responses in this fashion. Eight of these words were dropped from analyses because they were never used more than ten times on a single day in the news corpus, leaving a total of 309 relevant terms.

These terms were then sorted based on the date that they were most frequently mentioned by survey respondents and then linked to a series of events that occurred during the campaign. Events that were described by only a single term as well as terms that could not be linked to a unique event were dropped from the dataset. These processes yielded a total of 237 terms related to 38 unique events (though some combinations of similar events, such as the Democratic and Republican conventions and the three debates, were bundled because they were related to similar terms).

Events, the Candidates, and the Public

The words that were identified tapped events ranging from an attack on police officers in Dallas on July 7, 2016, to the Comey letters sent on October 28 and November 6. The events identified and the terms used to identify them are shown in table 7-1, which also contains the peak number of references to event-related terms in the open-ended responses to both candidates as well as across news outlets. Although the number and sensitivity of the keywords used to identify these events varied considerably, we can still use this information to make a number of observations about the campaign.

One interesting trend is that campaign events appeared to be far more salient for voters in thinking about Donald Trump as compared to Hillary Clinton. When an event occurred, more people tended to mention that event in relation to Donald Trump than they did in relation to Hillary Clinton. For 29 of the 38 events, peak references to the event in answering the Trump-retained information question were higher than peak references in answering the Clinton question. Similarly, event-related keywords were mentioned in 29.3 percent of the open-ended responses about Trump compared to 19.3 percent for Clinton ($p < 0.001$ difference).[2] The difference between the proportion of open-ended responses mentioning each candidate was relatively consistent across the campaign period, as can be seen by the difference in the proportion of daily mentions of each candidate that included event-related terms. The red line in figure 7-1 indicates the proportion of open-ended responses about Donald Trump that used event-related terms, while the blue line presents that same proportion for Hillary Clinton.

Much of the explanation for the added relevance of events for Donald Trump may be due to the fact that many seminal campaign events involved his own actions. In late July, when Mr. Trump insulted Khizr Khan, the father of a Gold Star family, the resulting controversy only nominally included Secretary Clinton. It is not surprising, therefore, that terms related to this incident were brought up eight times as often when respondents were thinking about Trump as when they were thinking about Clinton. Events ranging from Trump's suggestion

Figure 7-1

Proportion of Open-Ended Responses Mentioning Terms

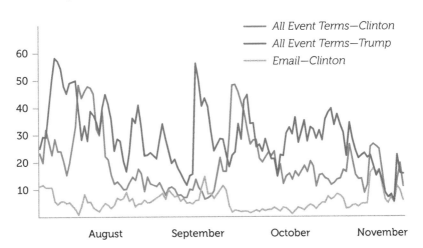

Table 7-1

Prevalence of Terms Associated with Campaign Events

Event	Terms	Date of Survey Maximum	Most Daily Mentions		
			Trump Survey Question	Clinton Survey Question	Newspaper Story Content
Dallas Shooting	Dallas; Officers; Police; Shooting; Shootings	7/10/2016	149	126	1463
Sanders Endorsement	Bernie; Endorsed; Endorsement; Endorsing; Sanders	7/12/2016	50	242	2112
Supreme Court Pick	Court; Justice; Supreme	7/14/2016	46	5	662
Vp Announcements	Announced; Announcement; Announcing; Decision; Kaine; Mate; Mike; Pence; Pick; Picked; Picking; Selected; Tim; Vice; Vp	7/16/2016	451	354	2612
Nice Attack	Attack; Attacks; France; Happened; Nice; Terrorist	7/15/2016	137	123	643
Baton Rouge Shooting	Baton; Rouge	7/18/2016	15	23	348
Conventions	Acceptance; Convention; Democratic; Democrats; Dnc; Gop; Nominated; Nomination; Nominee; Rnc; Wifes	7/26/2016	274	283	4529
Ted Cruz	Cruz; Ted	7/23/2016	60	3	1143
Trump Asks Russia To Hack Emails	Hack; Hacked; Hacking; Russia; Russian; Russians	7/28/2016	168	19	1182
Khizr Khan	Died; Father; Gold; Heart; Khan; Killed; Lost; Mother; Mr; Muslim; Muslims; Parents; Purple; Soldier; Soldiers; Son; Star; Tour; Veteran; War	8/1/2016	366	44	3956

Event	Keywords	Date			
Trump Invokes Second Amendment	2nd; Amendment; Gun; Rights; Second	8/10/2016	291	31	1136
Trump Claims Obama Started Isis	Founder; Founders; Isis; Started	8/12/2016	187	9	304
Biden Campaigns	Biden; Joe; Pennsylvania	8/15/2016	9	39	314
Trump Staff Shakeup	Changed; Fired; Hired; Manager; Staff	8/19/2016	79	11	301
Louisiana Flood	Flood; Louisiana; Victims	8/20/2016	103	15	128
Trump Meets Mexican Pres	Meet; Meeting; Met; Mexican; Mexico; Trip; Visit; Visiting	8/31/2016	436	37	800
Trump Visits Detroit Church	African; Black; Church; Detroit; Visited	9/4/2016	200	13	534
Trump Says He Knows More Than Generals	Chief; Commander; Forum; Generals; Hall; Iraq	9/8/2016	101	81	694
Matt Lauer Forum	Lauer; Matt	9/9/2016	24	22	288
Clinton Faints	9/11; Ceremony; Gets; Half; Ill; Illness; Leave; Memorial; Passed; Pneumonia; Sick	9/12/2016	59	284	540
Basket Of Deplorables	Deplorable; Supporters	9/13/2016	42	40	554
Trump Childcare Policy	Child; Childcare	9/14/2016	38	6	130
Candidates Release Medical Records	Doctor; Dr; Medical; Oz; Records	9/14/2016	111	36	423
Jimmy Fallon Touches Hair	Fallon; Hair; Jimmy	9/16/2016	52	9	96
Trump Ends Birther Claim	Admitted; Barack; Birth; Birther; Born; Citizen	9/17/2016	192	28	486
NY/NJ Bombings	Bomb; Bombing; Bombings; Jersey	9/19/2016	103	62	174
Charlotte Riots	Carolina; Charlotte; North; Riots	9/23/2016	51	51	542
Debate Prep	Preparation; Preparing; Ready; Tomorrow; Tonight; Upcoming	9/26/2016	83	90	185
Debates	Debates; Performance; Won	9/28/2016	49	68	640

Table 7-1 continued

Event	Terms	Date of Survey Maximum	Trump Survey Question	Clinton Survey Question	Newspaper Story Content
					Most Daily Mentions
Attacks Former Ms Universe	Beauty; Fat; Girl; Miss; Ms; Pageant; Tweeting; Tweets; Universe	9/30/2016	210	38	437
Trump Partial Tax Return	18; Dollars; Federal; Hasnt; Income; Paid; Paying; Return; Returns	10/3/2016	189	44	1128
Access Hollywood	2005; Audio; Billy; Bus; Bush; Hollywood; Hot; Leaked; Locker; Recorded; Recording; Room; Street; Tape; Tapes	10/8/2016	170	59	1142
Allegations	Accusations; Accusing; Allegations; Assault; Assaulted; Groping; Harassment; Inappropriate; Sex; Sexual; Sexually	10/15/2016	249	14	854
Rigged Elections	Accept; Claiming; Elections; Results; Rigged	10/17/2016	93	7	684
Al Smith Dinner	Al; Catholic; Charity; Dinner; Event; Smith	10/21/2016	155	153	269
Trump Hotel Opens	Dc; Hotel; Opened; Washington	10/26/2016	84	8	580
Comey Reopens Investigation	Anthony; Case; Cleared; Comey; Computer; Director; Found; Investigating; Letter; Opening; Reopening; Weiner	10/29/2016	40	162	1501
Trump Whisked Offstage in NV	Nevada; Secret; Service; Stage	11/6/2016	98	9	433

that President Obama was the founder of ISIS (August 11), his meeting with the Mexican president (August 31), and his criticism of former Ms. Universe contestant Alicia Machado (September 27), among others, uniquely implicated Donald Trump.

The prominence of these Trump-related events speaks to one key element in how Mr. Trump's presidential election campaign operated. As he had in much of his prior public life, he seemed to embrace a "there is no such thing as bad publicity" approach. Rather than minimize controversy, Trump appeared to largely embrace it. Among terms that were considered in the current analysis, approximately half of the event-related answers to the Trump "read, seen, or heard" question were related to self-induced (and often self-promoted) controversies.

The lack of salient events related to Secretary Clinton's candidacy may, in fact, have cost her. With the sole exception of the Comey letter, individuals were more likely to report that they had read, seen, or heard something about emails on the days when event responses were lower. The general pattern can be seen by comparing the blue and gray lines in figure 7-1, where most email mentions occur when people were not discussing other events. Overall, these trends were correlated at −0.22 over the entire time period; the correlation before the release of the Comey letter was −0.33. That is, prior to the Comey letter, for every 100 individuals who mentioned a recent salient event about Clinton in relation to the read, seen, or heard measure, nine fewer people would be expected to mention emails.[3] This result implies that emails may have filled the vacuum when individuals didn't have something else to say about Hillary Clinton.

Attention to Notable Campaign Events

To better understand the trajectories of some key events over the course of the 2016 campaign, figure 7-2 plots the volume of survey and newspaper mentions for keywords related to six of the salient events (plots for the other thirty-two events can be found online at https://dx.doi. org/10.17605/OSF.IO/JS7FT). For each event, two trend lines present

Figure 7-2a

Volume of Survey and Newspaper Mentions for Keywords Related to Six Salient Events

Conventions: *Acceptance; Convention; Democratic; Democrats; Dnc; Gop; Nominated; Nomination; Nominee; Republicans; Rnc; Wifes*

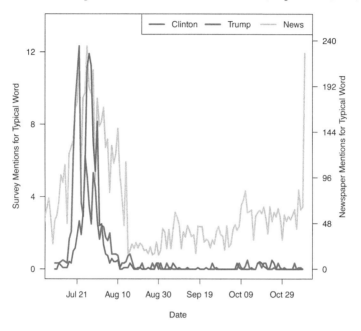

SHORT TIME WINDOW

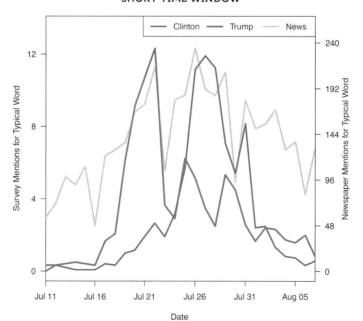

Figure 7-2b

Volume of Survey and Newspaper Mentions for
Keywords Related to Six Salient Events

Trump Asks Russia To Hack Emails: *Hack; Hacked; Hacking; Russia; Russian; Russians*

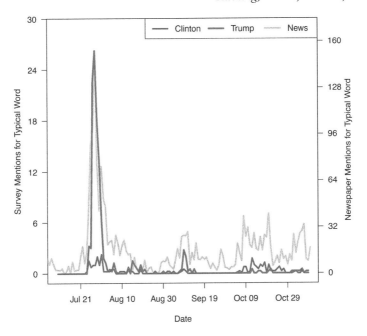

SHORT TIME WINDOW

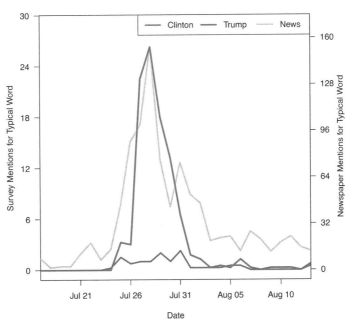

Figure 7-2c

Volume of Survey and Newspaper Mentions for Keywords Related to Six Salient Events

Khizr Khan : *Died; Father; Gold; Heart; Khan; Killed; Lost; Mother; Mr; Muslim; Muslims; Parents; Purple; Soldier; Soldiers; Son; Star; Tour; Veteran; War*

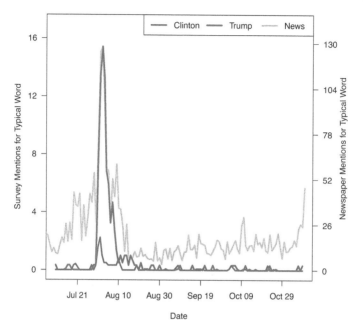

SHORT TIME WINDOW

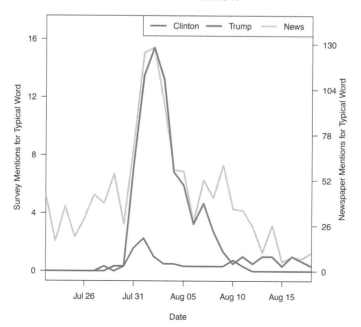

Figure 7-2d

Volume of Survey and Newspaper Mentions for Keywords Related to Six Salient Events

Clinton Faints: *9/11; Ceremony; Gets; Ill; Illness; Leave; Memorial; Passed; Pneumonia; Sick*

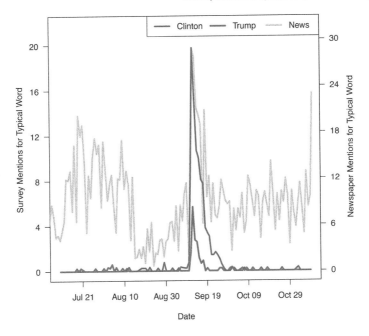

SHORT TIME WINDOW

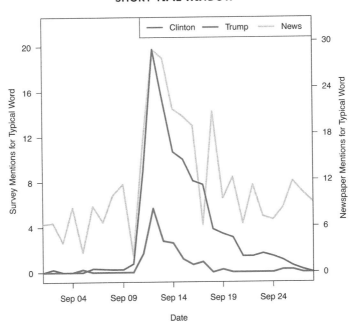

Figure 7-2e

Volume of Survey and Newspaper Mentions for Keywords Related to Six Salient Events

Allegations: *Accusations; Accusing; Allegations; Assault; Assaulted; Groping; Harassment; Inappropriate; Sex; Sexual; Sexually*

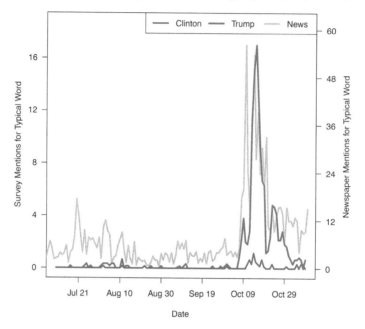

SHORT TIME WINDOW

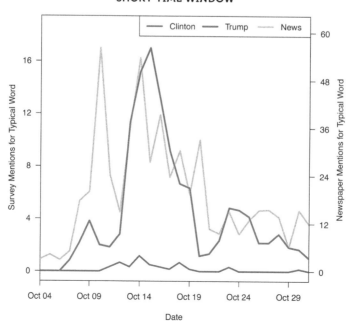

Figure 7-2f

Volume of Survey and Newspaper Mentions for
Keywords Related to Six Salient Events

Comey Reopens Investigation: *Anthony; Case; Cleared; Comey; Computer; Director; Found; Investigating; Letter; Opening; Reopening; Weiner*

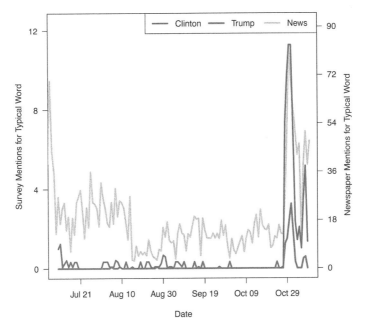

SHORT TIME WINDOW

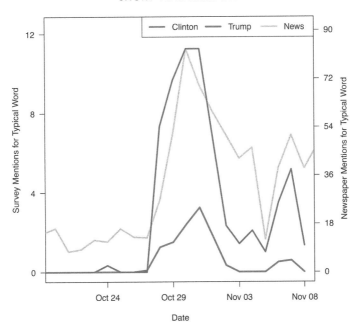

the frequency of mentions for a typical keyword[4] related to that event in survey responses and news articles over the entire timeline (top panels) and for twenty-day periods spanning the date with the most total survey attention to each set of words (bottom panels). In each figure, the gray line tallies newspaper mentions, the blue line presents the number of mentions in response to the retained information questions about Hillary Clinton, and the red line indexes mentions related to retained information questions about Donald Trump. All figures are scaled to capture the highest observed number of survey mentions (from either candidate) and associated newspaper mentions.

Patterns of attention to words related to the convention are shown in the first row of figure 7-2. The gray line shows the buildup of convention-related newspaper coverage before the convention began, two separate multiday peaks of coverage during the Democratic and Republican conventions, and a slow decline in mentions of convention-related words until they hit a low mark in mid-August. Convention-related mentions by survey respondents were principally associated with Hillary Clinton during the Democratic convention and with Donald Trump during the Republican convention, as might be expected. Although convention-related words could describe other events, and many appeared throughout the campaign, words such as *acceptance*, *nomination*, and *Democratic* tended to track these events far more than other moments. Also notable, news attention to convention-related words was elevated for a few weeks before and after the conventions even though these terms were rarely mentioned as content that respondents had read, seen, or heard in relation to the candidates. It therefore seems that only contemporaneous convention coverage was associated with respondents' open-ended expressions.

Distinct patterns of attention between news media and retained information questions can be identified for many of the events examined. For example, when Donald Trump suggested on July 27 that Russia would be rewarded for hacking and publicizing 30,000 emails supposedly missing from Hillary Clinton's personal server, words related to hacking and Russia spiked in both open-ended mentions about Donald

Trump and newspaper stories. Attention to these terms dissipated in both data streams over the course of the following week, and they were rarely raised again for the rest of the campaign cycle. In contrast, when Khizr Khan—the patriarch of a Muslim Gold Star family whose son was killed during the Iraq War—challenged Donald Trump's policies during the Democratic National Convention and elicited a controversial response from the nominee, survey and newspaper mentions of related words spiked during the controversy. As was the case for the Russia comments, public attention to this event faded after a few days, but newspaper coverage remained substantial for weeks after the speech, and the event reemerged in occasional media coverage through the election cycle.

As noted in earlier chapters, concerns about Hillary Clinton's health emerged as an important focus of public attention in September. This followed a particularly prominent event where Secretary Clinton fainted as she left a 9/11 memorial service and was later diagnosed with pneumonia. It is perhaps unsurprising that this was one of only four events for which the bulk of the attention was focused on Hillary Clinton (the others were Bernie Sanders's endorsement, Joe Biden's decision to campaign on Clinton's behalf, and the Comey letter). Also notable are the high levels of public attention to this event. Where the average event was mentioned four times as often in the newspaper coverage as in open-ended responses on the peak day, there was nearly a 1:1 ratio of newspaper mentions to survey mentions of the fainting incident. This implies a very high impact of this story on the public compared to most others.

Trump's "October surprise"—the *Access Hollywood* tapes followed by a series of allegations of sexual harassment—yielded a series of media spikes as each woman's claims were aired. This generated a lot of public attention as well. And the attention paid to these allegations lasted somewhat longer than many other notable media events. But even though this was a significant story, its impact appeared to have faded before Election Day. The proportion of individuals mentioning any of the eleven terms in open-ended responses about Donald Trump dropped from an average of over 30 percent for the week starting on October 13 to around 2 percent in the week preceding Election Day.

In some ways, Comey's letter about additional emails from Hillary Clinton found on a computer retrieved during an unrelated investigation was similar to the allegations of sexual harassment toward Donald Trump. Media stories quickly spiked on the news and talked about the incident for a period of around two weeks. But despite the fact that the Comey letter elicited a similar level of attention to Trump's allegations, accounting for around 30 percent of Clinton mentions for the four days from October 28 through 31, it differed from the allegations in the fact that its salience had not completely faded by Election Day. Instead, Comey-related news stories spiked a second time on the day before the election and accounted for around 7 percent of responses mentioned in the four days immediately prior to the election and 14 percent of Clinton-related mentions the day before voters went to the polls.

General Patterns

There are a number of important patterns that emerge from this attempt to catalog attention to key events during the 2016 campaign. One consistent story across the events in the dataset is that, when the two differ, newspaper coverage of events appears to outlast the salience of those events for members of the public. On some level, this is surprising; we know that respondents had the opportunity to see these messages given that they were present in contemporaneous news media and yet did not report seeing or hearing about them. Another consistent pattern is that both media attention and public attention to events were relatively short-lived. Both media outlets and ordinary individuals simply stopped talking about things within a week or two of their occurrence.

Patterns in media responses to events appeared to depend, at least somewhat, on the extent to which aspects of those events could be known in advance. Stories about scheduled/expected/anticipated conventions and debates, for instance, generate increasing newspaper coverage well before they occur; and this coverage seems to continue for some period thereafter. This differs from most surprise events (e.g., breaking news), for which coverage appears rapidly and often dissipates quickly. Interestingly, these patterns were not apparent for the open-ended responses, which displayed a rapid rise and fall even when events were predictable.

To understand the general patterns of responsiveness to events, we combined information across all identified events. This allowed us to compare how news and retained information streams related to one an-

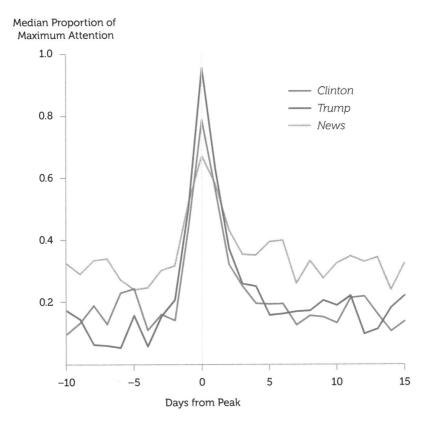

Figure 7-3

Pattern of Attention to All Events

other. Figure 7-3 shows the average pattern for mentioning key terms, with a gray line for the news stream, a blue line for the Clinton-retained information stream, and a red line for the Trump-retained information stream rescaled so that the maximum-observed attention in either the news or the retained information streams was set to 1.

In general, across all identified events, retained information tended to peak at around the same time as did news mentions. Retained information tied to events in relation to Trump or Clinton tended to follow similar patterns over time, with both spiking for a period of only a few days before returning to baseline levels. Differences in the height of Trump and Clinton peaks can be attributed to the tendency for individuals to mention more events in relation to Trump than in relation to Clinton. Patterns of news responsiveness to events were also typically short-lived, but these tended to be somewhat more prominent even a few days from their peaks.

What to Make of Campaign Events

The story of any campaign, and the 2016 election was no exception, can be understood as a series of events that capture the attention of the media and the public. To the extent that campaigns serve to guide voters' decisions and set the public issue agenda, these events are important. This chapter shows that real-time recollections about the candidates in the 2016 campaign were dominated by events generated by the candidates themselves. These events tended to displace longer-standing narratives about the candidates, most notably the attention to Hillary Clinton's emails. The events we observed were also disproportionately associated with Donald Trump, as opposed to Hillary Clinton. Even though many of these events did not reflect particularly positively on Mr. Trump, his victory may serve to validate an "all news is good news" approach to politics.

Finally, the findings of this study suggest that the events that most capture public attention are not a mirror image of the events that are reported in the news media. Although the distribution of attention to specific events is similar in its peaks, the level of salience for different events is inconsistent between news mentions and survey responses. Similarly, attention to events in survey responses tends to fade more quickly than corresponding media mentions.

At this point, it is unclear the extent to which the events that mattered in the 2016 election reflect a larger picture of contemporary campaigns or instead some idiosyncrasy of the particular candidates who were running. Nonetheless, the distinction between the constant refrain of email associated with one candidate and a smorgasbord of issues connected to the other created what was fundamentally imbalanced coverage of the campaign and attention to that coverage. This raises serious concerns about the extent to which contemporary journalistic norms might contribute to qualitatively different assessments of one candidate versus another as voters are making their decisions.

8

Fake News Production and Consumption

The spread of fake news was one of the defining characteristics of the 2016 election, with some even going as far as claiming the election results were a consequence of the spread of fake news (Dewey 2016a; Parkinson 2016; Jamieson 2018). While the spread of misinformation on social media platforms is nothing new, the 2016 election surely highlighted its extent and raised fears that this new paradigm of news consumption is misinforming voters and corroding our democracy. Given the significance of this phenomenon for the 2016 election—and for news media production and consumption more generally—it is crucial to carry out a retrospective analysis and determine the role of fake news production and consumption. This chapter does exactly that, and it focuses on several important queries about the spread of fake news during the 2016 presidential election: What was the prevalence of content produced by fake news publishers and how did this prevalence change over time? What were the fake news publisher stories about? Who shared them and whose perception of the election campaign was better aligned with them? We will answer these questions using various datasets—some we have introduced earlier in the book, some used here for the first time to examine the spread of low-quality news content during the election season. Before we delve into our analysis, let us first start with a broad summary of the fake news ecosystem before the 2016 election and enumerate conditions that might have led to the proliferation of fake news publisher content during the 2016 election.

A Complex Fake News Ecosystem: Actors and Causes

The news ecosystem in 2016—historically thought to be regulated by the gatekeeping capabilities of traditional news organizations—included many low-quality news producers (devoid of journalistic standards of traditional news outlets) that created and disseminated a broad range of low-quality news content for a broad range of reasons. The 2016 presidential election spurred significant discussion on the changes in the news ecosystem and the role that fake news plays in our democracy. There have been considerable research and investigative efforts following the 2016 U.S. elections that resulted in important findings worth noting here. The problems identified and actors involved are varied, highlighting the complexity of the information ecosystem online.

State Actors

There is strong evidence that the Russian government interfered in the 2016 presidential election. These efforts have been acknowledged by various government agencies and are assessed to have been aimed at increasing political instability in the United States and damaging Hillary Clinton's presidential campaign (Director of National Intelligence 2017). The efforts even included intrusions into state voter-registration systems, though cyber actors were not able to manipulate individual votes or vote totals (Demirjian 2018). Most related to the topic of this chapter, Russian interference used dissemination of fake news and its promotion on social media as a significant meddling tactic (Nakashima,

Demirjian, and Rucker 2017). In September 2017, Facebook told congressional investigators that fake accounts linked to a shadowy Russian company with links to the Kremlin bought 3,000 divisive ads on hot-button issues viewed by between four and five million Facebook users prior to the election (Shane and Goel 2017).

Overall, investigations by the U.S. government and international agencies revealed significant vulnerabilities of and missteps taken by platforms such as Facebook (Cadwalladr 2018). Investigations of the Russian government's efforts to interfere in the 2016 presidential election were carried out as part of the Special Counsel investigation, including an investigation of any possible links or coordination between Donald Trump's presidential campaign and the Russian government. This investigation culminated in a report that provided detailed accounting of various Russian interference attempts. Most relatedly to the theme of this chapter, the report (Mueller 2019) lays out a significant social media influence and infiltration operation led by the Internet Research Agency (IRA). This operation, which started in 2014 and reached its peak in 2016, included efforts to impersonate U.S. citizens, create pages and groups for causes related to polarizing U.S. issues, and purchase advertisements to promote its pages. By February 2016, internal IRA documents referred to support for the Trump campaign and opposition to candidate Clinton. As was noted by Mueller (2019), instructions to the IRA stated, "Main idea: use any opportunity to criticize Hillary [Clinton] and the rest (except Sanders and Trump—we support them)." This leaning is in line with other fake news producers—as we will later demonstrate in this chapter.

Private Firms

Facebook data privacy and security problems were revealed in March 2018 when the *New York Times* and the *Guardian* reported that Cambridge Analytica—a political data firm hired by Trump's 2016 election campaign—was improperly provided access to private information of more than fifty million Facebook users by Aleksandr Kogan, a Russian-

American psychology professor (Rosenberg et al. 2018). The following investigation and reports revealed that there were an additional thirty-seven million users whose information was obtained by Cambridge Analytica (Solon 2018). Such data were used to identify personalities of American voters with the goal of influencing their behavior and opinions. This revelation resulted in an apology by Facebook director Mark Zuckerberg (Chaykowski 2018), changes to Facebook data use (Ivanova 2018) and Zuckerberg's testimony in two separate congressional committee hearings (New York Times 2018; Kang et al. 2018). This scandal—while not directly related to low-quality news—spurred discussion on the role social media platforms play in our democracy, and such conversations included further debate and investigation into fake news.

Other Agents

In addition to the government agents and companies connected with them, there were other agents with monetary incentives involved in the spread of fake news during the 2016 U.S. election campaign season. Large fake news businesses were identified at both national and international levels. For instance, significant efforts emanating from Macedonia were linked to apolitical teenagers with pure monetary goals (Subramanian 2017). Despite the apparent apolitical incentives, such efforts commonly favored right-wing messages (Bhatt et al. 2018).

There is currently insufficient evidence to determine how much of the fake news content was created and distributed by each of the types of agents listed here. Yet one thing is clear; the fake news ecosystem was varied and extensive. Next we discuss why this was the case and what conditions made this ecosystem as rich and powerful as it was.

Several factors likely contributed to the optimal conditions for the widespread production and consumption of fake news content. The first factor relates to the way individuals access and share news. People consume the news increasingly through social media. Currently, 62 percent of U.S. adults get news on social media, a considerable jump from

49 percent[1] that was observed in 2012 (Gottfried and Shearer 2016). This new form of consumption changes the news production and consumption in a drastic way. The decentralized nature of social media platforms means that small media outlets, blogs, or even ordinary individuals can reach an audience—at times even larger than traditional news outlets—and spread their ideas. The lack of a filtering mechanism and the impossible challenge of inferring the credibility of individuals and information online can too often result in widespread diffusion of misinformation. This, coupled with recent research showing that readers commonly do not pay attention to or remember the source of news they read online (Kalogeropoulos and Newman 2017), highlights a potential cause for the spread of low-quality news—if a news reader cannot tell the source, all sources have the same credibility. Indeed, we saw several examples of this during the 2016 election. One was the Pizzagate conspiracy theory and the events that followed it (Fisher et al. 2018). After WikiLeaks posted a dump of 20,000 hacked emails from John Podesta, subscribers of an Internet message board called 8chan started to spread a number of outlandish rumors using social media platforms. One of these rumors claimed that the Podesta emails contained coded messages referring to a ring of pedophiles operating out of a pizza parlor in Northwest D.C. Despite the dubious and irrational nature of such allegations, they spread through social media to far-right blogs and eventually to the mainstream media.

A second, and potentially related, reason for the prevalence of low-quality news is the declining trust in traditional news media outlets. According to a 2016 Gallup poll, Americans' trust in mass media "to report the news fully, accurately and fairly" dropped by 8 percentage points from 2015 and is at a low of 32 percent (Swift 2016). Republicans largely drive this decline—only 14 percent of Republicans say they have such trust in the media—down from 32 percent a year ago. While it is likely that the election campaign—and perhaps the production and consumption of fake and otherwise low-quality news—contributed to the drop in public trust in the mass media, it is clear that this trust has been eroding over time, long before fake news became prevalent. One plausible explanation is that news consumers who were left unsatisfied by the products of traditional news media looked for alternatives, and fake news producers likely filled that void.

There was a third factor—unique to the 2016 election—that provided an opportunity for low-quality news sites to reach a wide audience. Donald Trump gave voice to a number of conspiracy theories both before (Barbaro 2016) and during (Finnegan 2016) the election season. On a number of occasions, he cited sources that are commonly labeled as fake or hyperpartisan. As a public figure running for the highest office in the country, Trump citing such sites provided these sources with national exposure and potentially gave more weight to their claims (Marwick and Lewis 2017).

On the production side, one of the most important reasons for the proliferation of fake and otherwise low-quality news is undoubtedly the monetary incentives. In the era of the Internet and Web 2.0, the barriers to entry for producing fake news have dropped significantly (Allcott and Gentzkow 2017). Content producers can now easily set up a website and a social media page, share their web content through their media page, and monetize on the received traffic through advertising. Furthermore, by creating fake social media accounts that look like real people and sharing their fake news content through such accounts, these producers can easily create the illusion of wide acceptance of the content they produced and bring in further traffic. Indeed, interviews with fake news producers revealed that the revenue during the election campaign was roughly around $10,000 per month (Ohlheiser 2016)—a substantial amount of money, especially considering the ease with which such a business can be set up. The significance of monetary incentives is perhaps most apparent in the story of one of the fake news producers, Jestin Coler, a registered Democrat, who made large amounts of money producing fake content that catered to Donald Trump supporters (Sydell 2016).

Defining Fake and Traditional News

Ascertaining the credibility of news content is a challenging task. A recent publication by leading scholars in the field of misinformation advocates for classification at the outlet level (Lazer et al. 2018). The authors provide the following argument:

> In evaluating the prevalence of fake news, we advocate focusing on the original sources—the publishers— rather than individual stories, because we view the defining element of fake news to be the intent and processes of the publisher. A focus on publishers also allows us to avoid the morass of trying to evaluate the accuracy of every single news story.

We follow this guideline and define fake and traditional news at the producer (web domain) level.

Given the significant societal implications of fake news production and consumption, there has been an increasing interest—in academia and the industry alike—in identifying fake news publishers. Consequently, there are a number of publicly available lists of fake news publishers.[2] This book relies on the list shared by Allcott, Gentzkow, and Yu (2019), which contains 673 fake news publishers and is compiled by combining five previous lists. Three of those lists are retrieved from organizations that apply journalistic standards in evaluating the validity of news articles,[3] and two of them are products of scholarly research.[4]

We use the Allcott, Gentzkow, and Yu (2019) list for two main reasons. First, this list provides the widest coverage. Second, the authors provide the most detailed robustness checks of their list compared to other efforts (e.g., Zimdars 2016). A key concern with the use of fake news publisher lists is the potential selection bias in the list of sites gathered. Allcott, Gentzkow, and Yu (2019) perform two robustness checks. First, they focus on sites that are identified as fake news sites by at least two or three lists instead of one. Second, they consider lists of sites assembled from any four out of the five original lists. They show that the general trends of fake news coverage are consistent across these definitions.

We define traditional news outlets using the categorization provided by Alexa Internet, Inc. (1996)—an American company based in California that provides commercial web traffic data and analytics based on the web-browsing behavior of a panel of millions of Internet users. In addition to providing website rankings based on readership, Alexa provides a rich ontology of the web. Using this ontology, we identify the set of websites listed under the *news* category, which includes national, regional, as well as international news sources. There are in total 5,497 domains listed under this heading. We remove the set of web domains listed by Allcott, Gentzkow, and Yu (2019) and classify the rest of the sites as traditional news publishers.

The Prevalence of Fake News Leading Up to the 2016 Election

How prevalent was fake news content leading up to the 2016 election? A study published by BuzzFeed News following the election (Silverman 2016b) painted a dire picture—claiming that hyperpartisan and fake news articles attracted more attention than mainstream news articles on Facebook. These hyperpartisan and fake news sites had a strong ideological bias—of the twenty most popular false election stories, all but three were overtly pro–Donald Trump or anti–Hillary Clinton. What followed was a lot of public outrage and an interest in understanding and curtailing fake news that gained traction after the election. While this analysis, and others like it, was instrumental in bringing attention to this important issue, the findings should be taken with a grain of salt for a number of reasons.

First, while Facebook is the most popular social media site for news consumption, it is only part of the story. Here, we start completing this story by performing a similar analysis of Twitter messages, which is the third most popular social media site for news consumption— following Facebook and YouTube (Gottfried and Shearer 2016).[5.] Facebook and

Twitter have significantly different mechanisms for sharing information, and the monetary incentives for the spread of fake news are likewise distinct. Given such differences, it is crucial to determine whether the significance of fake and hyperpartisan sites was just as prevalent on Twitter.

Second, the analysis presented in these earlier investigations inspects a biased data sample of websites. While the top stories indeed are far from negligible, they are still a small fraction of all news consumption. It is entirely possible for the fake news viewership to be mostly concentrated on these top stories, with traditional news consumption being more evenly distributed across a much larger production—resulting in traditional news outperforming fake news producers in aggregate. Therefore, it is important to inspect a more representative news dataset to more confidently determine the prevalence of such content.

This is what we do here. We examine the average and aggregate popularity of all content shared by traditional and fake news producers, as opposed to focusing on the top few most commonly shared articles. Furthermore, given that our dataset is balanced over time due to random tweet sampling at the daily level, our results are not dominated by a few articles that were highly popular for a short period of time. To achieve this, we rely on the subset of the tweets in the Twitter Daily Random Sample Database described in chapter 3 that included a link to an external web page. Such tweets include external information resources Twitter users deemed worth sharing and thus provide a perfect dataset for characterizing the extent to which the Twitter population relied on traditional or fake news sites as a source of information during the campaign season. In our dataset, there were over five million unique URLs shared. For each of the five million shortened URLs (e.g., http://t.co/rFoSwr68Hi), we first identified the actual URL (e.g., http://www.redstate.com/streiff/2015/07/24/polls-indicate-trump-hurt-gop-hispanics/) using automated scripts and removed links internal to Twitter since such content signifies retweets as opposed to links to external resources. This resulted in over 2.1 million unique URLs, which were consequently used to retrieve the content of the corresponding web page, again through automated web scrapers.[6]

The Concerning Popularity of Traditional and Fake News Alike

Alarmingly, we find that traditional news and fake news articles have comparable popularity on average. Traditional news articles were shared by 2.8 users on average, whereas this number was 2.88 for articles published by fake news outlets, a statistically insignificant difference. Similarly, a traditional news article had a shelf life of 4.7 days, on average, whereas this number is 5.5 for articles published by fake news producers. These measures both point to comparable popularity per article produced by fake and traditional news producers and raise significant concerns. The fact that an average product (article) produced by traditional news outlets, which employ professional journalists, is indistinguishable from an average product of fake news outlets is rather surprising. This finding highlights the challenges faced by traditional news outlets and the complexity of the required effort to combat this problem.

The Dominance of Traditional News
Media Outlets as a Silver Lining

While the comparability of traditional and fake news article popularity is concerning, there is a silver lining. We find that traditional news collectively accounted for significantly more shares—the number of users sharing traditional news content outnumbered those who share content produced by fake news outlets roughly one to four. This was largely due to the larger production by traditional news compared to fake news publishers, and this effect was mostly due to a small number of big news organizations. For instance, there were no fake news producers that single-handedly received more than 30,000 shares in our dataset, while there were a number of traditional news sites (e.g., *New York Times*, Fox News) with that many shares. This highlights significant differences in production and consumption of fake and traditional news publishers and underscores the importance of large news institutions in the defense against fake news producers.

Fake News Publisher Prevalence over Time

Next, we determine how the reliance on fake news producers changed over time and how those changes relate to changes in favorability of the two candidates. Figure 8-1 presents our findings in the form of three curves, comparing the fraction of fake news articles for each candidate, and Clinton's lead in favorability. The blue curve denotes the prominence of fake news publisher content in tweets mentioning Clinton. Prominence was estimated as the ratio between fake news content and all news content, using the following formula: for each day, we counted the number of times articles published by fake news outlets were shared in tweets mentioning Clinton (x). Next, we counted the number of times articles published by traditional news outlets were shared in tweets mentioning Clinton (y). The fraction of fake news in Clinton tweets is then simply estimated as $x/(x + y)$. Since this fraction can fluctuate from day to day, we smooth out the curve by using a moving average of 15 days. This simply means that the number plotted on the graph is estimated over the articles shared 7 days before and after any given day. The red curve estimates a similar measure for the prevalence of fake news publisher content in tweets mentioning Trump. The gray curve denotes the net Clinton favorability over time, obtained from Gallup survey responses. Net Clinton favorability simply refers to the degree to which responders found Clinton to be more favorable than Trump. This time series is equally smoothed out to provide the 15-day running average for purposes of consistency.

Figure 8-1 provides a number of important insights. First, we see that the tweets mentioning Clinton had a higher relative rate of fake news prevalence compared to tweets mentioning Trump. Past research highlights the significance of negativity bias—the tendency to prioritize negative information over positive—in democratic politics (Soroka 2014). This is true for both the news outlets and the consumers. Furthermore, news outlets tend to show their ideological bias not by directly advocating for a preferred political party but by disproportionately criticizing the other side (Budak, Goel, and Rao 2016). In addition, news consumers are more likely to read and share news with extreme sentiment scores (Rieis et al. 2015). These observations provide a possible explanation as to why the prevalence of fake news was higher in Clinton tweets compared to Trump: fake news producers—which were predominantly pro–Donald Trump and anti–Hillary Clinton (Silverman 2016b)—likely focused their attention on publishing negative content about Clinton, as opposed to positive news about Trump, and such content was shared in tweets mentioning Clinton.

Second, we observe a general upward trend in the prominence of fake news over time. This trend is seen for both Trump- and Clinton-

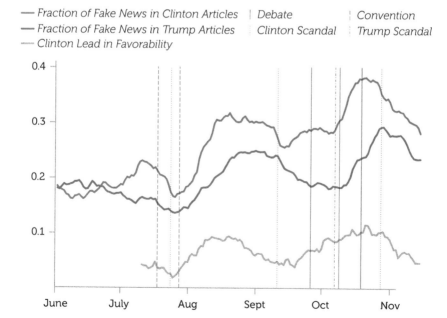

Figure 8-1

Fraction of Article Shares that are from Fake News Producers by Electoral Candidate, and Clinton Net Favorability over Time

— *Fraction of Fake News in Clinton Articles*   ⁞ *Debate*   ⁞ *Convention*
— *Fraction of Fake News in Trump Articles*   ⁞ *Clinton Scandal*   ⁞ *Trump Scandal*
— *Clinton Lead in Favorability*

related tweets but is most obvious in the case of Clinton. For instance, while the average fraction of low-quality news content is about 20 percent before the conventions, it jumps up to approximately 30 percent after the nominations. For both time series, we observe two peaks. The first upward trending starts after the Democratic and Republican conventions. The second upward trend starts after the second presidential debate. This overall trend can be a result of the production, the consumption, or a combination of the two. Fake news producers might have increased their production function over time, perhaps observing that there was enough public interest in such content. Twitter users could have increased their consumption of fake news content, or consumers of such content could have become more active over time—this result could have been exacerbated due to an increase in the number of automated political bots. Alternatively, the outcome can be a combination of all these effects. Although it is not possible to pinpoint the exact causal mechanism here, the increasing trend of fake news prominence, which means a relatively decreasing trend for traditional news, provides a cautionary tale for journalists because their output seems to have become less relevant as the campaigns progressed.

Finally, and most intriguingly, the net Clinton favorability measure computed through the Gallup surveys and the prevalence of low-quality news content in both Trump and Clinton tweets seem to follow a similar pattern. Indeed, the cross-correlation—a measure commonly used to estimate similarity between two time series data—between the time series for net Clinton favorability and the prevalence of fake news in Clinton tweets—is 0.8, suggesting a strong relationship. This could indicate one of the three following scenarios: fake news production and consumption could be *responding to* Clinton favorability polls; fake news production and consumption could be *leading to* changes in net Clinton favorability; or the two measures could be responding to a third measure not captured here, such as real-world events affecting the campaigns.

While ruling out the third option is not possible, we can determine whether the first or the second scenario is more likely by examining whether the changes in net Clinton favorability *lead* or *lag* changes in fake news production and consumption. Our analysis reveals that the changes in net Clinton favorability *precede* changes in fake news production and consumption. A focus on content shared in tweets mentioning Clinton shows the strongest relationship between net Clinton favorability at a given day d with the low-quality news article fraction on Twitter at day $d + 4$—the correlation in this case is 0.85. In other words, changes in the fraction of fake news articles shared in Clinton tweets lag changes in Clinton favorability by four days.[7]

What could generate such a relationship? One plausible explanation is that fake news producers with a pro-Trump and anti-Clinton agenda could have been responding to changes in public polling outcomes—increasing their production whenever an increase in Clinton support (or decrease in Trump support) was observed. Similarly, political bots with the same leaning could have been increasing the rate at which they tweet content in an effort to attack the Clinton campaign. Individuals who held unfavorable views of the Clinton campaign could have been increasing their consumption and sharing of fake news content, or individuals who were favorable to the Clinton campaign could have reduced their consumption and sharing of traditional news content, perhaps due to a sense of security. It is important to note that correlation is not causation. Even though our analysis suggests that fake news production and consumption might be responding to changes in net Clinton favorability, we cannot conclude a causal relationship. Yet the suggestive analysis is compelling. Regardless of the exact causal mechanism, this temporal analysis shows that fake news production and consumption were closely following election campaign dynamics.

The Content of Fake News during the 2016 Election Campaign

What was the appeal of fake news sites during the 2016 election campaign? To answer this question, we need to look at the content of the articles that were shared. Here, we start with a simple analysis by counting the number of times a word appears in articles published by fake and traditional news producers weighted by the number of times that the corresponding articles were shared on Twitter.[8] We do this separately for Trump and Clinton tweets to determine what words were most commonly observed in articles about the two candidates, and to identify how word usage differs between traditional and fake news producers. The results are given in table 8-1. Each row in this table gives the most frequently observed thirty words alongside the number of occurrences in parentheses within articles shared in one of the four categories: (1) articles from fake news producers shared in Trump tweets, (2) articles from traditional news producers shared in Trump tweets, (3) articles from fake news producers shared in Clinton tweets, and (4) traditional news articles shared in Clinton tweets.

There are several observations worth noting based on table 8-1. First, the focuses of discussion in fake and traditional news sites, as determined through the most commonly used words, look rather similar, although the similarity between the most common words for traditional and low-quality news articles shared in Trump tweets is more evident. We can see that no words associated with the controversies faced by Donald Trump show up among the most frequent top-30 words for either source. Perhaps, this is not surprising. One can argue that the subtleties of topical coverage cannot be revealed in the most common words. Yet a look at the Clinton results would show otherwise. Unlike for Donald Trump, *email*, which is associated with several Hillary Clinton controversies, is seen in the top-30 words for both traditional and fake news articles shared. In addition, articles shared from the fake news producers focus on other controversies, highlighted by the use of words such as *Benghazi* or *foundation* (likely related to the Clinton Foundation controversies).

Given the surprising similarity between the most common words used in traditional and fake news articles, we next identify topics, or rather words, that are most uniquely associated with traditional news as well as words that are unique to fake news articles. To do so, we first limit the vocabulary to frequent-enough words that voters read,

Table 8-1

Most Commonly Used Words on Fake and Traditional News Articles Shared in Tweets Mentioning Trump and Clinton.

Outlet Type	Focus	Most common words in articles
Fake	Trump	president (84,647), obama (78,065), republican (67,959), media (56,828), cruz (56,229), campaign (56,132), america (53,399), twitter (51,495), presidential (46,727), state (46,116), video (46,065), american (44,418), country (44,250), support (43,036), percent (42,833), candidate (42,480), gop (38,754), party (38,723), right (38,350), first (38,076), political (36,265), election (35,350), vote (32,999), continues (29,645), well (29,450), united (29,220), voters (28,990), government (28,553), national (28,180), life (28,107)
Traditional	Trump	republican (783,536), campaign (718,660), president (666,010), percent (525,712), presidential (505,957), voters (442,464), party (399,312), state (383,686), candidate (367,822), first (357,957), obama (346,452), political (320,780), country (317,964), gop (313,238), cruz (296,067), american (293,025), former (292,842), election (287,345), support (276,526), white (275,596), right (272,193), national (266,694), republicans (261,232), well (251,768), bush (246,874), million (244,883), america (238,151), house (230,517), media (229,153), business (228,621)

Outlet Type	Focus	Most common words in articles
Fake	Clinton	state (366,089), department (220,704), foundation (218,445), president (187,239), email (182,189), campaign (151,605), bill (149,733), secretary (146,429), obama (145,354), emails (141,270), former (135,271), posted (130,704), government (128,662), 2004 (110,888), kristinn (103,677), pdt (102,496), information (101,943), house (97,355), first (92,671), video (91,742), well (88,091), democratic (84,856), presidential (83,090), american (81,622), fbi (79,047), money (78,356), good (78,197), benghazi (77,328), election (76,196), million (76,099)
Traditional	Clinton	state (2,145,430), campaign (1,745,581), president (1,689,658), sanders (1,476,851), democratic (1,275,661), obama (1,198,803), former (1,075,099), department (1,054,652), percent (1,033,294), presidential (1,009,572), secretary (966,695), voters (876,391), first (871,344), mrs (858,860), email (782,138), bill (781,208), emails (768,223), republican (751,071), house (739,059), foundation (725,553), party (664,270), political (649,414), white (636,518), candidate (631,256), government (616,310), support (585,319), election (582,428), democrats (580,380), national (551,664), information (536,626)

Note: The most commonly used words for Clinton reveal that (1) emails were indeed among the most commonly discussed topics in both traditional news and low-quality news, and (2) the emphasis on emails as a topic was stronger for low-quality news.

saw, or heard about the candidates and remove general and domain-specific stop words and lemmatize the words. To measure how much a word in one of these sets is associated with fake news articles, we compute a "fakeness" score for each word (w), using the log-odds-ratio technique with informative Dirichlet priors (Monroe et al. 2008). Using this formulation, words with a high fakeness score are words that occur with much higher probability in fake news articles than all reviews, in general. We apply this method to identify words about Donald Trump and Hillary Clinton that are associated with low-quality news articles (words with the highest fakeness scores), as well as with traditional

Table 8-2

Words That Are Most Unique to Fake versus Traditional Articles for Trump and Clinton Tweets

News Outlet	Candidate	Most Unique Words
Fake	Trump	advertis, video, islam, continu, pleas, twitter, liber, obama, media, illeg, america, leav, establish, advanc, cruz, share, lie, support, christian, alien
Traditional	Trump	voter, campaign, republican, compani, casino, percent, photo, former, citi, iowa, advis, univers, hotel, tower, regist, month, busi, presidenti, chariti, build
Fake	Clinton	video, foundat, lawsuit, document, twitter, corrupt, huma, wikileak, lie, die, file, sex, court, death, report, email, content, forget, advertis, healthi
Traditional	Clinton	sander, percent, voter, campaign, democrat, photo, iowa, candid, republican, presidenti, primari, support, hampshir, senat, nomin, debat, poll, race, biden, gop

news articles (words with the lowest fakeness scores). The results are given in table 8-2.

Table 8-2 reveals some interesting differences. We see that a number of negative topics (e.g., *univers*, *chariti*[9]) are seen to be unique to traditional news articles about Trump. In comparison, words that are associated with fake news producer content seem to be related to topics such as immigration (related words: *illegal*, *alien*), religious concerns (related words: *islam*, *christian*), and antiestablishment populist topics (related word: *establish*). For Hillary Clinton, the words associated with fake news are all negative and focus on the email scandal as well as her health. In comparison, traditional news outlet words are more generally about the horse race. Note however, that the words given in table 8-2 are not necessarily frequent—they simply are significantly more frequent in traditional news compared to fake news and vice versa. Indeed, our earlier analysis revealed, to our dismay, that perhaps the focus of these two sources was rather similar. The email scandal was a popular topic for Clinton in both traditional and fake news, and no controversy about Donald Trump was really elevated to a significant popularity in either type of source.[10]

What Was Retained? Fake or Traditional News Content?

Was the public more likely to be exposed to the agenda set by traditional or fake news producers? To identify the topics related to Donald Trump mentioned by Gallup respondents, we compute the frequency with which words were uttered when respondents were asked *what they have read, seen, or heard about Donald Trump in the past day or two*.[11] We repeat the same process to identify the topics, or words, associated with Hillary Clinton in Gallup interviews. The result is a sorted list of words and the associated counts. We next compute the fakeness of each word using the log-odds ratio with the informed Dirichlet priors method mentioned earlier. Using this methodology, we will be able to determine whether the common themes revealed during the interviews are better aligned with a fake or a traditional news agenda. For instance, this method assigns a value of 68.2 for the word *emails* when used for Hillary Clinton—meaning that the word is more frequently observed in fake news articles and is therefore associated with a positive and large fakeness measure. The word *debate* on the other hand is more frequently observed in traditional news articles and has a fakeness measure of –48.5. Words like *foundation*, *lies*, and *liar* similarly have positive and high fakeness value. In comparison, words like *convention* and *issues* have low fakeness values.

Given the fakeness measure computed for each word, separately for Hillary Clinton and Donald Trump, we compute the fakeness of the most popular k words uttered in Gallup surveys for the two candidates, with k ranging between 1 and 100. When computing the fakeness of top-k words, we weigh the estimate by how frequently each word is observed. For instance, *emails* occurs three times more frequently than the word *debate*. Therefore, the fakeness of *email* will be accounted three times more heavily than the fakeness of the word *debate*. Using this methodology, we can measure the quality of all interview responses as well as responses given by Republican-leaning interviewees and Democrat-leaning interviewees, respectively. The empirical results of this analysis are presented in figure 8-2 for responses pertaining to Hillary Clinton, and in figure 8-3 for responses pertaining to Donald Trump.

A number of observations are worth noting with regard to figure 8-2. First, the top-100 words the interviewees uttered when asked what they had read, seen, or heard about Hillary Clinton consistently resemble fake news coverage more than traditional news coverage (with y-values greater than 0). Second, there is a clear divide between Republican- and Democrat-leaning respondents. Republican-leaning respondents consistently use words in line with those unique to fake news coverage, while the words used by Democrat-leaning respondents are more in line with traditional news coverage.

It is important to note, however, that this finding does not necessarily mean that the fake news coverage *resulted in* the topics individuals particularly remembered. The result we observe here might be due to fake news producers focusing more on topics that were more memorable (discriminately for the Republican-leaning voters). Indeed, the first analysis presented in this chapter already showed that the coverage by traditional and fake news outlets was rather similar. Traditional news outlets focused on Hillary Clinton controversies more than Donald Trump controversies, or at least the fact that there was a single controversial topic regarding Hillary Clinton (emails) resulted in this topic being elevated to the most frequently observed words. A similar observation was made in a recent study (Patterson 2016), which suggested that the traditional news outlets failed voters by creating false equivalencies. While we cannot establish causality using our observational data without a more careful causal inference framework, the overlap between the fake news coverage and retained information extracted from Gallup interviews is cause for concern and worthy of further exploration.

Figure 8-2

Fakeness of the Top-100 Words Uttered about Hillary Clinton in Gallup Surveys

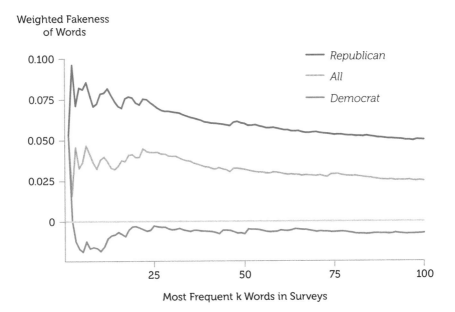

The results regarding Donald Trump, presented in figure 8-3, are rather distinct from what we observed for Hillary Clinton. We first see that the most frequent words across all interviewees were more in line with traditional news coverage. The fakeness only becomes slightly positive beyond the most popular topics and hovers only barely above zero. We also see that the difference between the Republican- and Democrat-leaning respondents is not distinguishable, while the directionality of the results is largely consistent between these two groups. What may explain the relatively low degree to which survey responses align with fake news content about Donald Trump? As mentioned earlier, fake news sites were predominantly pro–Donald Trump and anti–Hillary Clinton. Our findings therefore suggest that fake news producers showed their ideological leaning not by writing supportive articles about Donald Trump but by writing critical articles about Hillary Clinton. As a result, it is entirely reasonable that fake news outlets

Figure 8-3

Fakeness of the Top-100 words Uttered about Donald Trump in Gallup Surveys

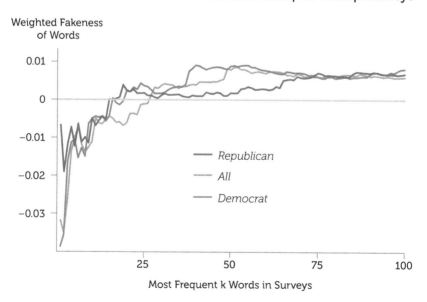

did not produce mass content about Donald Trump, resulting in a lack of alignment on this topic.

How do we interpret these findings overall? Which mechanisms are likely to have generated the alignment of retained information for Hillary Clinton and the fake news coverage about her? One possibility is that fake news consumption was widespread, dictating what information voters retained and consequently voted on. While this conjecture is in line with a number of bold claims that would have us believe fake news shaped the outcome of the 2016 election (Dewey 2016a; Parkinson 2016), while relieving traditional news media from much of the responsibility, one should not rush to this conclusion, it being merely one of many explanations. It is equally plausible that fake news producers focused more on topics that were more *memorable*. Take emails or health issues, for instance. These two topics were commonly mentioned in Gallup interviews, and both topics also had high fakeness values since fake news outlets, compared to traditional news media, covered them significantly more frequently. Similarly, it is entirely possible that even individuals who predominantly consumed traditional news content were more likely to remember controversial topics as opposed to information covered in common horse-race-style articles typical of traditional news reporting. Furthermore, the traditional news examined in this chapter is produced and consumed *online*—other forms of traditional news, such as cable news, might be more similar to fake news coverage.

How Our Analysis of Fake News May Be Limited

This chapter provides an analysis of the spread of fake news during the 2016 election. While important/significant, it is worthwhile to discuss some of the shortcomings arising from our analytic method. First, the Twitter population is not representative of the U.S. population. Yet, through an analysis of Twitter behavior online, we are able to capture the content individuals felt comfortable sharing publicly, as opposed to consuming privately. Furthermore, while Twitter is one of the popular social media sites used for sharing and consuming news content, it certainly is not the only one (Gottfried and Shearer 2016). Finally, bots generated a substantial fraction of Twitter content (Guilbeault and Woolley 2016).

Despite these shortcomings, Twitter still provides a rich window through which to observe public opinion online and determine to what extent conventional news media versus fake news outlets dominated the discussion in the digital space. Insights derived from Twitter analysis can help us make sense of how information propagated throughout the campaign process, and better understand the changes in public trust in, and reliance on, news media.

Identifying low-quality news at the domain level, as opposed to the article level, has certain shortcomings. First, domains classified as fake at times might publish real and reliable news. Second, even mainstream news sites exhibit ideological bias and at times might even disseminate misinformation due to unreliable sources. A recent example of such behavior was observed during the Boston marathon bombing, where highly respected organizations such as CNN, the Associated Press, Fox News, and the *Boston Globe*—with a desire to break the news early—falsely reported a nonexistent arrest. This mistake was followed by the *New York Post* printing the photo of two innocent men in a front-page picture as the perpetrators of the bombing (Carr 2013). This problem is perhaps even more relevant in today's publishing environment where news organizations are cutting expenses, and journalists are increasingly relying on social media to report on the news. However, credible news sites, unlike fake news outlets that consistently share misinformation, tend to correct such false reporting. Therefore, we believe that the focus on fake news at the outlet level provides a meaningful look into the news ecosystem.

Finally, and most notably, the findings presented in this chapter are purely correlational. Future research that identifies the causal mechanisms will be crucial in finding the path forward in combating fake news and misinformation online.

Conclusion

This chapter presents a number of empirical findings that are insightful to producers and consumers of traditional news and social media content alike. First, we found that fake news publishers produced a significant portion of content about the election in the Twitterverse, one of the most popular news media sites. While we cannot determine to what extent this pattern affected the election outcome, we can deduce that traditional news media face a significant challenge of becoming/staying relevant in the age of an expanding relevance of social media platforms. This has important consequences. News consumption carries important implications for societal dynamics, such as political participation (Dilliplane 2011), voting (DellaVigna and Kaplan 2007), and charitable giving (Brown and Minty 2006). The results also demonstrate that, for various measures of prevalence, low-quality news production and consumption outperformed traditional news during the 2016 election campaign. We also show that the information retained by Republican voters about Clinton was more in line with fake news content than traditional news. This raises serious concerns for modern democratic systems.

At the same time, our findings offer a silver lining. In contrast to early reporting immediately following the election, we do not find that fake news outperformed traditional news in the aggregate. While an average fake and traditional news article have comparable popularity, traditional news outlets collectively outperformed fake news by a 4:1 ratio, thanks in large part to a small number of news producers with large production. This highlights the importance of well-known news organizations for potential future efforts to combat the spread of misinformation. With that said, it becomes clear that news producers have an opportunity and a responsibility to leverage their popularity and provide the public with reliable news information.

Where do we go from here? If fake news corrodes our democracy, what can and should be done about it? Social media platforms such as Facebook, while initially skeptical about their role in the election outcome (Kokalitcheva, 2016), have taken steps to identify fake news content and are starting to warn their consumers about questionable content (Mosseri 2016; Shelbourne 2017), mostly relying on independent organizations for fact checking. A similar step has been taken by companies like Google, which provides news aggregation tools (Wingfield, Isaac, and Benner 2016). These are undoubtedly important steps toward a more robust news ecosystem. However, these developments also raise the following important question: Is it reasonable or even wise to expect social media platforms to take on the role of media gatekeepers or arbiters of truth? After all, it was not so long ago that Facebook faced a significant backlash for its moderation of the trending news section (Nunez 2016). The criticism even drove Facebook to change how it moderated trending topics, resulting in an increase of hoax stories being elevated to trending status (Dewey 2016b).

The change in our growing demands for content regulation from sites like Facebook demonstrates the number and complexity of problems in the current news ecosystem. Fake news detection and containment are both hard problems—the fields of computer and information sciences are yet to develop methods that are sufficiently accurate and objective. As fake and otherwise low-quality news is here to stay, we need to invest in building strategic tools for traditional news organizations to stay relevant, enabling them to compete with a growing fake news industry. Likewise, there is a need for developing literacy tools that news consumers can use to distinguish credible news from unreliable content. Perhaps one of the positive outcomes of the 2016 campaign season is the attention it brought to this important issue, since the first step to solving a problem is to acknowledge its existence.

9

Conclusions

Determining What (Words) Mattered

The preceding chapters make clear the advantages and importance of studying the language of political campaigns. A comparison of the words used in traditional media, social media, and open-ended survey responses provides a unique and valuable account of the 2016 election campaign. Our findings have spoken to imbalances in the coverage of presidential candidates; the predominance of negative content throughout the campaign; the enduring significance of email-related scandals for voters, even when news content turns to other issues; the significant but also short life span of campaign-related events; and the circulation of fake news content. In each analysis, words played a starring role. Some words get into voters' minds and some don't. Of those that do, some persist in voters' minds over the course of the campaign and others are quickly forgotten.

Recognizing the significance of language to politics is by no means a new idea. Early quantitative content-analytic work, mobilized in large part by authors' experiences with communications during World War

II, made a strong case for the importance of understanding words in order to comprehend persuasion and political behavior (Lasswell and Leites 1965). Subsequent work, both quantitative and qualitative, has pressed further. Edelman (1985) asserts the following in "Political Language and Political Reality":

> It is language about political events and developments that people experience; even events that are close by take their meaning from the language used to depict them. So *political language is political reality* [italics in original]; there is no other so far as the meaning of events to actor and spectators is concerned. (10)[1]

We would not make quite as bold a claim ourselves. Reality is not entirely subjective—some things happen, and in certain cases the event itself is not entirely open to reframing through language. Yet the partial truth of Edelman's claim is that so much of modern electoral campaigns is experienced from afar. Average Americans do not experience "retail politics" by attending a campaign rally or meeting a candidate; rather they experience the campaigns through traditional and social media. The things most citizens know about election campaigns are therefore secondhand, and, importantly, mediated. Walter Lippmann's (1997 [1922]) famous words are truer now than ever:

> The world we have to deal with politically is out of reach, out of sight, out of mind. It has to be explored, reported, and imagined.[18] . . . Each of us lives and works on a small part of the earth's surface, moves in a small circle, and of these acquaintances knows only a few intimately. . . . Inevitably our opinions cover a bigger space, a longer reach of time, a greater number of things, than we can directly observe. They have, therefore, to be pieced together out of what others have reported and what we can imagine. (53)

The words used to describe campaigns on traditional and social media are thus of fundamental significance. And the words that citizens remember from media content are an especially valuable tool for understanding (mediated) campaign effects.

The preceding chapters have reflected an interest in doing exactly this—in using words to understand the 2016 campaign. Our initial analyses were performed in the months immediately following that campaign; and for the most part, the chapters reflect that early post-election thinking. However, writing roughly three years after that campaign and during the primary season for the 2020 election, we have some additional insights, related both to what happened in 2016 and what may happen in 2020. We focus on three: (1) the relevance of pre-campaign attitudes to campaign-period media effects, (2) the impact of a changing media environment on the circulation of campaign information, and (3) the growing prevalence of fake news. We finally consider some additional general findings regarding the study of political communication in 2020 and beyond.

The Importance of Precampaign Histories and the Public's Awareness of Them

A crucial aspect of the 2016 campaign was that, despite being packed with huge media stories, recollections of those stories were short-lived. The striking exception was the set of related stories that we collectively label Hillary Clinton's email scandal. Respondents reported hearing about the email scandal fairly consistently throughout the campaign. Other stories would have their temporary moments in the sun and partially distract from Clinton's emails, but as soon as those stories faded, the public's thoughts would return to the emails. This steady attention to email was compounded by the two Comey letters, which drew extra attention to the story in the very last days of the campaign. Thus, Clinton's email was a story that was inherently more resonant than others during the campaign, but it had also been heavily primed before the election.

This latter point may be critical. Past work suggests that the effects of political messages on the public tend to fade quickly (Gerber et al. 2011; Hill et al. 2013). There is also evidence that, in 2016, a substantial number of voters, especially in pivotal Electoral College states, made their decisions close to Election Day (Blake 2016; McKee, Smith, and Hood 2019). Thus all the major stories during the campaign, which briefly dominated the public's attention and then faded out, likely had minimal effects on this very close election. One can nevertheless make a case that the email story, persistent in the public's mind and especially dominant at the end, was decisive in Hillary Clinton's very narrow loss. Yet to what extent was this a product of the campaign?

Consider the following. The number of scandals connected to Donald Trump was remarkable, but the durability of the impact of any one of those scandals was typical of most political campaigns. There is little evidence that these Trump scandals had a lasting impact on voters. The impact of the email scandal for Clinton was, in contrast, remarkably enduring. Our suspicion is that this is because messages about email scandals were not just from the campaign—they built upon months and months (if not years) of news coverage of Hillary Clinton. Stories about email were not short-term events that just happened to occur during the campaign, like many of the events highlighted in chapters 2, 3, and 7 that emerged and then faded from national attention. Their impact was most likely to keep an already highly salient issue in the public eye. The 2016 campaign may be an example of the significance of attitudes toward Clinton held by the mass public and journalists *before* the campaign. The strength of the email stories may have been due to their ability to sustain already existing concerns about Clinton, not produce new ones. (New scandals about Trump, in contrast, appeared to have had only short-term effects.)

One lesson for future campaigns is that precampaign narratives about candidates can be critical. A central product of the 2016 campaign information environment was to keep email on the agenda. In the end, new information may have mattered very little. Transpose this dynamic to, for instance, the 2020 campaign, in which there are already many long-lasting scandals connected to Trump. One likely consequence is that media content about Trump is likely to matter primarily through priming these now well-established concerns. Trump in 2020 could face the same kind of problem that Clinton faced in 2016.

What advice can we offer for parties when selecting presidential nominees in the future, as the Democrats are doing as this book goes to print? While not the only consideration, voters and party elites may reasonably consider electability when selecting a nominee. There are lessons from 2016 that may be relevant to that choice. Candidates with long-standing public careers, especially those who accumulated potentially problematic records, will have a steeper hill to climb in the general election.[2] There are real advantages to political experience, to be sure; and the advantages of experience may well outweigh the disadvantages of a past in politics. Even so, 2016 highlights the difficulties of entering a campaign with a past that can be (and most likely will be) repeatedly reinforced in both traditional and social media. Even as campaign events may matter relatively little, precampaign histories, augmented by campaign-period reporting, can matter a lot.

A Media Landscape That Has Become More Social

A second important factor is that the media environment is unquestionably changing. In past elections, voters primarily relied upon traditional sources of campaign information, including newspapers, broadcast and cable television news, news/talk radio, and direct contact from campaigns (such as canvassing, direct mail, and television advertisements). All of these sources of information still exist, but they are now accompanied by the exploding availability of information from online-only outlets, including social media platforms like Facebook, Twitter, and YouTube. Two-thirds (68 percent) of Americans get news from social media (Matsa and Shearer 2018), and people do learn from the information to which they are exposed on these platforms (Bode 2016). Because 69 percent of Americans are Facebook users, 73 percent use YouTube, and 22 percent use Twitter, the type of news that proliferates on social media is important to understand (Perrin and Anderson 2019). Still, the nature of what constitutes news is somewhat murky in these spaces that blend social and informational content in one place (Vraga et al. 2016).

From 2016 to the publication of this book, the number of Americans using YouTube, Facebook, and Twitter has generally held steady. Notably, encrypted social media including Snapchat and WhatsApp have emerged on the scene and grown in importance, and use of Instagram has grown over this time as well. All of these platforms offer challenges for studying content, as access is essentially impossible for encrypted messages, and Instagram's visual format makes parsing information there more complicated.

Even in a more fractured media landscape, coverage still returns to the horse race more than issues, a trend that media scholars have lamented for decades. This includes a focus on who is ahead and behind as well as the day-to-day accusations and attacks of the campaign trail, all of which Patterson (1993, 2016) has called "game schema" news coverage, rather than coverage of candidates' policy proposals or the state of the country. Our analysis of Twitter suggests that content on social media is more negative than coverage overall, and no more likely to focus on policy substance.

One of our most crucial findings is thus that the imbalance in attention, which is tilted toward campaign attacks and scandals, is much more extreme in public perceptions than in the conventional media content we observe. This could be because this type of coverage is featured more prominently or accessibly in the overall media landscape (the combination of traditional and social media), or it could be because it is more memorable than other campaign information to people who do encounter it. Either way, even a slight skew toward this type of content tends to produce a big shift in the information people absorb and remember, exacerbating the extent to which this type of content dominates the public's thinking.

Fake News

Third, the public's growing use of social media likely implies a greater role for it in the 2020 campaign. Importantly, both the information to which people are exposed and their perceptions of it are different for social media than for more traditional news outlets. One notable difference is that a larger portion of the information on social media is not true and may even be disseminated to mislead intentionally. Although this misinformation is certainly a minority of the overall content (Guess, Nyhan, and Reifler 2018), its presence affects perceptions of social media content. About 57 percent of social media news consumers reporting that they expect news they see on social media to be "largely inaccurate" (Matsa and Shearer 2018). Some of this information is intended to portray certain candidates unfavorably, and other elements are designed to demoralize and demobilize certain members of the electorate. Disconcertingly, in 2016 we not only found that fake news sources predominantly focused on one candidate—Clinton—but also that the information right-leaning individuals retained about her was significantly more aligned with fake news coverage compared to that retained by left-leaning individuals. This finding draws attention to new concerns about knowledge divides in today's news ecosystem between those consuming fake and those consuming generally accurate news. Although both the amount of content and the effects may be relatively small, they can alter the outcome in a close election.

One consequence is that foreign intrusion into the campaign landscape through social media—with the use of bots and fake news content or through explicit attempts to divide social groups in the electorate—can have an enhanced role in the formation of candidate assessments (Jamieson 2018). In the future, there probably will be heightened attention to and scrutiny of fake news producers, who operated without much opposition in 2016.

Such attention can result in successful efforts in curtailing the spread of fake news. Indeed, while similar disinformation campaigns took place in elections across the world following 2016, effective anticipation and reaction have—in at least some cases—resulted in successfully limiting their impact (Schmidt 2018). This heightened attention will also place added pressure on the platforms on which content is created and through which it is disseminated to detect and remove it early and often. We do not know yet whether governmental institutions are well organized to take on this role. The Trump administration has resisted investigations into how misinformation was produced and disseminated in 2016 and is expected to continue to fight such attempts in the future. Furthermore, constant societal and technological changes make confronting this increasingly difficult. Indeed, both the administrations that introduced fake news bans (Serhan 2018) and the companies that implemented technological solutions to curtail the spread (Chowdry 2017; Abril 2019) faced significant pushback from those citing freedom of speech concerns. Voices citing concerns about fake news were perhaps not as loud as they could have been in 2016. Looking forward, more vigilance is necessary and will require an extraordinary effort to produce disclosures and elimination of such content in close to real time.

This may be especially true given that we find that fake news prevalence in 2016 closely followed campaign dynamics—with changes in the fraction of news that was fake following changes in candidate favorability. This suggests a significant level of sophistication among those producing and disseminating fake news. The need to curtail such production and dissemination is self-evident, and the effort must involve multiple stakeholders. Platforms should not only retroactively remove bad actors and information, as they are already doing, but also audit their algorithms that prioritize content based on engagement— engagement that can be driven by outrageous and engaging fake news articles. The decentralized nature of social media platforms and the lack of robust filtering mechanisms make it impossibly hard for news consumers to tell facts from fake news. Technologists need to invest in efforts to identify fake news at scale and inform news consumers in a timely and convincing fashion. Timeliness is of utmost importance here given research that shows the difficulty of combating misinformation after a long delay (Budak, Agrawal, El Abbadi 2011).

Implications for the Study of Political Communication

One important lesson of the preceding chapters is that the different streams of information examined do not simply mirror each other. While the same topics do appear in each stream, and all streams react to the same set of events, they have quite different properties. We cannot study political communication during campaigns—the streams of information that potential voters see and absorb—just by studying traditional media, such as newspapers, television, and radio. As mentioned in the previous section, there will often be a disconnect between the content of traditional media and what people report hearing about the campaign. This pushes back against traditional models of agenda setting.

Instead, those who study campaign communication should do two things. First, we should try to do a better job of measuring social media content. This is challenging because the content of many social media platforms is neither public nor usually available to researchers to study. The volume of such information is so great that capturing and analyzing the information in real time is a formidable task. But more interdisciplinary work to combine the strengths of social and computer sciences would be a step in the right direction. This type of work is necessary if we hope to get a more complete picture of what the public is encountering. Second, as we have mentioned, no account of political information transmission during campaigns can be complete without measuring in surveys what messages people are hearing and remembering.

We learned from our open-ended survey questions that citizens' recall of campaign news reflects a biased (nonrandom) subset of actual campaign news content. Some themes are more enduring than others. Scandal and negative content are more readily recalled. So too, as a consequence, is fake information. And messages on topics that have been connected to a candidate's image repeatedly, over a long time, seem to be more easily absorbed and recalled by the public. This has implications for candidates who are fresh faces running against those with a long public record. Those older, well-established themes resonate among journalists who produce media coverage and (even more so) in the public's thinking.

Responses to the open-ended "read, seen, or heard" survey question have several advantages over other measures of public opinion. First, by asking citizens what they remember, we can highlight differences between media content and recalled media content. Work on media effects has long recognized that not all media content matters to electoral behavior. Typically, we infer this by looking at measures of media content alongside trends in approval or vote intentions. Moments of correspondence between them, or a lack thereof, are a signal of when media do or do not matter. Alternatively, closed-ended survey questions ask what respondents think about a recent event, often with some delay. In both cases, we get only a partial picture of the varying impact of media content. The open-ended responses used here provide a much clearer picture of what does or does not find its way into the public consciousness. We rely on full-text analyses of media coverage as the indication of what appears in media; and we rely on open-ended recalls to identify, in a more direct but also more flexible way, what citizens remember. These measures are preferable to asking people to report about their exposure and attention to particular media and what they recall from that.

For this reason, the open-ended "read, seen, or heard" responses have played a starring role in the preceding chapters, and we are strong advocates of the use of these or similarly formatted open-ended questions in future work. This is the case in part because the strength of the open-ended approach extends beyond identifying differences in media and opinion trends. The literature in political communication has struggled with what is quite possibly its most important variable: media exposure. Recent work by de Vreese and Neijens (2016) highlights the many different ways in which this variable has been measured, and the many different flaws in existing approaches to measurement.

Matters are unquestionably worsening in our fast-changing technological environment. It is becoming increasingly difficult to identify the "news" part of social media, for instance; it is becoming equally complicated to measure time spent consuming news. Does a quick glimpse of Twitter on the bus count as media exposure? It often should. Citizens are increasingly consuming news in this way, though they are unlikely to include such incidents in their own estimations of time spent watching news. How, then, are we to trust responses to survey questions that ask about media consumption habits?

This is an important problem in studies of campaign effects so it is of some significance that the "read, seen, or heard" open-ended questions do not depend on any estimate of either time spent consuming news or recalled sources of news. By focusing only on the content of news, we can see what news finds its way into citizens' heads, and we are simultaneously able to identify citizens who can or cannot recall recent events. Most importantly, we can explore the impact of news content directly, without relying on notoriously noisy self-reports about media exposure.

Finally, it is worth noting that the phrasing of our question asking what people have read, seen, or heard actually combines media exposure with other sources of information. For instance, a conversation with a co-worker would fall into the "heard" category of the question, and its substance may well show up in our data. Although this complicates the concept—it is not just a measure of media exposure but rather a measure of recalled content—it does so in a manner that we regard as worthwhile. First, in this complicated media environment, it is hard to anticipate in advance all the ways that someone might encounter information. Second, the co-worker in that example likely received the information from the media. This could represent a classic example of the two-step flow (Katz 1957), or it could be a manifestation of communication through a trusted network (Mutz and Young 2011). Indeed, scholars have pointed out that social media might be best construed as a modern-day two-step flow (Turcotte et al. 2015). The measure we use therefore combines a wealth of measures that have been previously used independently—exposure to a dozen types of media; talk with friends, family, strangers, and colleagues; and direct contact from campaigns themselves. What we argue is that it may no longer make sense to think of distinct types of exposure, but, rather, it is worth thinking more about what people are actually internalizing as a result of that exposure, since the salient details they recall are what is likely to affect their broader attitudes and eventual vote choice (Zaller 1992). And a long-standing body of evidence raises questions about how often people are even aware of where they encountered particular pieces of information (Kumkale and Albarracín 2004).

We hope that preceding chapters have made the advantages of the open-ended "read, seen, or heard" question readily apparent. We note here that we believe this method could be of real value in future work as well. We hope that scholars will build on what we have done to measure even more information streams at once over the course of election campaigns, with one of those being open-ended questions measuring campaign information retention.

Final Thoughts

In an election as consequential as the 2016 U.S. presidential campaign, there were so many important pieces of information that could have been conveyed to the public. The two nominees had long and complicated biographies, many details of which were relevant to their future performance as president. The United States also faced many important looming challenges, including sustaining the economic recovery, managing America's many overseas military operations, and the looming threat of climate change. Coverage of the candidates' plans to address these challenges and their ability to successfully implement those plans could have provided citizens with potentially important information. Yet we saw little evidence that such content was widely covered. Americans reported hearing very little about any of this during the presidential campaign.

In this book, we have examined the information that *was* conveyed in the campaign and when people absorbed and remembered it. We found a disconnect between the content of traditional media and what information people retained from the campaign, suggesting that people got information from a variety of types of media, likely including social media, and also from interpersonal communication. Social media platforms contained substantial misinformation. Overall, what people grasped from the campaign was mostly recent events, such as the conventions and debates and the attacks and scandals of recent weeks—but most of this would soon be forgotten. The most persistent story in the public mind was the various controversies surrounding Hillary Clinton's emails.

In every American presidential campaign cycle, journalists have a long list of possible topics to cover, many of which arguably should matter when picking the president for the next four years. The United States is the world's wealthiest and most militarily powerful country. While the presidency shares power with other branches of government, it still has a vast ability to shape domestic policy and (in recent decades) almost unlimited power in diplomatic and military affairs. The presidency is arguably the most powerful job in the world.

Decades ago, Patterson (1993) indicted the political news media for greatly overemphasizing the horse race and day-to-day back-and-forth attacks of the campaign rather than the substance of the national policy and the candidate's positions and plans. He wrote in an era before social media and when radio and cable were a much less important part of political news.

We find evidence that, even as the news environment has dramatically changed since the early 1990s, the tendency for the information environment to be dominated by the game of politics and the short-term attacks from both sides rather than the policy challenges facing the country remains as serious a problem as ever. It is hard to argue that the issues that people thought about most during the 2016 campaign were the most important challenges facing the country or the most important facts about the candidates.

Does this matter? The content of campaign information often does not determine who wins presidential elections. Political scientists have demonstrated that you can predict whether a race will be close or whether one candidate or the other will win handily without knowing anything about the campaign information environment—simply by knowing the economy's growth rate in the election year and how long the incumbent president's party has held the White House. But 2016 was an extremely close election. Anything that had even a small effect could have changed the result, including the information environment's emphasis on the horse race and scandals, or even the proliferation of fake stories. There is a good deal of quality news coverage, of course. But the problem of news coverage that distracts from the most important issues may be as bad now as ever in the post–World War II era. Future analysis of the language of election campaigns is critically important.

Appendix: Data and Methods

The Text Data Streams

Much of the data available today are unstructured, in free text form. While we can ignore these data, they give important insight into the behaviors, actions, and opinions of different populations. They can therefore be an important source of information about public opinion. A number of different text data streams are available online, including content from news media, blog posts, social media posts, reviews and comments, and the like. Different methods can be used to extract, describe, and summarize these text data streams. This appendix explains the different text data sets used in many of the chapters in this book—the Gallup open-ended questions, different Twitter data streams, and newspaper articles related to the 2016 presidential election. We begin by describing the data we collected and explaining our data collection methods. We then explain the data variables and values we chose to extract from the text and the methods used to generate these different values for our text streams. The majority of this appendix focuses on the nuts and bolts of how we cleaned and processed these data streams. We will also explain the algorithms we used and how we calibrated them, providing insight into the strengths and limitations of our methods. Finally, we will show some simple statistics about the data streams to better frame the analyses in the preceding chapters. All the data streams described in this appendix were collected from July 2016 until November 2016 (Election Day), but some were collected for a longer period of time.

Data Source and Data Collection

After a pretest in August 2015, Gallup began systematic data collection on July 11, 2016. The company administered a large U.S. survey about the public's opinions of the presidential candidates. As part of that survey, open-ended response questions asked about what Americans had read, seen, or heard about the two presidential candidates during the last day or two. Verbatim responses were recorded by the interviewers. No constraints were placed on length, but in general, the responses were very short—consisting of a few words (e.g., *email*, or short phrases, e.g., "he wants to keep America safe"). The phone survey was conducted daily with a random sample of 500 adults (approximately 60 percent cell and 40 percent landline phone numbers). In total, there were 58,943 survey responses collected from July to November. The overall response rate for the full set of respondents to these open-ended questions was 73.3 percent for Clinton and 75.8 percent for Trump.

In order to understand traditional media coverage of the presidential election better, we also analyzed newspaper articles from a range of national and regional newspapers. Articles related to the presidential election (i.e., containing either candidate's name) were part of this news sample. These data were obtained from LexisNexis using the Web Services Kit (WSK). Through the interface, we did a simple full text search on both candidates' names. This resulted in 40,842 newspaper articles retrieved between July 2016 and November 2016. The articles collected were from the following newspapers: the *Chicago Sun-Times*, the *Denver Post*, the *Houston Chronicle*, the *Los Angeles Times*, the *New York Times*, the *Philadelphia Inquirer*, the *St. Louis Post-Dispatch* (Missouri), *USA*

Today, and the *Washington Post*. Table A-1 shows the number of articles collected from each of these sources between July 1, 2016, and Election Day. We see that the majority of articles appeared in the *Washington Post* and the *New York Times*. In fact, the *Washington Post* has over twice as many articles as any other newspaper. For the analyses in this book, we do not investigate variation between newspapers. While there are different types of articles (e.g., local news, op-eds, etc.), we also do not distinguish among the different article categories. We save both of these for future work.

To gain insight into public opinion shared online, we also collected data from Twitter. We focused on three different Twitter data streams: a daily random sample of the Twitter stream, the daily stream of tweets shared by a list of political journalists, and a daily stream of tweets shared by political journalists around the debates. The daily random sample consisted of 5,000 tweets about Donald Trump and 5,000 tweets about Hillary Clinton. The data sample was collected using the Sysomos Application Programming Interface (API) (Sysomos 2018). In total, the daily random stream resulted in over 760,000 tweets per

Table A-1

Number of Articles from Each Newspaper

Newspaper	Article Count
Chicago Sun-Times	1,219
Denver Post	1,583
Houston Chronicle	1,780
Los Angeles Times	2,133
New York Times	7,447
Philadelphia Inquirer	1,986
St. Louis Post-Dispatch (Missouri)	1,730
USA Today	2,495
Washington Post	20,469

candidate. The journalists' stream captured tweets from over 930 journalists and bloggers who had an influential social media presence, as identified by StatSocial (StatSocial 2015). We also used the Twitter API to collect these data. Since July 2014, we have collected over 7.1 million tweets written by these journalists. From July 2016 to November 2016, we collected 1.97 million tweets from these journalists and bloggers. The final tweet stream we collected focused on the presidential debates. During each presidential debate, we collected the tweets associated with the #debate hashtag. We used the Twitter stream API to collect these data. We began data collection 30 minutes before the beginning of each presidential debate and ended 30 minutes after the conclusion of each debate. We collected over 1.5 million tweets and retweets during the three presidential debates held during the general election campaign. In this book, we focus in on tweets sent by our list of journalists for each debate. Table A-2 shows the number of tweets and journalists' tweets related to each debate that we collected. The main text of this book does not analyze these debate streams. We leave that for future work. However, we use this final stream here in the appendix to explain network analysis concepts that are presented in chapter 4.

Extracting Variables from Text

So what insight could we glean from these data sets? As a starting point, to operationalize the main concepts associated with different hypotheses, we focus on three basic analyses—word frequencies, text tone, and topic frequency. Word frequency was computed by counting the number of respondents, newspaper articles, and tweets that contained a specific word or word phrase. Tone is a measure of sentiment in a response, newspaper article, or tweet. It can be positive, neutral, or negative. Table A-3 shows examples of anonymized tweets that are labeled positive, neutral, or negative. There are different approaches for computing tone. The most common is to create a dictionary of positive-tone words and negative-tone words that are specific to a domain and then use the tone dictionary to identify the tone words in the text. Once the

Number of Tweets Collected during the Three Presidential Debates

Debate Date	Number of Tweets Collected	Number of Journalist Tweets
September 27, 2016	677,508	13,669
October 9, 2016	580,561	19,244
October 19, 2016	394,390	20,956

tone words have been identified, the sums for the positive tone words, neutral tone words, and negative tone words are computed, and the text is labeled as positive, negative, or neutral based on the maximum sum of the tone words found in the text. For example, words like *lying* or *complicit* are examples of negative tone words, while words like *stand with* or *tirelessly* are examples of words with a positive tone. Finally, we assigned topics to each response, article, or tweet and then counted the absolute and relative frequency of topics through time. The last column of table A-3 shows the primary topic associated with each tweet. This is based on the presence of words that were associated with a particular topic (see the next section for methodology). The last column of table A-3 shows the primary topic associated with each tweet in our example.

While these steps sound straightforward, text data streams are inherently noisy and inconsistent. Data quality issues that arise in text data include misspellings, abbreviations, capitalization inconsistencies, coding differences of different data collectors for the Gallup responses, varying vocabulary of respondents referring to the same idea or person (e.g., *Hillary* instead of *Clinton*, *sarcasm*, and *online spam* to name a few. Therefore, prior to computing word frequency, tone, or topics, we need to *clean* and preprocess the initial text streams. We use the following preprocessing procedure for all the data streams unless otherwise specified in a particular chapter:

Example Tweets with Sentiment and Topic Labels

Tweet	Sentiment	Topic
The silent majority will stand with Trump this November. It is time to retake America. #gop #maga	Positive	Positive Remarks Trump
#Hillary has worked tirelessly for children. That speaks volumes about her values.	Positive	Domestic Policies
Trump is lying. A 2013 report found that stop-and-frisk does not decrease crime.	Negative	Crime
Oh come on! Hillary is hiding major health issues, and the media does not care - complicit.	Negative	Health Problems
Donald Trump just had a speech in Miami.	Neutral	In the Media
Hillary Clinton rally in Des Moines, IA	Neutral	In the Media

1. *Remove all punctuation and replace it with a blank space.* Punctuation can be useful for understanding parts of speech or emotion, but neither of those are used in these analyses.

2. *Remove emojis.* Again, this is useful for emotion. Another approach is to replace emojis with their text equivalent. We chose not to do that for two reasons. First, our goal was to identify content-rich words specific to the presidential election for topics and word frequency counts. Second, the only data streams containing emojis were the Twitter ones. For consistency across data streams, we ignored them.

3. *Remove all single-letter words.* These words have little insight into the content of the text and are sometimes an artifact of removing punctuation (e.g., apostrophe *s* becomes *s*).

4. *Remove stop words.* Stop words are words that occur frequently, but are content-poor, meaning that they do not give sufficient insight into the meaning of the text. Examples of stop words include *in, the, and,* or *as.*

5. *Remove flood words.* Flood words (Churchill, Singh, and Kirov 2018) are domain-specific words that occur so frequently that they are relevant to almost every topic or are uninteresting to maintain for frequency counts. Example flood words for this domain are *Hillary, Trump,* and *election.*

6. *Remove words that begin with* http. Web links are important for certain analyses related to fake news (see chapter 8) and information about external articles and sites. However, they do not give insight into word, tone, or topic frequencies of the specific text being analyzed. Future work will look at the relationship between content associated with the web link and content of the specific text.

7. *Replace words with synonyms, if applicable.* Because we focus on frequency analysis, we need to consider that different people may use different words that mean the same thing, or that words may be misspelled. For example, *email, emails, e-mail,* and *emale* are all updated to *email,* and *trump, donald trump,* and *donald* are all updated to *trump.* We use synonyms sparingly, but for some words, multiple variations of the same word impact the overall accuracy of the frequency count if the counts are not merged.

8. *Lemmatize words.* Lemmatization is the process of removing endings on words and maintaining only the base of the word. This results in different forms of a word being reduced to a single form (e.g., *run, running, runs,* and *ran* will all be reduced to *run*). Again, this is important for capturing more accurate frequency counts.

Once data cleaning and preprocessing were complete, we began to look at word frequency, tone, and topic dynamics at different points throughout the election cycle. Much of this is discussed in the preceding chapters, but figures A-1 and A-2 illustrate one small example. Figures A-1 and A-2 show the most frequent words each month for Clinton and Trump, respectively, across the different streams. The first row of boxes shows the words that are common across streams. The remaining rows of boxes show the five most frequent words used for each data stream. For this example, we focus on nouns and remove common election words that do not give us insight into the specifics of the response, post, or article.[1] There are a few important takeaways. First, the most dominant word for Clinton across all of the streams is *email*. In contrast, the dominant words for Trump change month by month until the election. Not only is there more variability through time, there is also more variability across the streams. The word *woman* shows up as frequent for both Clinton and Trump, but for different reasons. For Clinton, there is discussion about her being the first woman president. For Trump, the discussion is related to his *Access Hollywood* scandal. Finally, the conventions and debates were consistently dominant across streams for both candidates, highlighting one focus on significant campaign events.

While words give some initial insight into the data, they miss broader themes that are captured by the use of many different words and vocabulary variations. This is where topics can provide additional insight since a topic is broader than a single word.

Determining Topics

It can be useful to classify Gallup responses, newspaper articles, and tweets by topic. We define a topic to be a set of words that describe a specific theme. Different algorithms exist for automatically identifying topics within a document collection. Most algorithms fall into two categories, probabilistic generative models and graph-theoretic models. A probabilistic generative model assumes that documents are generated following a known distribution of terms. Latent Dirichlet allocation (LDA) (Blei, Ng, and Jordan 2003) and its many variants (Blei and Lafferty 2006; Lafferty and Blei 2006; Teh et al. 2006; Wang and Mc-

Callum 2006) are the most widely used generative topic models. LDA finds the parameters of the topic/term distribution that maximizes the likelihood of the documents in the data set. Graph theoretic approaches use a word co-occurrence or semantic graph generated from the document collection to identify topics (Cataldi, Di Caro, and Schifanella 2010; Churchill, Singh, and Kirov 2018). A semantic graph is a network structure in which the nodes are words or phrases and the nodes are connected by edges if the words are in the same sentence or paragraph. Once the graph is constructed, the algorithms identify topics by finding clusters or groups of nodes that are well connected in the graph.

When we began topic analysis, we used the state-of-the-art methods to generate topics for the different text streams. We found that the topics were not coherent and contained many words that did not logically make sense as part of different topics. We believe this occurred because of the properties of our specific text streams. First, the Gallup open-ended responses and the Twitter tweets were very noisy. They involved a large vocabulary and words were used inconsistently. The generated topics were bogged down by noise words that polluted the topics. Second, many of the generative models assume knowledge of the underlying probability distribution for generating the terms and documents containing the terms. This is a reasonable assumption when the articles or documents are longer and the articles are written in a similar structure by different authors. However, these assumptions did not hold for social media data, for Gallup responses, or for many newspaper articles.

Because of these limitations, experts on the team manually curated a topic list using the following procedure. Looking at the list of frequent single words, pairs of words, and triples of words, we created a set of topics. We then added different words to the topics that logically fit into the topic. For example, words *wikileaks* and *Podesta* belonged to the *Clinton email* topic. Once this initial list was created, we used an automated program to identify the set of words and phrases that occurred frequently with one or more of the words already assigned to each topic. We used this same program to also identify frequently oc-

Figure A-1

Clinton—Comparison of Top Five Words Across Data Streams

	July	August
Common Words in at Least 3 Streams	Sanders	campaign emails
Gallup Survey Responses	emails convention speech VP Sanders	emails foundation campaign scandal Benghazi
Random Twitter	Sanders Obama DNC demsinphilly emails	emails Obama media video America
Journalists Twitter	Sanders demsinphilly speech Bill Kaine	poll campaign foundation emails Obama
Newspapers	democratic convention republican national campaign	campaign republican democratic national political

	September	October	November
	emails debate Obama	emails debate	emails FBI
	emails debate health pneumonia sick	emails debate Wikileaks FBI investigation	emails FBI investigation foundation scandal
	Obama emails FBI debate media	Wikileaks emails FBI woman debate	emails FBI Obama Wikileaks woman
	debate campaign emails polls Obama	debate emails campaign Bill polls	campaign Obama poll FBI emails
	campaign republican democratic Obama national	campaign republican political democratic debate	campaign republican political democratic voter

Trump—Comparison of Top Five Words Across Data Streams

	July	August
Common Words in at Least 3 Streams	convention speech	campaign
Gallup Survey Responses	convention speech VP emails Russia	immigration speech campaign ISIS Obama
Random Twitter	Pence Sanders speech America rncincle	media GOP Obama CNN America
Journalists Twitter	speech rncincle Pence convention campaign	campaign GOP immigration speech polls
Newspapers	republican convention national campaign democratic	republican campaign national democratic political

	September	October	November
	Obama debate	woman debate	
	debate mexico immigration speech Obama	woman debate sexual taxes emails	rally polls stage speech emails
	Obama debate media supporters polls	woman Pence debate media GOP	rally America Obama FBI Melania
	debate campaign Obama poll debatenight	debate woman campaign Pence GOP	campaign Obama rally voters polls
	campaign republican democratic national America	campaign republican political woman debate	campaign republican political voters democratic

curring words that seemed content rich and were not in any topics. Experts on the team then augmented the words associated with the initial topics based on these generated word lists. In some cases, words from the list helped experts identify new topics that they had not initially identified. The team went back and forth, adjusting topics in this way until we were comfortable with the topic word lists. We also want to point out that there are words that belong to more than one topic. For example, the word *policy* would be in all policy-related topics (e.g., domestic policy, foreign policy, immigration, etc.). Even though this word is related equally to all the topics, there are sometimes words that are more important to one topic than another. For example, *gun* is a more important concept for the gun rights topic than for the crime topic. But it is clearly relevant to both. Therefore, we use a simple weighting scheme that weighs the most important words associated with the topic higher than the rest of the words. We considered other more sophisticated weighting schemes but chose to maintain a simple topic model.

While we could have maintained separate topic lists for each text stream, we chose to maintain one cross-stream topic list for each candidate. This would allow us to compare topics across streams more easily. Doing this meant that hashtags and other stream-specific words were added to each list. Table A-4 gives an example of the words associated with the email topic for Hillary Clinton. The bolded words were given a higher weight than the other words. For all the phrases, many of the single terms were also considered associated words.

Once the topics were determined, the next step was to label each Gallup response, newspaper article, and tweet with one or more topics. While there are many different ways to assign topics to the text, we chose the simplest. For each document, we computed the weighted sum of the words appearing in the document that matched the words in the topic list. The topic having the highest weighted sum was considered the primary topic, and the document was labeled using that topic. We also considered variants where a weighted distribution of all the identified topics (or the two or three topics with the highest weights) was determined for each document. However, we found that the performance

Topic Word List

Words Associated with the Email Topic
email, private server, private email server, **Assange**, **FBI**, FBI
investigation, Comey, State Department, state, department, leak,
release, Russia, **hack**, Putin, delete, scandal, Congress investigation,
15000, more email found, classified, prosecute, private, server, Powell,
thousands, **WikiLeaks**, wiki, dnc, missing, speech, Goldman Sachs,
Goldman, Sachs, Wall Street, subpoena, cellphone, phone, 30000,
department, investigation

---

was inconsistent across the different data streams because of the variability in the streams themselves. Therefore, we chose to focus on only
the primary topic associated with each text document.

While we make no claim that these topics are comprehensive or
perfect in terms of word selection, we believe they fairly represent the
topics that were most dominant in the different data streams we have.
What would be useful for later analyses would be creation of a dynamic
topic list that adjusted the words and their importance associated with
the topic through time. While automated topic modeling algorithms are
getting better, the current state of the art does not elegantly handle
noise, flood words, subtopics, and the time dimension.

Figures 3-1 to 3-8 highlight the flow of the top twelve topics for each
candidate for each data stream through time. The x-axis shows the
date, week by week, through the campaign season until the election.
The y-axis represents the fraction of responses, tweets, or articles labeled with the specified topics. These top twelve topics generally summarized over 50 percent of the responses, tweets, or articles. While the
preceding chapters discuss these figures in more detail, it is interesting
to compare them to the monthly frequency shown in figures A-1 and
A-2. The comparison highlights that while some topics and words are
persistent (e.g., email) others are more visible when words are com-

bined to form a topic (e.g., immigration or taxes). Another important factor is the level of time granularity of the word and topic frequencies. The word frequencies are presented at a monthly granularity while the topic frequencies are daily. These different granularities give us different insight. The daily topic stream highlights the detailed topics that are emerging and falling each day of the campaign—these are more highly correlated to events of the day. The monthly word frequencies are highlighting the terms that persist or burst multiple times throughout the month. Considering both these dynamics gives us a more complete picture of the discussions taking place on the different streams.

Networks

When looking at social media, we can look at both the tweet content and the flow of tweet content through time. In Twitter, one unique way to look at information flow is to look at retweets of popular tweets. A retweet is a tweet that is reposted or forwarded by a Twitter user who is not the original author of the tweet. Chapter 4 considers the information flow of journalist tweets during a Republican debate. We use the tweets retweeted by journalists to identify journalists participating in online conversation during the debates and generate networks using subsets of these journalists. Generally, a network is created by identifying a set of entities and relationships between them. The entities are represented as nodes/vertices/circles in the network, and the relationships are represented as edges/links/lines between pairs of nodes having the relationship. As an accompanying example to the networks presented in chapter 4, we look at the flow of a single tweet among journalists in each of the three presidential debates. We do this to explain basic network concepts and metrics that are used in the main text of the book. We select the tweet that is retweeted the most among our journalist dataset. Any journalist that retweeted the tweet of interest is a node in the network.

While there are many relationships that exist between journalists, we look at the follower relationship. Suppose journalist B is following journalist A on Twitter. Then when journalist A posts a message, journalist B sees the message in his or her account. We are interested in capturing this relationship because it allows us to trace the flow of information through different journalist subnetworks. Edges exist in the network if a journalist follows another journalist. These edges are directed and the direction shown is the follower-to-followee relationship (i.e., the arrow is directed toward the journalist being followed). Figures A-3 through A-5 show the networks for the most frequently retweeted tweet across the journalists in our dataset for each of the three debates. Each node represents a journalist at an established media or news organization, freelance journalists, bloggers, academics, and the like. The tweet that was retweeted is shown on the upper left corner of each figure, and the timeline/order of the retweets by the journalists in the network are shown on the side of the network. Journalists with a name in blue received the tweet or retweet of the post from at least one other journalist in the network that they are following before they retweeted it. This timeline begins to give us insight into the flow of messages through these journalist subnetworks. The figures highlight the centrality of journalists in more established news organizations.

When analyzing a network, there are a number of metrics that can be used to evaluate its connectivity structure. Here we describe a few simple metrics and then discuss them for these three networks. Future work will present a more extensive network analysis of these journalist subnetworks based on retweets. Centrality metrics are used to identify the central individuals in the network. The simplest centrality metric is the degree of a node. The degree is the overall number of edges/connections a node has. The in-degree is the overall number of incoming edges in a directed network and the out-degree is the overall number of outgoing edges in the directed network. A node A's neighborhood is defined as the subset of nodes A is connected to. The clustering coefficient represents the amount of connectivity that exists among a node's neighbors. If all the neighbors are connected to each other, the clustering coefficient is one. If none of the node's neighbors are connected to each other, the clustering coefficient is zero. The density of the network

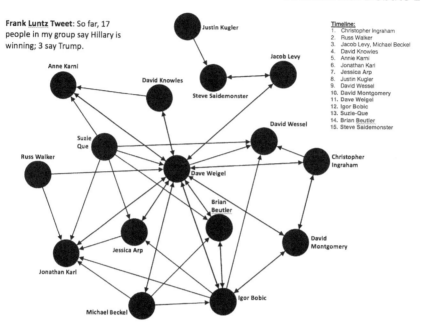

Presidential Debate 1

Frank Luntz Tweet: So far, 17 people in my group say Hillary is winning; 3 say Trump.

Timeline:
1. Christopher Ingraham
2. Russ Walker
3. Jacob Levy, Michael Beckel
4. David Knowles
5. Annie Karni
6. Jonathan Karl
7. Jessica Arp
8. Justin Kugler
9. David Wessel
10. David Montgomery
11. Dave Weigel
12. Igor Bobic
13. Suzie-Que
14. Brian Beutler
15. Steve Saidemonster

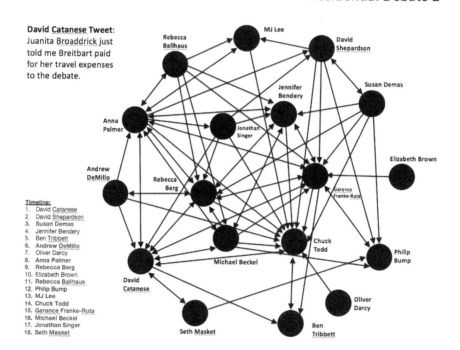

Presidential Debate 2

David Catanese Tweet: Juanita Broaddrick just told me Breitbart paid for her travel expenses to the debate.

Timeline:
1. David Catanese
2. David Shepardson
3. Susan Demas
4. Jennifer Bendery
5. Ben Tribbett
6. Andrew DeMillo
7. Oliver Darcy
8. Anna Palmer
9. Rebecca Berg
10. Elizabeth Brown
11. Rebecca Ballhaus
12. Philip Bump
13. MJ Lee
14. Chuck Todd
15. Garance Franke-Ruta
16. Michael Beckel
17. Jonathan Singer
18. Seth Masket

Figure A-5

Presidential Debate 3

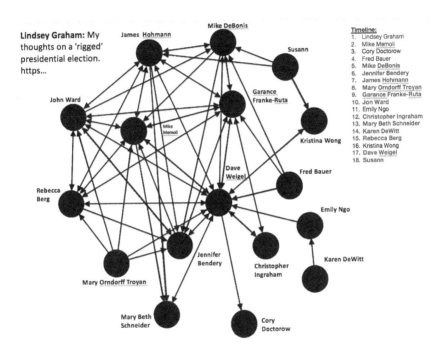

Lindsey Graham: My thoughts on a 'rigged' presidential election. https...

Timeline:
1. Lindsey Graham
2. Mike Memoli
3. Cory Doctorow
4. Fred Bauer
5. Mike DeBonis
6. Jennifer Bendery
7. James Hohmann
8. Mary Orndorff Troyan
9. Garance Franke-Ruta
10. Jon Ward
11. Emily Ngo
12. Christopher Ingraham
13. Mary Beth Schneider
14. Karen DeWitt
15. Rebecca Berg
16. Kristina Wong
17. Dave Weigel
18. Susann

is the proportion of possible edges in the network that actually exist. The higher a network's density, the more paths that exist throughout the network for information to flow. We focus on directed edge density, meaning that between every two nodes there may be zero edges (no follower relationship), one edge (one node follows the other), or two edges (both nodes follow each other). The diameter of the network is the shortest distance (number of edges) between the two nodes that are farthest from each other in the network. We measure the diameter by considering both directed edges and undirected edges. Finally, we also measure the average path length of the network, where the path length represents the number of edges that need to be traversed to get from any one node to any other node in the network.

Table A-5 shows the statistics for our three networks. They have a similar number of nodes, but the number of edges are more varied. The nodes are generally well connected with an average degree of 5.9, 8.2, and 8.5, respectively. The maximum degree of any node in the network is 23 (Dave Weigel), 17 (Dave Weigel), and 24 (Chuck Todd), respectively. All of them have a large number of journalists in these subnetworks that are following them (see maximum in-degree). To summarize, in each of these networks, there is a central node, but most of the nodes are well connected, and node neighborhoods are very connected given the high average clustering coefficient. From the density we see that about 20 percent to 30 percent of all possible directed connections exist in the network. These paths provide shortcuts through the network—this is clear from the low network diameter and average path length for all the networks. What we see is a set of subnetworks through which information flows very quickly.

This network analysis is an initial look into the journalist networks on Twitter. Future work will look at the retweeting pattern over time of journalists and bloggers with different political leanings, types of content that are retweeted more by these subnetworks, and how the flow of information impacts traditional understanding of influence.

Network Statistics for Journalist Retweet Networks

Network Metric	Edge Type	Debate 1	Debate 2	Debate 3
Number of nodes		16	18	17
Number of edges	Directed	47	74	72
Average degree	Undirected	5.9	8.2	8.5
Maximum degree	Undirected	23	17	24
Maximum in-degree	Directed	11	13	13
Average clustering coefficient	Undirected	0.56	0.60	0.66
Network density	Directed	0.20	0.24	0.27
Network diameter	Both	4 (4)	5 (3)	4 (3)
Average path length	Directed	2	2	1.7

Note: Numbers in parentheses represent **undirected network diameter.**

Final Data Thoughts

When working with text, there are a number of decisions that are made to simplify and clean the data, to improve the accuracy of different algorithms for determining variable values, and for analysis of the data. While we have paused to generate and analyze different text variables, we expect to continue to refine our methods and our lists to continue to improve the quality of variable extraction. Some future directions include removing spam from tweets, understanding the impact of fake accounts on our analysis, and considering different methods for generating topics from different types of text, such as those that are more coherent (newspaper articles) versus those that are just phrases (Gallup open-ended responses). Conducting text analysis is an active research area in computer science that we hope to continue to contribute to using these datasets.

Notes

Chapter 1

1. Researchers have debated whether media priming of issues changes people's votes to match their preferences or changes their preferences to match their vote choice, or some of each (Lenz 2012; Tesler 2015). These perspectives agree that the media environment focusing on some issues and not others does persuade people in some way.

Chapter 2

1. This is in 2018 dollars.

2. Twenty-two U.S. soldiers were killed in Afghanistan in 2015 and 14 in 2016, down from a peak of 599 in 2010. Additionally, 6 U.S. soldiers were killed in Iraq in 2015 and 17 in 2016. This was down steeply from the period 2004–2007, when casualties numbered over 800 every year ("iCasualties | Operation Iraqi Freedom | Iraq" 2017). On top of all this, while it produced no casualties, the United States also continued its involvement in a complex, multisided civil war in Syria, where it had gradually increased its intervention since first supplying rebels in 2011. Periodic manned and drone airstrikes against troops in Syria affiliated with ISIL began in September 2014 (Cooper and Schmitt 2014; McLaughlin 2016). In total worldwide (Syria, Iraq, Afghanistan, Libya, Yemen, Somalia, and Pakistan) in 2016, the U.S. military dropped 26,172 bombs from drones and manned aircraft.

3. Economic performance prior to the election year shows no correlation with votes (Sides and Vavreck 2013; Achen and Bartels 2016). The correlation

with the vote and the election year economy tends to be largest when the state of the economy is measured by either the gross domestic product (GDP) or real disposable income per capita (RDI).

4. These growth rates were 1.9 percent and 2.0 percent if you consider only the first three quarters of the year, which models often do because the election occurs 1 month into the fourth quarter. By quarter, the GDP annualized growth rate was 0.8 percent in the first quarter, 1.4 percent in the second quarter, 3.5 percent in the third quarter, and 2.1 percent in the fourth quarter of 2016. By quarter, the RDI annualized growth rate was 1.5 percent in the first quarter, 2.3 percent in the second quarter, 2.1 percent in the third quarter, and –1.0 percent in the fourth quarter of 2016. RDI per capita is including government transfers. RDI and GDP data are provided by the use of an inflation adjustment chained to 2009 dollars. They are from the Bureau of Economic Analysis, U.S. Department of Commerce.

5. Bureau of Labor Statistics, U.S. Department of Labor.

6. Calculated by the authors based on data from the Consumer Price Index, Bureau of Labor Statistics, U.S. Department of Labor. This was done by calculating the rate of change in the consumer price index between October 2016 and December 2015, adjusted to make an annual rate. The 2.1 percent rate excludes food and energy, which is how the inflation rate is customarily reported. It is 1.9 percent if they are included.

7. See Healy and Martin (2016). The previous day, before the results of the June 7 primary, the Associated Press's count of delegates won through primaries and caucuses plus public endorsements by super delegates, gave Hillary Clinton a majority of all Democratic Party convention delegates for the first time (Chozick and Healy 2016).

8. We examine a larger corpus of events in the news and open-ended survey data in chapter 7.

9. For more on convention bumps, see Campbell, Cherry, and Wink (1992).

10. This effect may have been exacerbated by Wikileaks, which, on the same day of the second Comey letter, released additional emails hacked from the DNC, including one in which a former aid to Bill Clinton appeared to accuse Bill and Hillary's daughter, Chelsea Clinton, of using Clinton Foundation money to pay for personal expenses (Datoc 2016; Hunter 2016).

11. See Sides, Tesler, and Vavreck (2018, 148).

Chapter 3

1. See also Byers (2015).

2. See the appendix for a description of the procedures used to code the topics in all of the datasets described in this chapter.

3. After a pretest of this question format in a single cross-sectional survey August 2015 (which we analyze in chapter 4), Gallup began systematic data collection on July 11, 2016.

4. The daily rolling cross-sectional survey was a mix of approximately 60 percent cell and 40 percent landline phone numbers in each day's sample. In total, there were 58,943 survey responses collected during this 2016 fall campaign period. The overall response rate for the full set of respondents to these open-ended questions was 73.3 percent for Clinton and 75.8 percent for Trump.

5. Though see Darr et al. (2019) for evidence that scandals did affect public opinion about President Trump once he had assumed office.

Chapter 4

1. While the use of polling data may seem objective as a precise statistical measure of eligibility, especially in the early phase of the campaign, name recognition has an inordinate role to play in the formation of popular assessments of contending candidates for the nomination (Kam and Zechmeister 2013). This inevitably affects their performance in the trial heat questions or assessments of their chances of securing the nomination.

2. By comparison, the Democratic Party organized nine debates and thirteen candidate forums, but their early schedule started later than the Republicans'.

3. The question wording took the following form: "Next, we'd like to get your overall opinion of some people in the news. As I read each name, please say if you have a favorable or unfavorable opinion of these people—or if you have never heard of them. How about . . . former Florida governor, Jeb Bush?" For a full report of the results, see www.gallup.com/poll/184499/republicans-view-rubio-walker-positively-debate-eve.aspx?g_source=name+familiarity&g_medium=search&g_campaign=tiles.

4. www.gallup.com/opinion/polling-matters/196730/americans-hear-read -trump-clinton.aspx?g_source=WWWV7HP&g_medium=topic&g_campaign =tiles.

5. Three days were selected for postdebate coverage because the event was held in the evening, and coverage in the day after might have been less than on the second day. The third day provided a way to check on extended coverage of any special topics that arose.

6. For the purpose of this analysis, the *New York Times* was also counted as Trump's local newspaper.

Chapter 5

1. Previous tests suggest that this measure is very highly correlated with other approaches (i.e., at $r > 0.95$).

Chapter 6

1. This is the difference between the sum of (Strongly favorable + Favorable) – (Strongly unfavorable + Unfavorable).

2. Given that the two candidates were widely known, their unfavorable ratings were generally the obverse of their favorable ratings.

Chapter 7

1. We set a cutoff such that words that appeared on fewer than 60 percent of days were eligible for inclusion. This number was determined by manually examining whether the list of words that would be included or excluded using each criterion could be identifiably linked to a single event. Increasing the stringency of this metric to 50 percent would have eliminated a number of event-linked places, such as Mexico, Russia, and Florida. The results were not sensitive to changes in these criteria.

2. If we used the 309 terms that produced an event-like pattern as opposed to the 237 that we could relate to specific events, these terms showed up in 34.2 percent of Trump responses versus 24.6 percent of Clinton responses ($p < 0.001$ difference).

3. Intercept = 0.71 (0.06), b = –0.89 (0.25), $ps < 0.001$.

4. Because many of the observed events were related to keywords that could emerge for other types of events as well, these plots were designed to estimate the frequency that any given keyword might be mentioned on a particular day. To do this, we calculated the distribution of keyword mentions on each day for each keyword and added together the number of mentions for keywords at the 25th, 50th, and 75th percentiles and divided this by three. Alternative approaches where all keyword mentions were summed on any given day or where the harmonic mean of mentions was used produced substantively similar results.

Chapter 8

1. Based on a survey with a slightly different question.

2. Examples include Silverman (2016a); Silverman and Singer-Vine (2016); Silverman, Lytvynenko, and Pham (2017); Gillin (2017); Schaedel (2018); Grinberg et al. (2018); Guess, Nyhan, and Reifler (2018).

3. The three organizations are PolitiFact, BuzzFeed, and FactCheck. These

lists include (1) the list of 223 publishers provided in the three articles published by BuzzFeed on fake news (Silverman 2016a; Silverman and Singer-Vine 2016; Silverman, Lytvynenko, and Pham 2017), (2) 325 publishers shared by PolitiFact (Gillin 2017), and (3) the publishers identified as posting fake and satirical stories by FactCheck (Schaedel 2018).

4. Grinberg et al. (2018) lists 490 publishers and Guess et al. (2018) lists 92. Grinberg et al. (2018) and Guess, Nyhan, and Reifler (2018) use a combination of these resources as well as lists published by Zimdars (2016) and Brayton (2016), with some further verification from Snopes.com.

5. Two other studies (Bovet and Makse 2019; Grinberg et al. 2019) also examined Twitter content, albeit through different data collection mechanisms. Their qualitative findings of fake news prevalence are comparable to ours despite different data collection choices.

6. The final dataset includes the following variables: (1) the shortened URL, (2) the original URL, (3) domain name (e.g., redstate.com), (4) title of the document, (5) text body of the document, (6) the date of the tweet, (7) Twitter ID of the user sharing the URL, (8) the number of followers of the Twitter user sharing the URL, and (9) the number of friends of the Twitter user sharing the URL.

7. The alignment between candidate favorability and fake news prevalence is weaker for Trump-related content. The cross-correlation is 0.48 when the time series are perfectly lined up and goes up to 0.79 with a lag of ten days. This pattern further suggests that the emphasis of fake news producers was on Clinton as opposed to Trump.

8. We remove English stop words (e.g., *a*, *the*, *at*), as well as domain-specific stop words (e.g., *Trump*, *Clinton*) for this analysis.

9. Please refer to https://www.cnn.com/2016/09/27/politics/alicia-machado -donald-trump-2016-election-anderson-cooper/index.html for background information about the Miss Universe scandal (related word is *univers*); and to https://www.vox.com/2016/9/13/12888492/ trump-foundation-sued-new-york-attorney-general for background information on the Trump charity–related scandal (related word is *chariti*).

10. We observe the same pattern when using semi-supervised machine learning techniques to parse text content and identify topics in Budak (2019).

11. These words are inspected to remove common English words, such as *the* that do not relate to any specific topic, as well as domain-specific stop words, such as the names of the candidates. Each word is lemmatized.

Chapter 9

1. For elaboration on this, see also Edelman (1988).

2. Earlier research suggests that electability will be an important element in these assessments (Abramowitz 1989), a factor heavily influenced by media portrayals and assessments of that likelihood.

Appendix

1. The common domain nouns we excluded were as follows: *candidate, day, election, news, nominee, party, people, president, public, story, time, today,* and *year.*

Bibliography

Abramowitz, Alan I. 1988. "An Improved Model for Predicting Presidential Election Outcomes." *PS: Political Science and Politics* 21, no. 4: 843–846.

———. 1989. "Viability, Electability, and Candidate Choice in a Presidential Primary Election: A Test of Competing Models." *Journal of Politics* 51, no. 4 (November): 977–992.

Abril, Danielle. 2019. "Google Introduces New Tools to Help Journalists Fight Fake News." *Fortune*, March 20, 2019. http://fortune.com/2019/03/20/google-new-tools-fight-fake-news/.

Achen, Christopher H., and Larry M. Bartels. 2016. *Democracy for Realists: Why Elections Do Not Produce Responsive Government.* Princeton: Princeton University Press.

Aldrich, John H. 1980. "A Dynamic Model of Presidential Nomination Campaigns." *American Political Science Review.* 74, no. 3 (September): 651–669.

Alexa Internet, Inc. 1996. Alexa–about us. www.alexa.com/about.

Allcott, Hunt, and Matthew Gentzkow. (2017). *Social Media and Fake News in the 2016 Election.* Technical Report. June 2017. Cambridge, MA: National Bureau of Economic Research.

Allcott, Hunt, Matthew Gentzkow, and Chuan Yu. 2019. *Trends in the Diffusion of Misinformation on Social Media.* Technical Report. January 2019. Cambridge, MA: National Bureau of Economic Research.

Anderson, Peter A., and Robert J. Kibler. 1978. "Candidate Valence as a Predictor of Vote Preference." *Human Communication Research* 5 (1): 4–14.

Ansolabehere, Stephen, and Shanto Iyengar. 1997. *Going Negative: How Political Advertisements Shrink and Polarize the Electorate.* New York: The Free Press.

Arango, Tim, and Michael S. Schmidt. 2011. "Last Convoy of American Troops Leaves Iraq, Marking a War's End." *New York Times*, December 18, 2011, sec. World.

Azari, Julia, and Seth Masket. 2017. "Presidential Primary Debates and Internal Party Democracy." Paper presented at the 88th Annual Meeting of the American Political Science Association, January 12–14, New Orleans, Louisiana.

Baker, C. Edwin. (1994). *Advertising and a Democratic Press.* Princeton: Princeton University Press.

Barbaro, Michael. 2016. "Donald Trump Clung to 'Birther' Lie for Years, and Still Isn't Apologetic." *New York Times*, September 17, 2016. www.nytimes.com/2016/09/17/us/politics/donald-trump-obama-birther.html.

———. 2016. "Trump Gives Up a Lie but Refuses to Repent." *New York Times*, September 1, 2016, A1, A10.

Barstow, David, Susanne Craig, and Russ Buettner. 2018. "Trump Engaged in Suspect Tax Schemes as He Reaped Riches from His Father." *New York Times*, October 2, 2018, sec. Special Investigations.

Barstow, David, Susanne Craig, Russ Buettner, and Megan Twohey. 2016. "Donald Trump Tax Records Show He Could Have Avoided Taxes for Nearly Two Decades, the *Times* Found." *New York Times*, October 2, 2016, sec. Politics.

Bartels, Larry M. 1985. "Expectations and Preferences in Presidential Nominating Campaigns." *American Political Science Review* 79, no. 3 (September): 804–815.

———. 1988. *Presidential Primaries and the Dynamics of Public Choice.* Princeton: Princeton University Press.

———. June 1993. "Messages Received: The Political Impact of Media Exposure." *American Political Science Review* 87 (2): 267–285.

———. 2002. "The Impact of Candidate Traits in American Presidential Elections." In *Leaders' Personalities and the Outcomes of Democratic Elections*, edited by Anthony King, 44–69. Oxford: Oxford University Press.

———. 2006. "Priming and Persuasion in Presidential Campaigns." In *Capturing Campaign Effects*, edited by Henry E. Brady and Richard Johnston, 78–112. Ann Arbor: University of Michigan Press.

———. 2008. *Unequal Democracy: The Political Economy of the New Gilded Age.* Princeton: Princeton University Press.

Bartels, Larry. M., and John Zaller. 2001. "Presidential Vote Models: A Recount." *PS: Political Science & Politics* 34, no. 1 (March): 8–20.

Basler, Robert. 2011. "Do We Get a Snack on This Flight, or What?" *Reuters Blogs* (blog). October 20, 2011. http://blogs.reuters.com/oddly-enough/2011/10/20/do-we-get-a-snack-on-this-flight-or-what/.

Bayagich, Megan, Laura Cohen, Lauren Farfel, Andrew Krowitz, Emily Kuchman, Sarah Lindenberg, Natalie Sochacki, Hannah Suh, and Stuart Soroka. 2017. "Exploring the Tone of the 2016 Campaign." *Center for Political Studies (CPS) Blog* (blog). January 2017. http://cpsblog.isr.umich.edu/?p=1884.

Becker, Jo, and Scott Shane. 2016. "Hillary Clinton, 'Smart Power' and a Dictator's Fall." *New York Times*, February 27, 2016, sec. Politics.

Belanger, Eric, and Stuart Soroka. 2012. "Campaigns and the Prediction of Election Outcomes: Can Historical and Campaign-Period Prediction Models Be Combined?" *Electoral Studies* 31 (December): 702–714.

Bennett, W. Lance. 1990. "Toward a Theory of Press-State Relations." *Journal of Communication* 40, no. 2 (Spring): 103–125.

———. 1996. An Introduction to Journalism Norms and Representations of Politics. *Political Communication* 13 (4): 373–384.

Berelson, Bernard, Paul F. Lazarsfeld, and William N. McPhee. 1954. *Voting: A Study of Opinion Formation in a Presidential Campaign*. Chicago: University of Chicago Press.

Berkowitz, Dan. 1987. "TV News Sources and News Channels: A Study in Agenda-Building." *Journalism Quarterly* 64, no. 2 (March): 508–513.

Bhatt, Shweta, Sagar Joglekar, Shehar Bano, and Nishanth Sastry. 2018. "Illuminating an Ecosystem of Partisan Websites." In *Companion Proceedings of the The Web Conference 2018, WWW '18*, 545–554. Republic and Canton of Geneva, Switzerland: International World Wide Web Conferences Steering Committee.

Blake, Aaron. 2016. "How America Decided, at the Last Moment, to Elect Donald Trump." *Washington Post*, November 17, 2016. www.washingtonpost.com/news/the-fix/wp/2016/11/17/how-america-decided-at-the-very-last-moment-to-elect-donald-trump/?utm_term=.05eb89f4b1a0.

———. 2016. "Welcome to the Next, Most Negative Presidential Election of Our Lives." *Washington Post*, July 29, 2016. www.washingtonpost.com/news/the-fix/wp/2016/07/29/clinton-and-trump-accept-their-nominations-by-telling-you-what-you-should-vote-against/?utm_term=.51b7cd946dfa.

Blei, David M., and John D. Lafferty. 2006. "Dynamic Topic Models." Paper presented at the 23rd International Conference on Machine Learning, June 2006, New York. DOI: doi.org/10.1145/1143844.1143859.

Blei, David M., Andrew Y. Ng, and Michael I. Jordan. 2003. "Latent Dirichlet Allocation." *Journal of Machine Learning Research* 3: 993–1022.

Boczkowski, Pablo J., Eugenia Mitchelstein, and Martin Walter. 2012. "When Burglar Alarms Sound, Do Monitorial Citizens Pay Attention to Them? The Online News Choices of Journalists and Consumers during and after the 2008 U.S. Election Cycle." *Political Communication* 29, no. 4 (October): 347–366.

Bode, Leticia. 2016. "Political News in the News Feed: Learning Politics from Social Media." *Mass Communication and Society* 19 (1): 24–48.

Bode, Leticia, and Kajsa E. Dalrymple. 2016. "Politics in 140 Characters or Less: Campaign Communication, Network Interaction, and Political Participation on Twitter." *Journal of Political Marketing* 15, no. 4 (October): 311–332.

Bovet, Alexandre, and Hernan A. Makse. 2019. "Influence of Fake News in Twitter during the 2016 US Presidential Election." *Nature Communications* 10, no. 1 (March): 7.

Boydstun, Amber E. 2013. *Making the News: Politics, the Media and Agenda Setting.* Chicago and London: University of Chicago Press.

Boydstun, Amber E., and Peter Van Aelst. 2018. "New Rules for an Old Game? How the 2016 U.S. Election Caught the Press Off Guard." *Mass Communication and Society* 21 (6): 671–696.

Brayton, Ed. 2016. "Please Stop Sharing Links to These Sites." *Patheos.* September 18, 2016. www.patheos.com/blogs/dispatches/2016/09/18/please-stop-sharing-links-to-these-sites/.

Brown, Philip, and Jessica Minty. 2006. "Media Coverage and Charitable Giving after the 2004 Tsunami." Working Paper 855. Ann Arbor, MI: William Davidson Institute, 2006.

Budak, Ceren. 2019. "What happened? The Spread of Fake News Publisher Content During the 2016 U.S. Presidential Election." In *The Proceedings of the World Wide Web Conference,* 139–150. New York: Association for Computing Machinery. DOI: doi.org/10.1145/3308558.3313721.

Budak, Ceren, Sharad Goel, and Justin M. Rao. 2016. "Fair and Balanced? Quantifying Media Bias through Crowdsourced Content Analysis." *Public Opinion Quarterly* 80 (S1): 250–271.

Budak, Ceren, Agrawal Divyakant, and Amr El Abbadi. 2011. "Limiting the Spread of Misinformation in Social Networks." In *Proceedings of the 20th International Conference on World Wide Web,* March 2011, 665–674. New York: Association for Computing Machinery. DOI: doi.org/10.1145/1963405.1963499.

Buettner, Russ, and Susanne Craig. 2019. "Decade in the Red: Trump Tax Figures Show Over $1 Billion in Business Losses." *New York Times*, May 7, 2019, sec. U.S.

Byers, Dylan. 2015. "Twitter's Most Influential Political Journalists." On Media (blog). April 14, 2015. www.politico.com/blogs/media/2015/04/twitters-most-influential-political-journalists-205510.

Cadwalladr, Carole. 2018. "A Withering Verdict: MPS Report on Zuckerberg, Russia and Cambridge Analytica. *Guardian*, July 28, 2018. https://amp.theguardian.com/technology/2018/jul/28/dcms-report-fake-news-disin formation-brexit-facebook-russia.

Campbell, James E. 2008. *The American Campaign: U.S. Presidential Campaigns and the National Vote.* College Station: Texas A&M University Press.

———. 2016. Introduction. *Political Science and Politics* 49, no. 4 (October): 649–654. DOI: doi.org/10.1017/S1049096516001591.

Campbell, James E., Lynna L. Cherry, and Kenneth A. Wink. July 1992. "The Convention Bump." *American Politics Quarterly* 20 (3): 287–307.

Cappella, Joseph N., and Kathleen Hall Jamieson. 1997. *Spiral of Cynicism: The Press and the Public Good.* New York: Oxford University Press.

Carlson, M. 2009. "Dueling, Dancing, or Dominating? Journalists and Their Sources." *Sociology Compass* 3, no. 4 (July): 526–542.

Carr, David. 2013. "The Pressure to Be the TV News Leader Tarnishes a Big Brand." *New York Times*, April 21, 2013. Sec. Business.

Cataldi, M., L. Di Caro, and C. Schifanella. 2010. "Emerging Topic Detection on Twitter Based on Temporal and Social Terms Evaluation." In *Proceedings of the Tenth International Workshop on Multimedia Data Mining*, no. 4, 1–10. New York: Association for Computing Machinery. DOI: doi.org/10.1145/1814245.1814249.

Chaddock, Gail Russell. 2003. "Clinton's Quiet Path to Power." *Christian Science Monitor*, March 6, 2003. www.csmonitor.com/2003/0310/p01s01-uspo.html.

Chaykowski, Kathleen. 2018. "Mark Zuckerberg Addresses "Breach of Trust" in Facebook User Data Crisis. *Forbes*, March 21, 2018. www.forbes.com/sites/kathleenchaykowski/2018/03/21/ mark-zuckerberg-addresses-breach-of-trust-in-facebook-user-data-crisis.

Chowdry, Amit. 2017. "Facebook Launches a New Tool That Combats Fake News." *Forbes*, March 5, 2017. www.forbes.com/sites/amitchowdhry/2017/03/05/facebook-fake-news-tool/%2366a9d7347ec1.

Chozick, Amy, and Patrick Healy. 2016. "Hillary Clinton Has Clinched Democratic Nomination, Survey Reports." *New York Times*, June 7, 2016, sec. Politics.

Churchill, Rob, Lia Singh, and Christo Kirov. 2018. "A Temporal Topic Model for Noisy Mediums." *PAKDD*. Sydney, Australia: Springer. DOI: doi. org/10.1007/978-3-319-93037-4_4.

Clinton, Hillary Rodham. 2017. *What Happened?* New York: Simon and Schuster.

Cogburn, Derrick L., and Fatima K. Espinoza-Vasquez. 2011. "From Networked Nominee to Networked Nation: Examining the Impact of Web 2.0 and Social Media on Political Participation and Civic Engagement in the 2008 Obama Campaign. *Journal of Political Marketing* 10, no. 1–2 (February): 189–213.

Colby, Edward B. 2017. "Trump vs. Clinton: Relive the Drama of Election Night 2016." *Newsday* (blog). November 8, 2017. https://projects.newsday.com/nation/trump-clinton-relive-election-night-2016/.

Collinson, Stephen, and Jeremy Diamond. 2016. "Trump Finally Admits It: 'President Barack Obama Was Born in the United States.'" CNN. September 16, 2016. www.cnn.com/2016/09/15/politics/donald-trump-obama-birther-united-states/index.html.

Collinson, Stephen, and Tal Kopan. 2016. "Obama to Leave More Troops than Planned in Afghanistan." CNN. July 7, 2016. http://edition.cnn.com/2016/07/06/politics/obama-to-speak-on-afghanistan-wednesday-morning/.

Confessore, Nicholas, and Jason Horowitz. 2016. "Clinton's Paid Speeches to Wall Street Animate Her Opponents." *New York Times*, January 21, 2016, sec. Politics.

Cook, Timothy E. (1998). *Governing with the News: The News Media as a Political Institution*. Chicago: University of Chicago Press.

Cooper, Helene, and Eric Schmitt. 2014. "U.S. and Allies Strike Sunni Militants in Syria." *New York Times*, September 23, 2014, sec. Middle East.

Crouse, Timothy. (1973). *The Boys on the Bus*. New York: Random House Press.

Darr, Joshua P. 2018. "Reports from the Field: Earned Local Media in Presidential Campaigns." *Presidential Studies Quarterly* 48, no. 2 (June): 225–247.

Darr, Joshua P., Nathan P. Kalmoe, Kathleen Searles, Mingxiao Sui, Raymond J. Pingree, Brian K. Watson, Kirill Bryanov, and Martina Santia. 2019. "Collision with Collusion: Partisan Reaction to the Trump-Russia Scandal." *Perspectives on Politics* 17 (3): 772–787.

Daku, Mark, Stuart Soroka, and Lori Young. 2015. Lexicoder, version 3.0. www.lexicoder.com.

Datoc, Christian. 2016. "Clinton Campaign FREAKING OUT about Final WikiLeaks Releases." *Daily Caller*, September 6, 2016. http://dailycaller.com/2016/11/06/clinton-campaign-freaking-out-about-final-wikileaks-releases/.

De Vreese, Claes, and Peter Neijens. 2016. "Measuring Media Exposure in a Changing Communications Environment." *Communication Methods and Measures* 10 (April): 69–80.

Dearing, James W. 1995. "Newspaper Coverage of Maverick Science: Creating Controversy through Balancing." *Public Understanding of Science* 4 (October): 341–361.

Delavande, Adeline, and Charles F. Manski. 2012. "Candidate Preferences and Expectations of Election Outcomes." *Proceedings of the National Academy of Sciences* 109 (10): 3711–3715.

DellaVigna, Stefano, and Ethan Kaplan. 2007. "The *Fox News* Effect: Media Bias and Voting." *Quarterly Journal of Economics* 122, no. 3 (August): 1187–1234.

Delli Carpini, Michael X. 2004. "Mediating Democratic Engagement: The Impact of Communications on Citizens' Involvement in Political Life." In *Handbook of Political Communication Research*, edited by L. L. Kaid, 395–434. Mahwah, NJ: Lawrence Erlbaum.

Delli Carpini, Michael X., and Scott Keeter. 1996. *What Americans Know about Politics and Why It Matters*. New Haven: Yale University Press.

DelReal, Jose. 2016. "Trump Bashes 'Disgusting' Former Beauty Queen Alicia Machado, Accuses Her of Having 'Sex Tape'—the *Washington Post*." *Washington Post*, September 30, 2016. www.washingtonpost.com/news/post-politics/wp/2016/09/30/trump-falsely-cites-sex-tape-in-latest-attack-against-former-miss-universe/?utm_term=.1102d7bb745e.

Demirjian, Karoun. 2018. Senate Intelligence Committee Releases Interim Report on Election Security. *Washington Post*, May 8, 2018. www.washingtonpost.com/powerpost/ senate-intelligence-committee-releases-inter im-report-on-election-security/2018/05/08/4b33d992-531e-11e8-9c91-7da b596e8252_story.html.

Desilver, Drew. 2016. "5 facts about Twitter at Age 10." Pew Research Center. March 18, 2016. www.pewresearch.org/fact-tank/2016/03/18/5-facts-about-twitter-at-age-10/.

———. 2018. "For Most U.S. Workers, Real Wages Have Barely Budged in Decades." Pew Research Center, August 7, 2018. www.pewresearch.org/fact-tank/2018/08/07/for-most-us-workers-real-wages-have-barely-budged-for-decades/.

Dewey, Caitlin. 2016a. "Facebook Fake-News Writer: 'I Think Donald Trump Is in the White House Because of Me.'" *Washington Post*, November 17, 2016. www.washingtonpost.com/news/the-intersect/wp/2016/11/17/facebook-fake-news-writer-i-think-donald-trump-is-in-the-white-house-because-of-me/.

———. 2016b. "Facebook Has Repeatedly Trended Fake News since Firing Its Human Editors." *Washington Post*, October 12, 2016. www.washingtonpost. com/news/the-intersect/wp/2016/10/12/ facebook-has-repeatedly-trended-fake-news-since-firing-its-human-editors.

Dilliplane, Susanna. 2011. "All the News You Want to Hear: The Impact of Partisan News Exposure on Political Participation." *Public Opinion Quarterly* 75, no. 2 (Summer): 287–316.

Dixon, Graham N., and Christopher E. Clarke. 2013. "Heightening Uncertainty around Certain Science: Media Coverage, False Balance, and the Autism-Vaccine Controversy." *Science Communication* 35, no. 3 (June): 358–382.

Druckman, James N. 2004. "Priming the Vote: Campaign Effects in a U.S. Senate Election." *Political Psychology* 25, no. 4 (August): 577–594. DOI: doi. org/10.1111/j.1467-9221.2004.00388.x.

Edelman, Murray. 1985. "Political Language and Political Reality." *PS: Political science and politics* 18, no. 1 (Winter): 10–19.

———. 1988. *Constructing the Political Spectacle*. Chicago: University of Chicago Press.

Enten, Harry. 2015. "Hillary Clinton Was Liberal. Hillary Clinton Is Liberal." *FiveThirtyEight* (blog). May 19, 2015. https://fivethirtyeight.com/datalab/ hillary-clinton-was-liberal-hillary-clinton-is-liberal/.

———. 2016. "Americans' Distaste for Both Trump and Clinton Is Record-Breaking." *FiveThirtyEight* (blog). May 5, 2016. https://fivethirtyeight. com/features/americans-distaste-for-both-trump-and-clinton-is-record-breaking/.

Entman, Robert M. 2003. "Cascading Activation: Contesting the White House's Frame after 9/11. *Political Communication* 20 (October): 415–432.

Erikson, Robert S., and Christopher Wlezien. 2012. *The Timeline of Presidential Elections: How Campaigns Do (and Do Not) Matter*. Chicago: University of Chicago Press.

Fahrenthold, David A. 2016. "Trump Recorded Having Extremely Lewd Conversation about Women in 2005," *Washington Post*, October 8, 2016. www. washingtonpost.com/politics/trump-recorded-having-extremely-lewd-conversation-about-women-in-2005/2016/10/07/3b9ce776-8cb4-11e6-bf8a-3d26847eeed4_story.html?utm_term=.96a18fe93940.

Fallows, James. M. 1997. *Breaking the News: How the Media Undermine American Democracy*. New York: Vintage Books.

Finnegan, William. 2016. "Donald Trump and the 'Amazing' Alex Jones." *New Yorker*, June 23, 2016. www.newyorker.com/news/daily-comment/donald-trump-and-the-amazing-alex-jones.

Fisher, Marc, John Woodrow Cox, and Peter Hermann. 2018. "Pizzagate:

From Rumor, to Hashtag, to Gunfire in D.C." *Washington Post*, December 6, 2016. www.washingtonpost.com/local/pizzagate-from-rumor-to-hashtag-to-gunfire-in-dc/2016/12/06/4c7def50-bbd4-11e6-94ac-3d3248 40106c_story.html.

Foreman, Tynesha, Alice Roth, and Erica Moriarty. 2017. "How 'The Apprentice' Manufactured Trump." Voices and Ideas about Politics (YouTube series). www.theatlantic.com/video/index/520821/how-the-apprentice-manu factured-trump/.

Frantzich, Steven E. 2013. "Are We Halfway There Yet?" In *Winning the Presidency 2012*, edited by W. J. Crotty, 90–102. New York: Paradigm Publishers.

Freedman, Paul, and Ken Goldstein. 1999. "Measuring Media Exposure and the Effects of Negative Campaign Ads." *American Journal of Political Science* 43, no. 4 (October): 1189–1208.

Gans, Herbert J. 1979. *Deciding What's News*. New York: Pantheon.

Gans, Herbert J. 2004 [originally published 1979]. *Deciding What's News: A Study of CBS Evening News, NBC Nightly News, Newsweek, and Time*. 25th Anniversary Edition. Evanston: Northwestern University Press.

Gass, Nick. 2016. "15 Most Revealing Moments from Comey's Testimony on Clinton Emails." Politico. July 7, 2016. www.politico.com/story/2016/07/ james-comey-testimony-clinton-email-225224.

Geer, John G. 2008. *In Defense of Negativity: Attack Ads in Presidential Campaigns*. Chicago: University of Chicago Press.

Gelman, Andrew. 2011. "There's No Evidence That Voters Choose Presidential Candidates Based on Their Looks." *Statistical Modeling, Causal Inference, and Social Science* (blog). April 9, 2011. http://andrewgelman. com/2011/04/09/political_pundi/.

———. 2016. "Trump-Clinton Probably Won't Be a Landslide. The Economy Says So." *Slate*, August 31, 2016. www.slate.com/articles/news_and_politics/politics/2016/08/why_trump_clinton_won_t_be_a_landslide.html.

Gelman, Andrew, and Gary King. 1993. "Why Are American Presidential Election Campaign Polls So Variable When Votes Are So Predictable?" *British Journal of Political Science* 23, no. 1 (January): 409–451.

Gerber, Alan S., James G. Gimpel, Donald P. Green, and Daron R. Shaw. 2011. "How Large and Long-Lasting Are the Persuasive Effects of Televised Campaign Ads? Results from a Randomized Field Experiment." *American Political Science Review* 105, no. 1 (February): 135–150.

Gerstein, Josh. 2016. "Clinton BlackBerry Photo Led to State Official's Query about Email Account." Politico, June 9, 2016. www.politico.com/blogs/under-the-radar/2016/06/hillary-clinton-emails-probe-blackberry-224 154.

Gillin, Joshua. (2017). PolitiFact's Guide to Fake News Websites and What They Peddle. PolitiFact, April 20, 2017. http://bit.ly/2o8kj3b.

Gold, Matea, Rosalind S. Helderman, and Anne Gearan. 2015. "Clintons Have Made More than $25 Million for Speaking since January 2014." *Washington Post*, May 15, 2015, sec. Politics.

Goldenberg, Suzanne, John Vidal, Lenore Taylor, Adam Vaughan, and Fiona Harvey. 2015. "Paris Climate Deal: Nearly 200 Nations Sign in End of Fossil Fuel Era." *Guardian*, December 12, 2015, sec. Environment.

Goldman, Adam. 2016. "Justice Dept. Grants Immunity to Staffer Who Set up Clinton Email Server." *Washington Post*, March 2, 2016. www.washingtonpost.com/world/national-security/in-clinton-email-investigation-justice-department-grants-immunity-to-former-state-department-staffer/2016/03/02/e421e39e-e0a0-11e5-9c36-e1902f6b6571_story.html.

Gottfried, Jeffrey, Michael Barthel, Elisa Shearer, and Amy Mitchell. 2016. "The 2016 Presidential Campaign—a News Event That's Hard to Miss." Pew Research Center. January 2016. www.journalism.org/wp-content/uploads/sites/8/2016/02/PJ_2016.02.04_election-news_FINAL.pdf.

Gottfried, Jeffrey, and Elisa Shearer. 2016. "News Use across Social Media Platforms." 2016. Pew Research Center, May 26, 2016. www.journalism.org/2016/05/26/news-use-across-social-media-platforms-2016.

Graber, Doris A., and Johanna Dunaway. 2017. *Mass Media and American Politics*. Washington, DC: CQ Press.

Gramlich, John. 2019. "10 Facts about Americans and Facebook." Pew Research Center. February 1, 2019. www.pewresearch.org/fact-tank/2019/02/01/facts-about-americans-and-facebook/.

Greene, Bob. 2012. "When candidates said 'no' to debates." CNN, October 1, 2012. www.cnn.com/2012/09/30/opinion/greene-debates.

Greenwood, Shannon, Andrew Perrin, and Maeve Duggan. 2016. "Social Media Update 2016." Pew Research Center. November 11, 2016. www.pewinternet.org/2016/11/11/social-media-update-2016/.

Grinberg, Nir, Kenneth Joseph, Lisa Friedland, Briony Swire-Thompson, and David Lazer. 2018. "Fake News on Twitter during the 2016 US Presidential Election." Technical report, working paper. Available from the authors.

———. 2019. "Fake News on Twitter during the 2016 US Presidential Election. *Science* 363 (6425): 374–378.

Grynbaum, Michael M., and Ashley Parker. 2016. "Donald Trump the Political Showman, Born on 'The Apprentice.'" *New York Times*, July 16, 2016, sec. Media.

Guess, Andrew, Brendan Nyhan, and Jason Reifler. 2018. "Selective Exposure to

Misinformation: Evidence from the Consumption of Fake News during the 2016 US Presidential Campaign." European Research Council. https://apo.org.au/sites/default/files/resource-files/2018/01/apo-nid126961-1162776.pdf.

Guest, Steve. 2016. "Klein: Comey and 'A Lot of Other FBI Agents' Will Resign If Hillary Is Not Indicted [VIDEO]." Daily Caller. April 1, 2016. http://dailycaller.com/2016/04/01/klein-comey-and-a-lot-of-other-fbi-agents-will-resign-if-hillary-is-not-indicted-video/.

Guilbeault, Douglas, and Samuel Woolley. 2016. "How Twitter Bots Are Shaping the Election. *Atlantic*, November 1, 2016. www.theatlantic.com/technology/archive/2016/11/election-bots/506072/.

Haberman, Maggie, and Alan Rappeport. 2016. "Trump Drops False 'Birther' Claim But Offers New One: Clinton Started It." *New York Times*, September 16, 2016, sec. Politics.

Hamby, Peter. 2013. "Did Twitter Kill the Boys on the Bus? Searching for a Better Way to Cover a Campaign." Shorenstein Center on Media, Politics, and Public Policy Paper. August 2013. https://shorensteincenter.org/wp-content/uploads/2013/08/d80_hamby.pdf.

Hardy, Bruce W., and Kathleen Hall Jamieson. 2005. "Can a Poll Affect Perception of Candidate Traits?" *Public Opinion Quarterly* 69 (5): 725–743. DOI: doi.org/10.1093/poq/nfi067.

Hattem, Julian. 2016. "Clinton BlackBerry Photo Prompted Questions about Email Setup." *The Hill*, June 9, 2016. http://thehill.com/policy/national-security/282970-clinton-blackberry-photo-prompted-new-look-at-email-setup.

Healy, Patrick, and Jonathan Martin. 2016. "After Victory in California, Hillary Clinton Turns toward Donald Trump." *New York Times*, June 8, 2016, sec. Politics.

Helderman, Rosalind S., and Tom Hamburger. 2016. "State Dept. Inspector General Report Sharply Criticizes Clinton's Email Practices." *Washington Post*, May 25, 2016, sec. Politics.

Herman, Edward S., and Noam Chomsky. 1988. *Manufacturing Consent: The Political Economy of the Mass Media*. New York: Pantheon Books.

Hetherington, Marc J. 1996. "The Media's Role in Forming Voters' National Economic Evaluations in 1992." *American Journal of Political Science* 40, no. 2 (May): 372–395.

Hibbs, Douglas A., Jr. July 2000. "Bread and Peace Voting in U.S. Presidential Elections." *Public Choice* 104, nos. 1–2 (July): 149–180.

———. 2007. "Voting and the Macroeconomy." In *Oxford Handbook of Politi-

cal Economy, edited by Barry R. Weingast and Donald Wittman, 565–586. Oxford, UK: Oxford University Press.

Hill, Seth J., James Lo, Lynn Vavreck, and John Zaller. 2013. "How Quickly We Forget: The Duration of Persuasion Effects from Mass Communication." *Political Communication* 30, no. 4 (October): 521–547.

Holbrook, Thomas M. 1996. *Do Campaigns Matter?* Thousand Oaks, CA: Sage Publications.

Holtz-Bacha, Christine, and Pippa Norris. 2001. "'To Entertain, Inform and Educate': Still the Role of Public Television." *Political Communication* 18 (2): 123–140.

Hunter, Derek. 2016. "Clinton Foundation Head Accused Chelsea of Using Funds for Wedding, Campaigning, and Avoiding Taxes." Daily Caller. September 6, 2016. http://dailycaller.com/2016/11/06/clinton-foundation-head-accused-chelsea-of-using-funds-for-wedding-campaigning-and-avoiding-taxes/.

"iCasualties | Operation Enduring Freedom | Afghanistan." n.d. iCasualties. http://icasualties.org/OEF/index.aspx.

"iCasualties | Operation Iraqi Freedom | Iraq." 2017. iCasualties. 2017. http://icasualties.org/Iraq/index.aspx.

"Insider Says Hillary Will Be Indicted." 2016. InfoWars. July 2, 2016. www.InfoWars.com/insider-says-hillary-will-be-indicted/.

Intergovernmental Panel on Climate Change (United Nations). 2014. "AR5 Synthesis Report: Climate Change 2014." United Nations. www.ipcc.ch/report/ar5/syr/.

Ivanova, Irina. 2018. 8 promises from Facebook after Cambridge Analytica. *CBS News*, April 10, 2018. www.cbsnews.com/news/facebooks-promises-for-protecting-your-information-after-data-breach-scandal/.

Iyengar, Shanto, and Donald Kinder. 1987. *News That Matters: Television and American Opinion*. Chicago: University of Chicago Press.

Iyengar, Shanto, Helmut Norputh, and Kyu S. Hahn. 2004. "Consumer Demand for Election News: The Horserace Sells. *Journal of Politics* 66, no. 1 (February): 157–175.

Iyengar, Shanto, and Adam Simon. 1994. "News Coverage of the Gulf Crisis and Public Opinion: A Study of Agenda Setting, Priming, and Framing." In *Taken by Storm: The Media, Public Opinion, and U.S. Foreign Policy in the Gulf War*, edited by W. Lance Bennett and David L. Paletz, 186–209. Chicago: University of Chicago Press.

———.2000. "New Perspectives and Evidence on Political Communication and Campaign Effects." *Annual Review of Psychology* 51, no. 1 (February): 149–169. DOI: doi.org/10.1146/annurev.psych.51.1.149.

Jackson, David. 2013. "Hillary Clinton Sends Her First Tweet." *USA Today*, June 10, 2013. www.usatoday.com/story/theoval/2013/06/10/hillary-rodham -clinton-twitter-bill-clinton-chelsea/2408341/.

James, Brendan. (2015). "How White and Male are Digital Newsrooms? New Media's Old Diversity Problem." *International Business Times*, August 17, 2015. www.ibtimes.com/how-white-male-are-digital-newsrooms-new-medias -old-diversity-problem-2056843.

Jamieson, Kathleen Hall. 2018. *Cyberwar: How Russian Hackers and Trolls Helped Elect a President: What We Don't, Can't, and Do Know*. New York: Oxford University Press.

Johnston, Richard, Andre Blais, Henry Brady, and Jean Crete. 1992. *Letting the People Decide: Dynamics of a Canadian Election*. Stanford: Stanford University Press.

Johnston, Richard, Michael G. Hagen, and Kathleen Hall Jamieson. 2004. *The 2000 Presidential Election and the Foundations of Party Politics*. New York: Cambridge University Press.

Judkis, Maura. 2012. "'Texts from Hillary' Blog Depicts Clinton as Phone Addict." *Washington Post*. April 5, 2012. http://archive.is/Xzeav.

Jungherr, Andreas, Harald Schoen, Oliver Posegga, and Pascal Jürgens. 2016. "Digital Trace Data in the Study of Public Opinion an Indicator of Attention toward Politics Rather Than Political Support." *Social Science Computer Review*. DOI: doi.org/10.1177/0894439316631043.

Kahn, Kim Fridkin, and Patrick J. Kenney. 1999. "Do Negative Campaigns Mobilize or Suppress Turnout? Clarifying the Relationship between Negativity and Participation." *American Political Science Review* 93, no. 4 (December): 877–889. DOI: doi.org/10.2307/2586118.

Kalogeropoulos, Antonis, and Nic Newman. 2017. "'I Saw the News on Facebook' Brand Attribution When Accessing News from Distributed Environments." Reuters Institute for the Study of Journalism.

Kaid, Lynda Lee, and Anne Johnston. 1991. "Negative versus Positive Television Advertising in U.S. Presidential Campaigns, 1960–1988." *Journal of Communication* 41, no. 3 (September): 53–64. DOI: doi.org/10.1111/j.1460-2466.1991.tb02323.x.

Kam, Cindy D., and Elizabeth J. Zechmeister. 2013. "Name Recognition and Candidate Support," *American Journal of Political Science* 57, no. 4 (October): 971–986.

Kamarck, Elaine. 2016. "Has a Presidential Election Ever Been as Negative as This One?" Brookings Institution, October 18, 2016. www.brookings.edu/ blog/fixgov/2016/10/18/the-most-negative-campaign/.

Kang, Cecilia, Tiffany Hsu, Kevin Roose, Natasha Singer, and Matthew Rosenberg. 2018. "Mark Zuckerberg Testimony: Day 2 Brings Tougher Questioning." *New York Times*, April 11, 2018. Sec. U.S.

Karni, Annie. 2015. "Hillary Clinton Formally Announces 2016 Run." Politico. April 12, 2015. www.politico.com/story/2015/04/hillary-clinton-2016-election-presidential-launch-116888.html.

Katz, Elihu. 1957. The Two-Step Flow of Communication: An Up-to-Date Report on an Hypothesis. *Public Opinion Quarterly* 21, no. 1 (Spring): 61–78.

Keith, Tamara. 2015. "Clinton Endures an 11-Hour Grilling Before Benghazi Committee." NPR. October 22, 2015. www.npr.org/sections/itsall politics/2015/10/22/451012235/clinton-endures-an-11-hour-grilling-before-benghazi-committee.

Kenski, Kate, Bruce Hardy, W. Bruce W. and Kathleen Hall Jamieson. 2010. *The Obama Victory*. New York: Oxford University Press.

Kim, Yeojin, William J. Gonzenbach, Chris J. Vargo, and Youngju Kim. 2016. "First and Second Levels of Intermedia Agenda Setting: Political Advertising, Newspapers, and Twitter during the 2012 U.S. Presidential Election." *International Journal of Communication*, 10: 4550–4569.

Kinder, Donald R. 2003. "Communication and Politics in the Age of Information." In *Oxford Handbook of Political Psychology*, edited by David O. Sears, Leonie Huddy, and Robert Jervis, 357–393. New York: Oxford University Press.

Klapper, Joseph. 1960. *The Effects of Mass Communication*. Glencoe, IL: Free Press.

Klein, Ezra. 2016. "Hillary Clinton's 3 Debate Performances Left the Trump Campaign in Ruins." Vox. October 19, 2016. www.vox.com/policy-and-politics/2016/10/19/13340828/hillary-clinton-debate-trump-won.

Koehler, D. J. 2016. "Can Journalistic 'False Balance' Distort Public Perception of Consensus in Expert Opinion?" *Journal of Experimental Psychology, Applied* 22, no. 1 (March): 24–38.

Kokalitcheva, Kia. 2016. "Mark Zuckerberg Says Fake News on Facebook Affecting the Election Is a 'Crazy Idea.'" *Fortune*, November 11, 2016. http://fortune.com/2016/11/11/ facebook-election-fake-news-mark-zuckerberg/.

Koran, Laura, Dan Merica, and Tom LoBianco. 2016. "WikiLeaks Posts Apparent Excerpts of Clinton Wall Street Speeches." CNN. October 8, 2016. www.cnn.com/2016/10/07/politics/john-podesta-emails-hacked/index.html.

Koury, Ken, and Dick Raspa. 1999. "The Business of Media: Organizing Carnival by the New Entrepreneurs." In *Modern Organizations and Emerging Conundrums: Exploring the Postindustrial Subculture of the Third Millennium*, edited by Richard A. Goodman. Lanham, MD: Lexington Books.

Kramer, Katherine. 2016. *The Politics of Resentment: Rural Consciousness in Wisconsin and the Rise of Scott Walker.* Chicago: University of Chicago Press.

Kraus, Sidney. 1979. *The Great Debates: Carter vs. Ford 1976.* Bloomington: Indiana University Press.

Kreutz, Liz. 2015. "Clinton on Private Email: 'That Was a Mistake. I'm Sorry.'" *ABC News.* September 9, 2015. http://abcnews.go.com/Politics/hillary-clinton-private-email-mistake-im/story?id=33608970.

Krieg, Gregory. 2016. "14 of Trump's Most Outrageous 'Birther' Claims—Half from after 2011." CNN. September 16, 2016. www.cnn.com/2016/09/09/politics/donald-trump-birther/index.html.

Krosnick, Jon A., and Donald R. Kinder. 1990. "Altering the Foundations of Support for the President through Priming." *American Political Science Review* 84, no. 2 (June): 497–512.

Krugman, Paul. 2014. "On Income Stagnation." *New York Times*, November 12, 2014. sec. Opinion.

Kwak, Haewoon, Changhyun Lee, Hosung Park, and Sue Moon. 2010. "What Is Twitter, a Social Network or a News Media?" In *Proceedings of the 19th International Conference on World Wide Web*, 591–600. New York: Association of Computing Machinery. DOI: doi.org/10.1145/1772690.1772751.

Ladd, Jonathan M. 2007. "Predispositions and Public Support for the President during the War on Terrorism." *Public Opinion Quarterly* 71, no. 4 (Winter): 511–538.

Lafferty, John D., David M. Blei. 2006. "Correlated Topic Models." In *Proceedings of the 18th International Conference on Neural Information Processing Systems*, 147–154. Cambridge: MIT Press.

LaFranchi, Howard. 2011. "Hillary Clinton: More 'Smart Power' Needed in Terrorism Fight." *Christian Science Monitor*, September 9, 2011. www.csmonitor.com/USA/Foreign-Policy/2011/0909/Hillary-Clinton-more-smart-power-needed-in-terrorism-fight.

Landler, Mark. 2013. "Scare Amplifies Fears That Clinton's Work Has Taken Heavy Toll." *New York Times*, January 4, 2013.

———. 2016. "H Is for Hawk." *New York Times*, April 21, 2016, sec. Magazine.

Landler, Mark, and Eric Lichtblau. 2016. "F.B.I. Director James Comey Recommends No Charges for Hillary Clinton on Email." *New York Times*, July 5, 2016, sec. U.S.

Lasswell, Harold Dwight, and Nathan Constantin Leites. 1965. *Language of Politics Studies in Quantitative Semantics.* Cambridge, MA: Massachusetts Institute of Technology Press.

Lau, Richard R., Lee Sigelman, Caroline Heldman, and Paul Babbitt. 1999.

"The Effects of Negative Political Advertisements: A Meta-Analytic Assessment." *American Political Science Review* 93, no. 4 (December): 851–875.

Lawrence, Regina G., Logan Molyneux, Mark Coddington, and Avery Holton. 2014. "Tweeting Conventions: Political Journalists' Use of Twitter to Cover the 2012 Presidential Campaign." *Journalism Studies* 15, no. 6 (September): 789–806.

Lazarsfeld, Paul F., Bernard Berelson, and Hazel Gaudet. 1948. *The People's Choice: How the Voter Makes Up His Mind in a Presidential Campaign.* New York: Columbia University Press.

Lazer, David M. J., Matthew A. Baum, Yochai Benkler, Adam J. Berinsky, Kelly M. Greenhill, Filippo Menczer, Miriam J. Metzger, Brendan Nyhan, Gordon Pennycook, David Rothschild, Michael Schudson, Steven A. Sloman, Cass R. Sunstein, Emily A. Thorson, Duncan J. Watts, and Jonathan L. Zittrain. 2018. "The Science of Fake News." *Science* 359, no. 6380 (March): 1094–1096.

Lee, Carol E., and Felicia Schwartz. 2016. "Obama to Slow Troop Withdrawal from Afghanistan." *Wall Street Journal*, July 7, 2016, sec. World.

Lee, Michelle. 2016. "Fact Check: Has Trump Declared Bankruptcy Four or Six Times?" *Washington Post.* www.washingtonpost.com/politics/2016/live-updates/general-election/real-time-fact-checking-and-analysis-of-the-first-presidential-debate/fact-check-has-trump-declared-bankruptcy-four-or-six-times/.

Lenz, Gabriel S. 2012. *Follow the Leader? How Voters Respond to Politicians' Performance and Policies.* Chicago: University of Chicago Press.

Leonhardt, David. 2014. "The Great Wage Slowdown, Looming Over Politics." *New York Times*, November 11, 2014. www.nytimes.com/2014/11/11/upshot/the-great-wage-slowdown-looming-over-politics.html.

Lewis, Paul, Spencer Ackerman, and Kamali Dehghan Saeed. 2014. "Iraq Crisis: Barack Obama Sends in US Troops as ISIS Insurgency Worsens." *Guardian*, June 17, 2014, sec. World News.

Lewis-Beck, Michael S. 1990. *Economics and Elections: The Major Western Democracies.* Ann Arbor: University of Michigan Press.

Lewis-Beck, Michael S., and Mary Stegmaier. 2000. "Economic Determinants of Electoral Outcomes." *Annual Review of Political Science* 3 (June): 183–219.

Lippmann, Walter. 1997 [1922]. *Public Opinion.* New York: Simon & Schuster.

Lowe, Will, Kenneth Benoit, Slava Mikhaylov, and Michael Laver. 2011. "Scaling Policy Preferences from Coded Political Texts." *Legislative Studies Quarterly* 36, no. 1 (February): 123–155.

Lowrey, Annie. 2014. "Will the Economy Ever Be As Good As It Was in the

'90s?" *New York Magazine*, September 19, 2014. http://nymag.com/intelligencer/2014/09/will-the-economy-ever-be-as-good-as-the-90s.html.

Lupia, Arthur. 1994. "Shortcuts versus Encyclopedias: Information and Voting Behavior in California Insurance Reform Elections." *American Political Science Review* 88 (1): 63–76.

Lupia, Arthur, and Tasha S. Philpot. 2005. "Views from Inside the Net: How Websites Affect Young Adults' Political Interest." *Journal of Politics* 67, no. 4(November): 1122–1142.

Lynch, Patrick. 2016. "2016 Climate Trends Continue to Break Records." Global Climate Change: Vital Signs of the Planet. July 18, 2016. https://climate.nasa.gov/news/2465/2016-climate-trends-continue-to-break-records.

Martinez, Michael. 2015. "U.S. Troops Are in Afghanistan—and Will Be into 2016." CNN. October 15, 2015. www.cnn.com/2015/10/09/world/us-troops-military-still-in-afghanistan-doctors-without-borders/index.html.

Marwick, Alice, and Rebecca Lewis. 2017. "Media Manipulation and Disinformation Online." Data and Society. May 15, 2017. https://datasociety.net/output/media-manipulation-and-disinfo-online/.

Matsa, Katarina Eva, and Elisa Shearer. 2018. "News Use across Social Media Platforms 2018." Pew Research Center. September 10, 2018. www.journalism.org/2018/09/10/news-use-across-social-media-platforms-2018/.

Mayhew, David R. 2008. "Incumbency Advantage in U.S. Presidential Elections: The Historical Record." *Political Science Quarterly* 123, no. 2 (Summer): 201–228.

Mazzetti, Mark, and Katie Benner. 2018. "12 Russian Agents Indicted in Mueller Investigation." *New York Times*, July 13, 2018. www.nytimes.com/2018/07/13/us/politics/mueller-indictment-russian-intelligence-hacking.html.

McChesney, Robert W. 2008. *The Political Economy of Media: Enduring Issues, Emerging Dilemmas*. New York: Monthly Review Press.

McCombs, Maxwell. 2014. *Setting the Agenda: The Mass Media and Public Opinion*, 2nd ed.. Malden, MA: Polity Press.

McCombs, Maxwell E., and Donald L. Shaw. 1972. "The Agenda-Setting Function of Mass Media." *Public Opinion Quarterly* 36, no. 2 (Summer): 176–187.

McCombs, Maxwell E., and Donald L Shaw. 1993. "The Evolution of Agenda-Setting Research: Twenty-Five Years in the Marketplace of Ideas." *Journal of Communication* 43 (2): 58–67.

McCombs, Maxwell E., Donald L. Shaw, and David H. Weaver. 2014. "New Directions in Agenda-Setting Theory and Research." *Mass Communication and Society* 17, no. 6(November): 781–802. DOI: doi.org/10.1080/15205436.2014.964871.

McKee, Seth C., Daniel A. Smith, and M. V. (Trey) Hood. 2019. "The Comeback Kid: Donald Trump on Election Day in 2016." *PS: Political Science and Politics* 52, no. 2 (April): 1–4.

McLaughlin, Elizabeth. 2016. "Two Years of U.S.-Led Airstrikes on ISIS in Syria and Iraq in Numbers." *ABC News*. August 8, 2016. http://abcnews.go.com/International/years-us-led-airstrikes-isis-syria-iraq-show/story?id=41206050.

McLeary, Paul. 2017. "More U.S. Troops Bound for Afghanistan, As Marines, Commandos, Arrive In Syria." *Foreign Policy* (blog). March 9, 2017. https://foreignpolicy.com/2017/03/09/more-us-troops-afghanistan-marines-syria-commandos-iraq/.

Milita, Kerri, and John B. Ryan. 2018. "Battleground States and Local Coverage of American Presidential Campaigns." *Political Research Quarterly* 72, no. 1 (June 13): 104–116. DOI: doi.org/10.1177/1065912918781752.

Monroe, Burt L., Michael P. Colaresi, and Kevin M. Quinn, Kevin M. 2008. "Fightin' Words: Lexical Feature Selection and Evaluation for Identifying the Content of Political Conflict. *Political Analysis* 16, no. 4(Autumn): 372–403.

Morrongiello, Gabby. 2016. "Former House Oversight Chairman: 'FBI Director Would Like to Indict Clinton and Abedin.'" *Washington Examiner*, January 29, 2016. www.washingtonexaminer.com/former-house-oversight-chairman-fbi-director-would-like-to-indict-clinton-and-abedin.

Mosseri, A. 2016. "News Feed FYI: Addressing Hoaxes and Fake News. Facebook. December 15, 2016. http://newsroom. fb.com/news/2016/12/news-feed-fyiaddressing-hoaxes-and-fake-news.

Mueller, Robert S. 2019. *Report on the Investigation into Russian Interference in the 2016 Presidential Election*. Washington, DC: U.S. Department of Justice.

Mullainathan, Sendhil, and Andrei Shleifer. 2005. "The Market for News." *American Economic Review* 95 (4): 1031–1053.

Mutz, Diana C., and Lori Young. 2011. "Communication and Public Opinion." *Public Opinion Quarterly* 75 (5): 1018–1044.

Nakashima, Ellen, Karoun Demirjian, and Philip Rucker. 2017. "Top U.S. Intelligence Official: Russia Meddled in Election by Hacking, Spreading of Propaganda." *Washington Post*, January 5, 2017. www.washingtonpost.com/world/national-security/top-us-cyber-officials-russia-poses-a-major-threat-to-the-countrys-infrastructure-and-2017/01/05/36a60b42-d34c-11e6-9cb0-54ab630851e8_story.html.

NASA's Goddard Institute for Space. 2016a. "NASA Analysis Finds August 2016 Another Record Month." Climate Change: Vital Signs of the Planet.

September 11, 2016. https://climate.nasa.gov/news/2490/nasa-analysis-finds-august-2016-another-record-month.

———. 2016b. "September Was Warmest on Record by Narrow Margin." Climate Change: Vital Signs of the Planet. October 17, 2016. https://climate.nasa.gov/news/2503/september-was-warmest-on-record-by-narrow-margin.

New York Times. 2015. "Full Transcript: Democratic Presidential Debate." *New York Times*, October 14, 2015. www.nytimes.com/2015/10/14/us/politics/democratic-debate-transcript.html.

New York Times. 2018. "Mark Zuckerberg Testimony: Senators Question Facebook's Commitment to Privacy." *New York Times*, April 10, 2018. www.nytimes.com/2018/04/10/us/ politics/mark-zuckerberg-testimony.html.

Nie, Norman H., Darwin W. Miller III, Saar Golde, Daniel M. Butler, and Kenneth Winneg. 2010). "The World Wide Web and the U.S. Political News Market." *American Journal of Political Science* 54, no. 2(April): 428–439.

Norris, Pippa. 2000. *Virtuous Circle: Political Communication in Post-industrial Societies*. New York: Cambridge University Press.

Nunez, Michael. (2016). Former Facebook Workers: We Routinely Suppressed Conservative News. Gizmodo. May 9, 2016. http://gizmodo.com/former-facebook-workers-we-routinely-suppressed-conser-1775461006.

Office of Director of National Intelligence. 2017. *Assessing Russian Activities and Intentions in Recent US Elections*. Intelligence Community Assessment. January 6, 2017. Washington, DC: Office of the Director of National Intelligence.

O'Harrow, Robert. 2016. "Trump's Bad Bet: How Too Much Debt Drove His Biggest Casino Aground." *Washington Post*. January 18, 2016. www.washingtonpost.com/investigations/trumps-bad-bet-how-too-much-debt-drove-his-biggest-casino-aground/2016/01/18/f67cedc2-9ac8-11e5-8917-653b65c809eb_story.html.

Ohlheiser, Abby. 2016. This Is How Facebook's Fake-News Writers Make Money. *Washington Post*, November 18, 2016. www.washingtonpost.com/news/the-intersect/wp/2016/11/18/this-is-how-the-internets-fake-news-writers-make-money/.

Orren, Gary R., and Nelson W. Polsby, eds. 1987. *Media and Momentum: The New Hampshire Primary and Nomination Politics*. Chatham, NJ: Chatham House.

Parkinson, H. J. 2016. "Click and Elect: How Fake News Helped Donald Trump Win a Real Election." *Guardian*, November 14, 2016. www.theguardian.com/commentisfree/2016/nov/14/fake-news-donald-trump-election-alt-right-social-media-tech-companies.

Pasek, J., L. O. Singh, Y. Wei, S. N. Soroka, J. M. Ladd, M. W. Traugott, C. Budak, L. Bode, and F. Newport. 2019. "Attention to Campaign Events: Do Twitter and Self-Report Metrics Tell the Same Story?" *BIGSURV Big Data Meets Survey Science.*

Pasek, Josh, Colleen A. McClain, Frank Newport, and Stephanie Marken. 2019. "Who's Tweeting about the President? What Big Survey Data Can Tell Us about Digital Traces?" *Social Science Computer Review.* DOI: doi. org/10.1177/0894439318822007.

Patterson, Thomas E. 1993. *Out of Order.* New York: Knopf.

———. 2016. "News Coverage of the 2016 General Election: How the Press Failed the Voters." Shorenstien Center on Media, Politics and Public Policy. Shorenstein Center. December 7, 2016. https://shorensteincenter. org/news-coverage-2016-general-election/.

———. 2016a. "Pre-primary News Coverage of the 2016 Presidential Race: Trump's Rise, Sanders' Emergence, Clinton's Struggle." Shorenstein Center. June 13, 2016. https://shorensteincenter.org/pre-primary-news-coverage-2016-trump-clinton-sanders/.

———. 2016b. "News Coverage of the 2016 General Election: How the News Media Failed the Voters." Shorenstein Center. December 7, 2016. https:// shorensteincenter.org/news-coverage-2016-general-election/.

Perrin, Andrew, and Monica Anderson. 2019. "Share of U.S. Adults Using Social Media, Including Facebook, Is Mostly Unchanged since 2018." Pew Research Center. April 10, 2019. www.pewresearch.org/fact-tank/2019/04/10/ share-of-u-s-adults-using-social-media-including-facebook-is-mostly-unchanged-since-2018/.

Pew Research Center. 2016. "2016 Campaign: Strong Interest, Widespread Dissatisfaction." Pew Research Center. July 7, 2016. www.people-press. org/2016/07/07/2016-campaign-strong-interest-widespread-dissatis faction/.

Pickard, Victor. 2014. *America's Battle for Media Democracy: The Triumph of Corporate Libertarianism and the Future of Media Reform.* Cambridge, UK: Cambridge University Press.

Picketty, Thomas, and Emmanual Saez. 2003. "Income Inequality in the United States, 1913–1998." *Quarterly Journal of Economics*, 118, no. 1 (February).

Popkin, Samuel L. 1991. *The Reasoning Voter.* Chicago: University of Chicago Press.

Prior, Markus. 2005. "News vs. Entertainment: How Increasing Media Choice Widens Gaps in Political Knowledge and Turnout." *American Journal of Political Science* 49, no. 3 (July): 577–592.

———. 2007. *Post-broadcast Democracy: How Media Choice Increases Inequality in Political Involvement and Polarizes Elections.* New York: Cambridge University Press.

Prior, Markus. 2018. *Hooked: How Politics Captures People's Interest.* New York: Cambridge University Press.

Proksch, Sven-Oliver, Will Lowe, Jens Wäckerle, and Stuart Soroka. 2019. "Multilingual Sentiment Analysis: A New Approach to Measuring Conflict in Legislative Speeches," *Legislative Studies Quarterly* 44, no. 1 (February): 97–131.

Qiu, Linda. 2016. "Yep, Donald Trump's Companies Have Declared Bankruptcy . . . More than Four Times." PolitiFact. June 21, 2016. www.politifact.com/truth-o-meter/statements/2016/jun/21/hillary-clinton/yep-donald-trumps-companies-have-declared-bankrupt/.

Quandt, Thorsten, Martin Loffelholz, David H. Weaver, Thomas Hanitzsch, and Klaus-Dieter Altmeppen. 2006. "American and German Online Journalists at the Beginning of the 21st Century. *Journalism Studies* 7 (2): 171–186.

Rieis, Julio, Fabricio de Souza, Pedros O. S. Vas de Melo, Raquel Prates, Haewoon Kwak, and Jisun An. 2015. "Breaking the News: First Impressions Matter on Online News." In *Proceedings of the Ninth International AAAI Conference on Web and Social Media*, 357–366. Menlo Park, CA: Association for the Advancement of Artificial Intelligence.

Robinson, Michael J. 1976. "Public Affairs Television and the Growth of Political Malaise: The Case of 'Selling the Pentagon.'" *American Political Science Review* 70, no. 2 (June): 409–432.

Rosenberg, Matthew, Nicholas Confessore, and Carole Cadwalladr. 2018. "How Trump Consultants Exploited the Facebook Data of Millions." *New York Times*, March 17, 2018. www.nytimes.com/2018/03/17/us/ politics/cambridge-analytica-trump-campaign.html.

Saad, Lydia. 2016. "Trump and Clinton Finish with Historically Poor Images." Gallup. November 8, 2016. https://news.gallup.com/poll/197231/trump-clinton-finish-historically-poor-images.aspx.

Schaedel, Sydney. 2018. "Websites That Post Fake and Satirical Stories. FactCheck. November 12, 2018. www.factcheck.org/2017/07/websites-post-fake-satirical-stories.

Scheufele, Dietram A. 2000. "Agenda-Setting, Priming, and Framing Revisited: Another Look at Cognitive Effects of Political Communication." *Mass Communication and Society* 3 (2–3): 297–316.

Schmidt, Christine. 2018. "How France Beat Back Information Manipulation (and How Other Democracies Might Do the Same)." NeimanLab. September

19, 2018. www.niemanlab.org/2018/09/how-france-beat-back-information-manipulation-and-how-other-democracies-might-do-the-same/.

Schmidt, Michael S. 2015. "Hillary Clinton Used Personal Email Account at State Dept., Possibly Breaking Rules." *New York Times*, March 2, 2015, sec. Politics.

Schmidt, Michael S., and Matt Apuzzo. 2015. "Hillary Clinton Emails Said to Contain Classified Data." *New York Times*, July 24, 2015.

Schober, Michael F., Josh Pasek, Lauren Guggenheim, Cliff Lampe, and Frederick G. Conrad. 2016. "Social Media Analyses for Social Measurement." *Public Opinion Quarterly* 80, no. 1 (Spring): 180–211. DOI: doi.org/10.1093/poq/nfv048.

Schrodt, Paul. 2016. "Why 'The Apprentice' Made Donald Trump's Presidential Campaign Possible." Business Insider. November 8, 2016. www.businessinsider.com/the-apprentice-paved-way-for-donald-trump-presidential-campaign-2016-11.

Schwarz, Hunter. 2015. "The 'Texts from Hillary' Meme Isn't So Funny Anymore." *Washington Post*, March 6, 2015, sec. The Fix.

Schwartz, Ian. 2015 "Trump: I Will Not Pledge To Endorse Republican Nominee, Not Run As Independent." RealClearPolitics. August 6, 2015. www.realclearpolitics.com/video/2015/08/06/trump_i_will_not_pledge_to_endorse_republican_nominee.html.

Searles, Kathleen, and Kevin K. Banda. 2019. "But Her Emails! How Journalistic Preferences Shaped Election Coverage in 2016." *Journalism* 20 (8): 1052–1069. DOI: doi.org/10.1177/1464884919845459.

Serhan, Yasmeen. 2018. "Macron's War on 'Fake News.'" *Atlantic*, January 6, 2018. www.theatlantic.com/international/archive/2018/01/macrons-war-on-fake-news/549788/.

Shane, Scott, and Vindu Goel. 2017. "Fake Russian Facebook Accounts Bought $100,000 in Political Ads. *New York Times*, September 6, 2017. www.nytimes.com/2017/09/06/technology/ facebook-russian-political-ads.html.

Shaw, Daron R. 1999. "The Impact of News Media Favorability and Candidate Events in Presidential Elections." *Political Communication* 16 (2): 183–202.

Shearer Elisa, and Jeffrey Gottfried. 2016. "News Use across Social Media Platforms 2016." Pew Research Center. May 26, 2016. www.journalism.org/2016/05/26/news-use-acrosssocial-media-platforms-2016/.

Shelbourne, Mallory. 2017. "Facebook Rolls Out Feature to Combat Fake News." *The Hill*, March 5, 2017. http://thehill.com/policy/technology/ 322427-facebook-begins-to-introduce-new-feature-to-combat-fake-news.

Sides, John. 2016. "Never Forget: The 2016 Presidential Election Is Supposed to Be One That Republicans Can Win." *Washington Post*, August 23, 2016. www.washingtonpost.com/news/monkey-cage/wp/2016/08/23/never-forget-the-2016-presidential-election-is-supposed-to-be-one-that-republicans-can-win/.

Sides, John, and Lynn Vavreck. 2013. *The Gamble: Choice and Chance in the 2012 Presidential Election.* Princeton: Princeton University Press.

Sides, John, Michael Tesler, and Lynn Vavreck. 2018. *Identity Crisis: The 2016 Presidential Campaign and the Battle for the Meaning of America.* Princeton: Princeton University Press.

Silver, Nate. 2011. "What Do Economic Models Really Tell Us About Elections?" FiveThirtyEight. June 4, 2011. https://fivethirtyeight.com/features/what-do-economic-models-really-tell-us-about-elections/.

Silverman, Craig. 2016a. "Here Are 50 of the Biggest Fake News Hits on Facebook from 2016." BuzzFeed News. December 30, 2016. www.buzzfeed.com/craigsilverman/top-fake-news-of-2016.

———. 2016b. "This Analysis Shows How Fake Election News Stories Outperformed Real News on Facebook. BuzzFeed News. November 16, 2016. www.buzzfeed.com/craigsilverman/ viral-fake-election-news-outperformed-real-news-on-facebook.

Silverman, Craig, Jane Lytvynenko, and Scott Pham. 2017. "These Are 50 of the Biggest Fake News Hits on Facebook in 2017. BuzzFeed News. December 28, 2017. www.buzzfeednews.com/article/craigsilverman/ these-are-50-of-the-biggest-fake-news-hits-on-facebook-in.

Silverman, Craig, and Jeremy Singer-Vine. 2016. Most Americans Who See Fake News Believe It, New Survey Says. BuzzFeed News. December 6, 2016. www.buzzfeed.com/craigsilverman/fake-newssurvey.

Soloski, J. 1989. "Sources and Channels of Local News." *Journalism Quarterly* 66: 864–870.

Solon, Olivia. 2018. Facebook Says Cambridge Analytica May Have Gained 37m More Users' Data. *Guardian*, April 4, 2018. www.theguardian.com/technology/2018/apr/04/ facebook-cambridge-analytica-user-data-latest-more-than-thought.

Soroka, Stuart N. 2014. *Negativity in Democratic Politics: Causes and Consequences.* Cambridge, UK: Cambridge University Press.

Soroka, Stuart, Marc Andre Bodet, Lori Young, and Blake Andrew. 2009. "Campaign News and Vote Intentions." *Journal of Elections, Public Opinion and Parties* 19, no. 4 (October): 359–376.

StatSocial. 2015. "Twitter's Most Influential Journalists." Dataset provided from StatSocial to the authors.

Stelter, Brian. 2015. "Fox's GOP Debate Had Record 24 Million Viewers." CNN. August 7, 2015. https://money.cnn.com/2015/08/07/media/gop-debate-fox-news-ratings/.

Strömbäck, Jesper, and Benjt Johansson. 2007. "Electoral Cycles and the Mobilizing Effects of Elections: A Longitudinal Study of the Swedish Case." *Journal of Elections, Public Opinion and Parties* 17, no. 1 (February): 79–99.

Strömbäck Jesper, and Adam Shehata. 2010. "Media Malaise Or a Virtuous Circle? Exploring the Causal Relationships between News Media Exposure, Political News Attention and Political Interest. *European Journal of Political Research* 49, no. 5 (July): 575–597.

Subramanian, Samanth. 2017. "The Macedonian Teens Who Mastered Fake News." Wired. February 15, 2017. www. wired.com/2017/02/veles-macedonia-fake-news/.

Sultan, Niv M. 2017. "Election 2016: Trump's Free Media Helped Keep Cost Down, But Fewer Donors Provided More of the Cash." Open Secrets. April 13, 2017. www.opensecrets.org/news/2017/04/election-2016-trump-fewer-donors-provided-more-of-the-cash/.

Summers, Joana. 2015. "Bernie Sanders: Americans Are 'Sick and Tired' of Hillary Clinton's 'Damn Emails.'" Mashable. October 13, 2015. https://mashable.com/2015/10/13/bernie-sanders-clinton-emails/#6sCxFQprFiqY.

Summers, Lawrence. 2013. "Why Stagnation Might Prove to Be the New Normal." *Financial Times*, December 15, 2013. http://larrysummers.com/commentary/financial-times-columns/why-stagnation-might-prove-to-be-the-new-normal/.

Swift, Art. 2016. "Americans' Trust in Mass Media Sinks to New Low. Gallup. September 14, 2016. https://news.gallup.com/poll/195542/americans-trust-mass-media-sinks-new-low.aspx.

Sydell, Laura. 2016. "We Tracked Down a Fake-News Creator in the Suburbs. Here's What We Learned." NPR, *All Tech Considered*. November 23, 2016. www.npr.org/sections/alltechconsidered/2016/11/23/503146770/npr-finds-the-head-of-a-covert-fake-news-operation-in-the-suburbs.

Sysomos API. 2018. https://sysomos.com/services/api/.

Tacopino, Joe. 2016. "This Photo Was the Beginning of the End for Hillary." *New York Post*, June 10, 2016. https://nypost.com/2016/06/10/was-this-photo-the-beginning-of-the-end-for-hillary/.

Tandoc, Edson C. 2014. "Journalism Is Twerking? How Web Analytics Is Changing the Process of Gatekeeping. *New Media and Society* 16, no. 4 (April): 559–575.

Teh, Yee Whye, Michael I. Jordan, Matthew J. Beal, and David M. Blei. 2006.

"Hierarchical Dirichlet Processes." *Journal of the American Statistical Association* 101 (476): 1566–1581.

Tesler, Michael. 2015. "Priming Predispositions and Changing Policy Positions: An Account of When Mass Opinion Is Primed or Changed." *American Journal of Political Science* 59, no. 4 (October): 806–824.

The Smoking Gun. 2013. "Hacker Begins Distributing Confidential Memos Sent to Hillary Clinton on Libya, Benghazi Attack." The Smoking Gun. March 18, 2013. www.thesmokinggun.com/buster/sidney-blumenthal/hacker-distributes-memos-784091.

Trende, Sean. 2016. "RealClearPolitics—2016 Presidential Race." RealClearPolitics. November 8, 2016. www.realclearpolitics.com/epolls/2016/president/2016_presidential_race.html.

Trump, Donald J., and Tony Schwartz. 2015. *Trump: The Art of the Deal*. Reprint edition. New York: Ballantine Books.

Turcotte, Jason, Chance York, Jacob Irving, Rosanne M. Scholl, and Raymond J. Pingree. 2015. "News Recommendations from Social Media Opinion Leaders: Effects on Media Trust and Information Seeking." *Journal of Computer-Mediated Communication* 20, no. 5 (June): 520–535.

Vance, J. D. 2018. *Hillbilly Elegy: A Memoir of a Family and Culture in Crisis*. New York: HaperCollins.

Vargo, Chris J., Lei Guo, Maxwell McCombs, and Donald L. Shaw. 2014. "Network Issue Agendas on Twitter during the 2012 U.S. Presidential Election." *Journal of Communication* 64, no. 2 (March): 296–316. DOI: doi.org/10.1111/jcom.12089.

Vavreck, Lynn. 2009. *The Message Matters: The Economy and Presidential Campaigns*. Princeton: Princeton University Press.

Vergeer, Maurice, and Philip Hans Franses. 2015. "Live Audience Responses to Live Televised Election Debates: Time Series Analysis of Issue Salience and Party Salience on Audience Behavior." *Information, Communication and Society* 19, no. 10 (October): 1390–1410. DOI: doi.org/10.1080/1369118X.2015.1093526.

Viñas, Maria-José. 2016. "Arctic Sea Ice Annual Minimum Ties Second Lowest on Record." Global Climate Change: Vital Signs of the Planet. September 14, 2016. https://climate.nasa.gov/news/2496/arctic-sea-ice-annual-minimum-ties-second-lowest-on-record.

Vraga, Emily K., Leticia Bode, Anne-Bennett Smithson, and Sonya Troller-Renfree. 2016. "Blurred Lines: Defining Social, News, and Political Posts on Facebook." *Journal of Information Technology and Politics* 13, no. 3 (May): 272–294.

Wallace, Gregory. 2016. "Negative Ads Dominate in Campaign's Final Days." CNN. November 8, 2016. www.cnn.com/2016/11/08/politics/negative-ads-hillary-clinton-donald-trump/index.html.

Wang, Xuerui, and Andrew McCallum. 2006. "Topics over Time: A Non-Markov Continuous-Time Model of Topical Trends." *In Proceedings of the 12th ACM SIGKDD International Conference on Knowledge Discovery and Data Mining*, 424–433. New York: Association for Computing Machinery. DOI: doi.org/10.1145/1150402.1150450.

Warner, Benjamin R., and Mary C. Banwart. 2016. "A Multifactor Approach to Candidate Image." *Communication Studies* 67, no. 3 (April): 259–279.

Watson, Steve. 2016. "Judge: FBI Is Ready to Indict Hillary over Emails 'This Is Enough to Shake the American Political System to Its Foundation.'" Info-Wars. March 3, 2016. www.InfoWars.com/judge-fbi-is-ready-to-indict-hillary-over-emails/.

Wihbey, John, Kenneth Joseph, Thalita Dias Coleman, and David Lazer. 2017. "Exploring the Ideological Nature of Journalists' Social Networks on Twitter and Associations with News Story Content." https://arxiv.org/pdf/1708.06727.pdf.

Wingfield, Nick, Mike Isaac, and Katie Benner. 2016. Google and Facebook Take Aim at Fake News Sites. *New York Times*, November 14, 2016. www.nytimes.com/2016/11/15/technology/google-will-ban-websites-that-host-fake-news-from-using-its-ad-service.html.

Wlezien, Christopher. 2002. "On Forecasting the Presidential Vote." *PS: Political Science and Politics* 34 (01): 25–31. DOI: doi.org/10.1017/S104909650100004X.

Wlezien, Christopher, and Robert S. Erikson. 2008. "The Timeline of Presidential Election Campaigns." *Journal of Politics* 64 (4): 969–993. DOI: doi.org/10.1111/1468-2508.00159.

Wooten, Sarah McIntosh. 2009. *Donald Trump: From Real Estate to Reality TV*. Berkeley Heights, NJ: Enslow Publishers.

Yan, Xiaohui, Jiafeng Guo, Shenghua Liu, Xueqi Cheng, and Yanfeng Wang. 2013. "Learning Topics in Short Texts by Non-negative Matrix Factorization on Term Correlation Matrix." In *Proceedings of the SIAM International Conference on Data Mining*, 749–757. DOI: doi.org/10.1137/1.9781611972832.

Young, Lori, and Stuart Soroka. 2012. "Affective News: The Automated Coding of Sentiment in Political Texts." *Political Communication* 29 (2): 205–231.

Zaller, John R. 1992. *The Nature and Origins of Mass Opinion*. New York: Cambridge University Press.

———. 2003. "A New Standard of News Quality: Burglar Alarms for the

Monitorial Citizen." *Political Communication* 20 (2): 109–130. DOI: doi.org/10.1080/10584600390211136.

Zengerle, Jason. 2015. "Why Hillary Clinton Is Doubling Down on Her Black-Berry Picture." *GQ*, March 13, 2015. www.gq.com/story/hillary-clinton-texting-origin-story.

Zenko, Micah, and Jennifer Wilson. 2017. "How Many Bombs Did the United States Drop in 2016?" *Politics, Power, and Preventive Action Blog, Council on Foreign Relations.* January 5, 2017. www.cfr.org/blog-post/how-many-bombs-did-united-states-drop-2016.

Zimdars, Melissa. 2016. "False, Misleading, Clickbait-y, and Satirical 'News' Sources." https://docs.google.com/document/u/1/d/10eA5-mCZLSS4MQY5QGb5ewC3VAL6pLkT53V_81ZyitM/mobilebasic.

About the Authors

LETICIA BODE is a Provost's Distinguished Associate Professor in the Communication, Culture, and Technology master's program at Georgetown University. Her work lies at the intersection of communication, technology, and political behavior, emphasizing the role communication and information technologies may play in the acquisition and use of political information. This covers a wide area, including exposure to political information on social media, correction of misinformation on social media, effects of exposure to political comedy, use of social media by political elites, selective exposure and political engagement in new media, and the changing nature of political socialization given the modern media environment.

CEREN BUDAK is assistant professor of information and assistant professor of electrical engineering and computer science in the College of Engineering at the University of Michigan, Ann Arbor. Her research interests lie in the area of computational social science. She utilizes network science, machine learning, and crowdsourcing methods and draws from scientific knowledge across multiple social science communities to contribute computational methods to the field of political communication.

JONATHAN M. LADD is an associate professor at Georgetown University, where he holds appointments in the McCourt School of Public Policy and the Department of Government. He is the author of *Why Americans Hate the Media and*

How It Matters, which won the Goldsmith Book Prize from the Shorenstein Center on the Press, Politics and Public Policy at Harvard University. His research examines partisan polarization, the changing nature of the news industry, the causes and consequences of declining public confidence in national institutions, and the effects of partisan news outlets on political preferences.

FRANK NEWPORT is a senior scientist at Gallup, Inc., and served as Gallup editor-in-chief from 1990 to 2018. Newport holds a PhD in sociology from the University of Michigan and was 2010–2011 president of the American Association for Public Opinion Research. He is the author of *Polling Matters—Why Leaders Must Listen to the Wisdom of the People* and *God Is Alive and Well: The Future of Religion in America*, and the editor of the long-standing *Gallup Poll Public Opinion* volumes.

JOSH PASEK is associate professor of communication and media, faculty associate in the Center for Political Studies, Institute for Social Research, and core faculty for the Michigan Institute for Data Science at the University of Michigan. His research explores how new media and psychological processes each shape political attitudes, public opinion, and political behaviors. He also examines issues in the measurement of public opinion, including techniques for reducing measurement error and improving population inferences. His work has been published in *Public Opinion Quarterly, Political Communication, Communication Research,* and the *Journal of Communication,* among other outlets.

LISA O. SINGH is a professor in the Department of Computer Science and a research professor in the Massive Data Institute at Georgetown University. Broadly, her research interests are in data-centric computing—data mining, data privacy, data science, data visualization, and databases. Her current research focuses on understanding ways to blend new forms of organic data with established forms of traditional data to begin tackling societal scale problems in a more holistic way.

STUART N. SOROKA is the Michael W. Traugott Collegiate Professor in Communication Studies and Political Science, and research professor in the Center for Political Studies at the Institute for Social Research, University of Michigan. His research focuses on political communication, the sources and/or structure of public preferences for policy, and the relationships between public policy, public opinion, and mass media.

MICHAEL W. TRAUGOTT is Professor Emeritus of Communication Studies and Political Science and Research Professor Emeritus in the Center for Political Studies at the University of Michigan. He studies campaigns and elections, political communication, and survey methodology. He is a past president of the American Association for Public Opinion Research and World Association for Public Opinion Research. He has received an award for distinguished lifetime achievement from each organization. He assisted Gallup in a review of their 2012 polling and was a Gallup senior scientist.

Index

Note: Figures and tables are indicated by "f" and "t" following page numbers.